From Rousseau to Lenin

From Rousseau to Lenin

Studies in
Ideology and Society

Lucio Colletti

*Translated by John Merrington
and Judith White*

Monthly Review Press
New York and London

First published as *Ideologia e Società* by
Editori Laterza, Rome, Italy. Copyright
© 1969 by Editori Laterza.

First Printing

Library of Congress Cataloging in Publication Data
Colletti, Lucio
 From Rousseau to Lenin
 Translation of Ideologia e società.
 1. Communism and society.   I. Title.
HX542.C6213   335.43   72-92035   ISBN 0-85345-278-4

Monthly Review Press
116 West 14th Street, New York, N.Y. 10011
33/37 Moreland Street, London, E.C.1

Manufactured in the United States of America

Bibliographical Note: 'Marxism as Sociology' was originally delivered as a paper to a conference on Marxism and Sociology organized by the Gramsci Institute of Rome in 1958; it was published in 1959 in *Società*. 'Bernstein and the Marxism of the Second International' was written as the introduction to an Italian edition of Bernstein's *Socialism and Social-Democracy*, published in 1968. 'Rousseau as Critic of "Civil Society" ' and 'From Hegel to Marcuse' first appeared in the March and June 1968 issues of the journal *De Homine*. 'Mandeville, Rousseau and Smith' was previously unpublished. 'Lenin's *State and Revolution*' appeared in the August 1967 issue of *Problemi del Socialismo*, and 'Marxism: Science or Revolution?' in the July 1969 issue of *Il Manifesto*.

Part One

Marxism as a Sociology

THE OBJECT OF 'CAPITAL'

We may start by turning to the preface written for the first edition of *Capital*. Two important circumstances stand out straight away, the first of which is as follows. Unlike all the economists who had discussed society 'in general' before him, Marx is concerned with *one* society only, modern *capitalist* society. He claims to have examined the laws of development of *this* society and none other. In other words, *Capital* is not a study of society as such, that is of the *abstraction* society 'in general', but a study of *this* particular society. Which means that the analysis concerns not an *idea* (an ideal object) but a *materially determined* or real object. This is the first point of departure. Since this first point is already thought-provoking it is worth pausing to consider it more closely.

In the first place, who are those reduced to discussing society *in general*? The answer can be given: those who regard the factor of 'consciousness' as the specific element of human society and history, and accordingly hold that societies should be investigated exclusively at the level of *ideological* social relations. For in this perspective the juridical and political forms of such societies (ideological forms in general) must inescapably appear, remarked Lenin, as 'originating in this or that idea of humanity' and hence as mere *products or moments of thought*. It follows that analysis cannot engage with a *real* object, but only with an ideal objectivity. The relation between the theory and its object contracts, due to the ideal character of the latter, into a mere relation of idea to idea, an internal monologue within thought itself. The object of analysis thus slips through our fingers; it is, as Lenin pointed out, impossible for us to undertake any study of the *facts*, of social processes, precisely because we are no longer confronting *a* society, a real object, but only the *idea* of society, society *in general*. This is the hypostasis which reaches its high point in bourgeois sociology. The sociologists talk of society 'in general', they argue with Spencer about 'the nature of society in general, about the aim and essence of society', i.e. about how society *should* be organized to satisfy this or that 'requirement' of 'human nature'; they cannot see, Lenin wrote, that 'such theories are useless because of the very fact that they exist, they are useless because of their basic methods, because of their solid unrelieved metaphysics'. Indeed, the most obvious sign of metaphysics, from which every science originated but always by contrast, is precisely this: so long as men did not know how to approach the study of the facts, they invented *a priori* general theories which always remained sterile. In other words, they *substituted* or superimposed a *generic* or *ideal* object for the *real* object to be explained. In short, metaphysics never produces an effective analysis since for it, strictly speaking, facts no longer exist; or, more precisely, because in the place of concrete historical phenomena it has interpolated the *idea*; in the place of a concrete, determinate society it has substituted society 'in general'.[1]

Lenin makes this point most acutely:

The metaphysician-chemist, still unable to make a factual investigation of chemical processes, concocts a theory about chemical affinity as a force. The metaphysician-biologist talks about the nature of life and the vital force. The metaphysician-psychologist argues about the nature of the soul. Here it is the method itself that is absurd. You cannot argue about the soul without having explained psychical processes in particular: here progress must consist precisely

[1] Lenin, 'What the "Friends of the People" Are', *Collected Works*, Vol. I, pp. 136–45. The quotations which follow are also taken from the first part of this work. The hypostasis or substitution of 'ideas' for 'facts' discussed here is a critique which goes well beyond positivist sociology of the Spencerian type, contrary to what some might believe. On this question, cf. the following interesting admission of Alfred Weber, from *Wesen und Aufgabe der Soziologie*. In considering the general characteristics of sociology after Marx, he observes how at this point a 'rupture' occurred. 'Major forces governing historical development' such as capitalism, modern science, etc., disappeared from the scope of analysis. Instead, there emerged 'a myriad of sociologies, which, however diverse they may be, for the most part no longer pose for themselves the task of providing an analysis – an analysis of the present – as a *particular* historical epoch. . . . On the contrary, these sociologies, in their treatment of "society" substitute for a historical reality a "concept" or, more precisely, a concept applicable only to the everyday situation as they represent it.' (*Einführung in die Soziologie* von A. Weber in Verbindung mit Herbert von Borch, Nicolaus Sombart, Hanno Kesting, Graefin Leonore Lichnowsky, Heinz Markmann, Götz Roth, Erwin Faul, Hans-Joachim Arndt, Heinz Hund; Munich 1955, pp. 13–14.)

For a clear testimony to the spiritualist and irrationalist orientations of modern *Konstellationssoziologie* and of 'subjectivism in sociology' in general, see the above quoted *Einführung* and especially the essays in it by Alfred Weber; *Wesen und Aufgabe der Soziologie, Geistige Einordnung der Soziologie, Allgemeine Probleme.*

in abandoning general theories and philosophical discourses about the nature of the soul, and in being able to put the study of the facts about particular psychical processes on a scientific footing.

Progress, then, consists in restoring and re-establishing these 'facts', these *real processes*, eluded and transcended by metaphysics, and opposing the hypostasis that conceal them. Their objective existence is, in short, the indispensable premiss for any kind of scientific enquiry.

However, if an analysis of society limited to the *ideological* level necessarily involves eluding the *real* object and hence the contraction of the analysis into an *a priori* mode of reasoning, it clearly follows, at least hypothetically, that the sole way of guaranteeing the possibility of a scientific analysis can only be that of investigating society at its *material* level, i.e. at the level of the real basis which specifies it and prevents its dissolution into an idea. Which means, in turn (since only *this* object is material and not *the* object in general, only *this* process, not *the* process *in general*) that Marx, in order to study the determinate object 'society', had inevitably to study precisely *this* society. The first circumstance emerging from the preface of *Capital* seems, therefore, to be more or less clarified.

However, there is also the other side of the coin. If limiting the study of society to the ideological level implies the contraction of the analysis into an *a priori* and metaphysical discourse, can we conclude that for a scientific approach it suffices to concentrate *exclusively* on the material level? And indeed, is it sufficient to say that an object is *material* because it can be said to be *determinate*, and thus to be *this* object?

To start with, we can state that everything is material, any thing *exists*, not excluding even the most hopelessly spiritualist philosophies. The 'spirit' is not the 'letter', but these philosophies are determinate philological entities none the less. They *are* (exist) insofar as they are *expressed*; in other words, as Marx wrote, insofar as 'the element of the vital manifestation of thought, *language*, is of a sensory nature'. To say, therefore, that an object is material is still to say nothing. Materiality as such does not specify, it is rather a *generic* attribute, a property common to *all* things. Indeed, however strange it may seem, and at the risk of provoking protest from some over-zealous 'materialist', it should be said loud and clear that *matter* as such is itself only an *idea*, a mere *flatus vocis*. In one of the most brilliant passages in the *Dialectics of Nature*, where Engels, arguing as a consistent materialist, provides arguments (even though involuntarily) for rejecting all the *idealist* generalizations to which he himself resorts quite frequently in other parts of this same work; and where, for instance, he puts us in a position to understand that it is meaningless to speak (as he himself does elsewhere) of 'motion in the most general sense, conceived as the mode of existence, the inherent attribute of matter', which 'comprehends all changes and processes occurring in the universe, from mere changes of place right to thinking'; and that therefore it is also meaningless to speak of a law of this motion in general, of any 'general law of development of nature, society, and thought'; in one of these passages he writes:

Matter as such is a pure creation of thought and an abstraction. We leave out of account the qualitative differences of things in lumping them together as corporeally existing things under the concept matter. Hence matter as such, as distinct from definite existing pieces of matter, is not anything sensuously existing.

Elsewhere he writes:

. . . matter as such and motion as such have not yet been seen or otherwise experienced by anyone, but only the various, actually existing material things and forms of motion. Matter is nothing but the totality of material things from which this concept is abstracted, and motion as such nothing but the totality of all sensuously perceptible forms of motion; words like matter and motion are nothing but *abbreviations* in which we comprehend many different sensuously perceptible things according to their common properties. Hence matter and motion *can* be known in no other way than by investigation of the separate material things and forms of motion.[2]

Thus in conclusion, while it is impossible to specify without matter, *as such* and of itself matter itself awaits its specification. This in turn implies that the same transformation of a determinate society into society 'in general' must occur whether we examine the *ideological* level to the exclusion of (without) *material* relations of production, or, conversely, if we consider only material production, excluding ideological relations. Indeed, in the latter case, to what is 'production' reduced when one abstracts from the element which makes that *material* production simultaneously a production of *ideas* and hence a production of human relations (for which however, precisely, thought, language, and communication exist)? This could only reduce it to a relation between *individual* man and nature (the notorious bourgeois Robinsonades), that is to a *presocial* or *asocial* fact. The result, in other words (remembering that here *society* precisely is the object of our study), is to remove 'production' from the field of enquiry

[2] Engels, *Dialectics of Nature*, Moscow, 1966, pp. 255, 235–6.

altogether, evading the very object in question. In the first case we have considered, society was eluded by transcending it. In the second, it is also eluded, insofar as it is never even touched, insofar as the social 'level' is simply not attained. With ideological relations alone, society dissolved into the *Spirit* or Ideal; now, with the material level alone, it dispersed into the great framework of *Nature*.

As *The German Ideology* already had it:

In the whole conception of history up to the present, this real basis of history (i.e. production) has either been totally neglected or else considered as a minor matter, quite irrelevant to the course of history. History must, therefore, always be written according to an extraneous standard; *the real production of life appears to be beyond history* (i.e. pre-social), *while the truly historical appears as something extra- and superterrestrial.* With this the relation between man and nature is excluded from history and the antithesis of nature and history, of nature and the spirit, is created.[3]

If we *isolate*, that is abstract, either the ideological alone or the material alone, the result as we can see is a dualistic separation between production as production of *things* on the one hand and production as production of *human relations* on the other. Or else a division of *production* and *distribution*[4] (the latter understood here above all as the distribution of human labour-power in the various branches and sectors of production). Or else a division between *production* and *society*. Or, finally, the separation of a relation (assumed to be) purely *material* or natural on the one hand, and a relation (assumed to be) exclusively human or better still exclusively *spiritual* on the other. In other words the relationship of man to nature is thereby excluded from relations between man and man; and in man, so to speak, mind and body are divided, considering only as a body the worker, the man who is in a relationship to nature (and hence the entire productive process as a process regulated by 'natural', eternal laws), and inversely, only as mind, only as consciousness, the man who is in relation with other men (and hence the entire historical process as an exclusively spiritual or ideal process).

Clearly, we cannot have a *concrete* society without taking both together: production and distribution; relations of production and social relations; economic structure and the ideological-political level; structure and superstructure. This in turn, however, is only possible on one condition:

[3] Marx and Engels, *The German Ideology*, London, 1965, p. 51.
[4] For analysis of this relation, cf. Marx, '1857 Introduction' to *A Contribution to the Critique of Political Economy*, London, 1971, the whole of the second section.

that we reach reality, that we break with the method of *generic* or *in-determinate abstraction* from which, as we have seen, arises the double abstraction of *Monsieur l'Esprit* and *Madame la Matière*. Hence the need for a new method, a new type of abstraction. More precisely, on the one hand the need for an approach which can encompass the *differences* presented by one object or *species* with respect to all the others – for example bourgeois society as against feudal society – and which does not, therefore, arrive at the *generic*, idealist notion of society 'in general', but rather hangs on to this determinate society, the particular object in question. (The need for a method which does not give us abstractions, but facts.) On the other hand, however, the individual fact, in its unique, absolute singularity, is as generic as the abstract genus. Hence the need for a non-empiricist method which is also – as well as fact – abstraction, and does not preclude the specific *identity*, the *species*, and hence that typicality by which each object is what it is precisely because it is an expression of its 'class'. On one side, therefore, the need for observation-induction; in this respect an object or process is inconceivable if it is not this particular process, this particular *nature*. Yet on the other side, the need for hypothesis-deduction, i.e. a particular process or phenomenon is inconceivable for us if it is not itself a *model* or typical phenomenon. For us, 'this' determinate *natural* event is impossible unless it is not simultaneously a natural *law*, and hence simultaneously individual and *repeatable*.

The same applies when we turn to the example quoted above. Neither abstraction from the differences between bourgeois society and other social regimes; nor abstraction, in examining a particular case such as nineteenth- and twentieth-century Britain, from what is the specific or *essential* aspect of this case – namely, its *capitalist* organization. The need, in sum, for the method of *determinate*, specific or scientific abstraction; i.e. the need for a method which (forgive the paradox) is no longer nor exclusively a method – at least in the traditional, formalist sense in which thought and logic are still assumed to be self-enclosed, autonomous spheres. In the latter case, we can discern the classic alternative: on the one hand of those who believe that discourse on method need not in itself be a mode of implicating reality (Kant and the Neocritical School); on the other, of those who resolve discourse on reality into discourse on logic (Hegel and Company).[5] For Marx, on the contrary, the discourse on method implies also a particular assumption of reality; but without ever

[5] In my view, the whole debate some years ago between the partisans of Marxism as a 'method' and Marxism as a 'world-view' was still framed by these alternatives.

resolving reality into itself or negating it. For Marx, in fact, the theoretical requirements we have elaborated are fulfilled. *A parte objecti*, the necessity of grasping both production and distribution, *the economy and politics*, since only thus is the object *determinate* and 'society' *this* society. *A parte subjecti*, the necessity that 'this' society nevertheless be a specific *generalization*, a *type* or 'model' – i.e. not Britain, but the capitalist *socio-economic formation* (or, better still, Britain only *insofar* as it is the 'classical' example of one phase of capitalist development). In this case, it is clear how a particular methodological assumption implies a particular structuration of the object, and vice versa. Hence Marx's method can never be divorced from the particular objective patterns which are reflected in it (still less, therefore, from materialism). Nor can any serious Marxist substitute or integrate these objective material patterns with 'objects', as offered him by the procedures of other methodologies.

Here (finally) we encounter the second circumstance which should emerge just by reading the preface to *Capital*. Marx indeed studies this society *hic et nunc*; but this society is 'modern' society, the capitalist mode of production and exchange, not Britain, France, etc., as such.

The physicist either observes physical phenomena where they occur in their most typical form and most free from disturbing influence, or, wherever possible, he makes experiments under conditions that assure the occurrence of the phenomenon in its normality. In this work I have to examine the *capitalist mode of production* and the conditions of production and *exchange* corresponding to that mode. Up to the present, their classic ground is England. That is the reason why England is used as the chief illustration in the development of my theoretical ideas. If, however, the German reader shrugs his shoulders at the conditions of the English industrial and agricultural labourers, or in optimist fashion comforts himself with the thought that in Germany things are not nearly so bad; I must plainly tell him, *De te fabula narratur!*

England does indeed enter the analysis, but, as Marx says, for a *particular* reason: only because, and insofar as, within it, at a certain historical moment, an objective situation was produced such as to realize the 'model' conditions indispensable for a scientific analysis. The subject of Marx's enquiry is not, in fact, England as such, but *the development of the capitalist mode of production*, which, in a particular phase, found in that country the conditions and theatre for its dynamic and parabola to unfold in a 'classic' or 'typical' form.[6] 'Intrinsically', Marx immediately goes on, 'it is

---

[6] cf. G. Pietranera, 'La Struttura Logica del "Capitale"', in *Società*, August 1956. We note this study in particular here for the important considerations it offers on the

not a question of the higher or lower degree of development (in different countries) of the social antagonisms that result from the natural laws of capitalist production. It is a question of *these laws themselves.* . . . The country that is more developed industrially only shows, to the less developed, the image of its own future.'

On one side, then, *Capital* is not a study of 'society' but of *this* society; not an abstraction, but rather a real process (a natural process), not an *Objekt* but a *Gegenstand*. On the other side, however, 'this' society is 'the typical, generalized form of all existing capitalist societies' (Dobb), that is, it is an abstraction reached by 'distinguishing, to use an example, the differences between each capitalist country from what is common to them all' (Lenin). On one side we have a natural phenomenon; on the other, this *nature* is a *law* of nature. On the one hand, this society *hic et nunc*; but on other, this *hic et nunc* is a socio-economic formation.

THE UNITY OF ECONOMICS AND SOCIOLOGY

The term 'socio-economic formation' is a vivid linguistic expression of the fact that the object of *Capital* has the character of a 'whole', and this is so, as we have seen, because of the impossibility of any dualistic separation between the *material* and *ideological* levels, or because the object only really becomes an object and hence something *determinate* through the contribution of both of these its two modalities. It is, therefore, a *totum*, i.e. something including in its scope both social *being* and social *conscious-ness*, or rather both conditions *a parte objecti* and conditions *a parte subjecti*.

But this in turn raises the question of how subject and object are combined within this whole. One mode of combination is clearly as follows: the subject is *part* of the object, a moment within the object, and hence is itself *objective*. Both subject and object are part of an *objective* object-subject process. The superstructure is itself an aspect and articu-lation of the structure; consciousness is itself a mode of being; the know-ledge of life is itself a mode and manifestation of life. From this stand-point, art, philosophy or science are realities, social institutions, i.e. expressions or articulations of society. Criticism of them, reflection on them, is already an investigation of society, i.e. a sociology. In Marx's

---

historical character even of Marx's assumption of an 'equal organic composition of capital in all branches of production' – which is, of course, the condition for the validity of the labour theory of value, but which is still often considered (even at times by Dobb) as an abstraction of the Ricardian type.

early work, for example, we find that in studying Hegel, and in particular (not by chance) his *Philosophy of Right*, Marx was studying not only the bourgeois *theory* of the state but the bourgeois *state* itself. Similarly, in the *1844 Manuscripts*, in Smith, Ricardo or Say, he was studying not only bourgeois economic theory but (if only as a first attempt) also the objective relations between capital and ground rent on the one hand and wage labour on the other.

Granted this, it is, however, equally true that the superstructural or ideological level, though it may be *part* of the structure and of social being, nonetheless is so as *consciousness* or ideology; i.e. it has a *specific* role *vis-à-vis* other parts of the structure. A work of art or science, such as Balzac's *Comédie Humaine*, is not the French railway system. Indeed, precisely and solely because of this is it part of society: because through it society realizes one of its functions that could not be otherwise realized (for example, by producing bolts). Hence what makes it a *part* is precisely what *distinguishes* it from the *totum* to which it belongs. The distinguishing feature of consciousness is, as we know, that while it is part of social being and is therefore internal to life, at the same time it *reflects* on the latter and embraces it mentally within itself. While it embraces society within itself it is also *part* of society, i.e. it is only *one* of its functions and has the others *outside itself*. Marx wrote: 'Thought and being are *united*, it is true, but are also *distinct* from one another.' Consciousness does indeed belong to being, to social practice; theory is itself life, practice; there is a unity and inter-relationship of the two. However, consciousness belongs to life insofar as it is *one* of its parts. Theory is practice insofar as it is *one* aspect or moment of practice: i.e. insofar as it is reincorporated within the latter as one of its specific functions – and hence insofar as it does not absorb practice within itself, but is instead surrounded by it, and has it outside itself. Similarly, production, in one sense, is distribution, exchange and consumption; but the latter are nonetheless only moments of the former and presuppose production as their antecedent. Once understood correctly, therefore, it is precisely the unity of being and consciousness, their inter-relation, which implies the fundamental character or priority of being over thought, i.e. *materialism*.[7]

[7] For the relationship production-distribution-consumption, see again: Marx, 'Introduction' to *A Contribution to the Critique of Political Economy*, op. cit., second paragraph. Hans Kelsen claims to have identified a 'contradiction' in the Marxist conception of law in that it is understood both as a *social relation*, or reality, and a form of consciousness or *reflection upon* this social relation. But this is merely a result of his own failure

However, if this is correct, then two consequences clearly follow. The first concerns *method*: since the superstructure reflects the structure and is *part* of it, the content of theoretical generalization can only be *verified* as a determination or aspect of the object of analysis. Secondly, as a *structural* consequence, if the structure always includes both 'structure and superstructure' and 'society' is always an objective object-subject process, the objective terms of analysis must also themselves be seen as *active*, as objects capable of referring theoretically to one another, and hence as objects susceptible to description in purely *physical* terms on the one hand and also social *agents* on the other. The process is a *natural* one, but this nature is *socio-historical*.

In other words, the analysis of the *structure*, of the real basis of capitalism, does indeed constitute the *skeleton* of *Capital*. However, as Lenin pointed out: 'The whole point is that Marx did not content himself with this skeleton, that he did not confine himself to "economic theory" in the usual sense of the term, that, while explaining the structure and development of a given social formation *exclusively* through productive relations he nevertheless everywhere and incessantly scrutinized the superstructure corresponding to these productive relations and clothed the skeleton in flesh and blood'; that is, his analysis encompassed both economics and history, economics and sociology.

Obviously Marx did not attain this result by a mere work of juxtaposition. He did not start with a *purely* economic analysis and then fill the data of this analysis out with historical and political elements. He did not work with *two* criteria, but with categories which represented from the outset, in their most intimate structure, at once *factors* (objects, conditions) of production and socio-historical agents. His categories were *both* economic and historical.

In the last pages of *Capital* we read:

Scientific analysis of the capitalist mode of production demonstrates . . . that the distribution relations essentially coincident with these production relations are their opposite side . . . the wage presupposes wage-labour, and profit – capital.

---

to grasp the central nexus of Marx's thought: that the superstructure is at once a *part* or moment of the structure and a form of the latter. This nexus or unity of heterogeneous elements seems a contradiction to Kelsen because his own approach is based on the old neo-critical separation between 'fact' and 'value'. Contemporary juridical *sociologism* and *normativism* derive precisely, but in opposite ways, from this same separation. (H. Kelsen, *The Communist Theory of Law*, London, 1955.)

These definite forms of distribution thus presuppose definite social characteristics of productive conditions and definite social relations of productive agents. . . .

Never in Marx do we find economic categories that are *purely* economic categories. All his concepts, on the contrary, are both economic and sociological. The most abstract and simplest capitalist relationship, M-C-M, is already the relation between capital and labour power. In other words, it is already a relationship between two *social classes*.

As Schumpeter writes:

We have seen how in the Marxian argument sociology and economics pervade each other. In intent and to some degree also in actual practice, they are one. All the major concepts and propositions are hence both economic and sociological and carry the same meaning on both planes – if, from our standpoint, we may still speak of two planes of argument. Thus the economic *category* 'labour' and the social *class* 'proletariat' are, in principle at least, made congruent, in fact identical. Or the economist's functional distribution – that is to say, the explanation of the way in which incomes emerge as returns to productive services irrespective of what social class any recipient of such a return may belong to – enters the Marxian system only in the form of distribution between social classes and thus acquires a different connotation.[8]

This 'wholeness', and the stupendous effect even as literature thereby achieved in the pages of *Capital*, is not, therefore, the result of any mechanical superimposition of 'levels'. To use Lenin's metaphor, the 'skeleton' is not analysed *first* and *then* clothed in 'flesh and blood'. Rather, it is achieved by the end, because it is already there in that initial, so abstract and rarified relationship M-C-M, with which *Capital* commences and which is the true 'sphinx' of the entire gigantic construction. On the one hand, the relationship money-commodity (M-C), or capital-labour power, expresses the relation between *constant* and *variable capital*, i.e. a relation between simple *objects*, raw materials and machinery on the one hand and the rest of the means of production on the other, under capitalism. Yet on the other hand, this relation between the mere *objective conditions* of production, between the mere means or instruments by which the objective *material* process of production proceeds, is indeed a relationship between objects, but one between *active* objects, i.e. between capital and labour-power, between the employer and the wage worker: in short, a relationship between socio-historical *agents*.

We can now understand how this *unity* of economics and sociology,

---

[8] J. A. Schumpeter, *Capitalism, Socialism and Democracy*, London, 1954, p. 45.

of nature and history in Marx does *not* signify an identity between the terms. It involves neither a reduction of society to nature, nor of nature to society; it does not reduce human society to an ant-hill, nor human life to philosophical life. But we can also understand, conversely, how the avoidance of these two unilateral antitheses on Marx's part is due precisely to their organic composition, i.e. to their unification in a 'whole'. This whole is a totality, but a *determinate* totality; it is a synthesis of *distinct* elements, it is a unity, but a unity of *heterogeneous* parts. From this vantage point, it is easy to see (if in foreshortened form) both Marx's debt to Hegel and the real distance that separates them.[9]

In other words, *Capital* does indeed analyse a process between men, relations that are social and not between objects; but this social process is itself a natural-objective process. So, if it is true that *Capital* deals with a human social process, it by no means follows that this process is simply reducible to *ideological* social relations, i.e. to merely intentional conscious patterns of behaviour, to a mere relation of ideas. Rather, the relation is between subjects who are *objective entities*, despite the fact that these entities in their turn have the peculiarity of being *subjects*.

The historical subject then is neither Idea, World-Spirit, Vico's Providence, nor a transcendental subject. Nor is the subject conceived as Evolution, Struggle for Existence, Societal Instinct, Race, etc. Against these generic abstractions, all equally fruitless, Marx produces a new concept of the subject as a historical-natural entity, as a *species* or collectivity of empirical formations – such, precisely, as are social *classes*. He analyses these species in the light of determinate or scientific concepts, precisely those 'pseudo-concepts' so abhorred by the theological leanings of idealist historicism. The organic unity of economics and sociology lies here: in the concept of class. 'Class' has a double significance: firstly as factors or *objective conditions* of production (as a certain historical phase of the division of labour, of course); and secondly as the *political agents* of the whole human social process. Classes are precisely sections which cut vertically and horizontally through the entire society, from top to bottom. Hence the profound and organic unity between Marx's historical-*economic* work and his historical-*political* work. Lenin said as much when he observed that *Capital* 'shows the whole capitalist social formation as a living thing, with its everyday aspects, with the actual social manifestation of the class antagonism inherent in production relations, with the

---

[9] For this fundamental concept of a unity of heterogeneous elements, see G. della Volpe, *Logica come scienza positiva*, Messina and Florence, 1956.

bourgeois political superstructure that protects the rule of the capitalist class, with the bourgeois ideas of liberty, equality and so forth'.

Schumpeter supports the same point:

Marx's synthesis embraces all those historical events – such as wars, revolutions, legislative changes – and all those social institutions – such as property, contractual relations, forms of government – that non-Marxian economists are wont to treat as disturbing factors or as data. The trait peculiar to the Marxian system is that it subjects these historical events and social institutions themselves to the explanatory process of economic analysis or, to use the technical lingo, that it treats them not as data but as variables.[10]

The conclusion is evident. *Capital* is itself and above all a great *historical* work. All the so-called 'historical' works of Marx, the *Eighteenth Brumaire*, the *Class Struggles in France* and so on, not only have their roots in *Capital*, not only presuppose it and have it as a foundation but, far from representing a 'passage to a different genre' in Marx's research, are located within the same horizon. To fail to see this (as even many Marxists still do) means in practice to fail to grasp the historico-social pregnancy of all the economic categories in *Capital*, including the most 'abstract' ones. It means to reproduce the bourgeois separation of economics and politics, of nature and history. This is to ignore that for Marx the movement of society is 'a movement in its base and not merely on its base';[11] it is a *natural-historical* process, rather than one still to be simply relegated to the sphere of 'ideological social relations'.

We are confronted, then, by an organic unity of both these 'levels'. This is proved by the fact that the four volumes of *Capital* present not only the analysis of the capitalist *economic structure*, i.e. the history and dynamics of the mode of production of bourgeois society, but also the analysis of bourgeois political economy (*Theories of Surplus Value*), in other words the history of *economic thought*. It is proved even more incontrovertibly by the original plan of the work, according to which it was to have extended to embrace the following themes: 'the state as the epitome of bourgeois society. The "unproductive" classes, taxes, National debt. Public credit. Population. Colonies. Emigration. International conditions of production. International division of labour. International exchange. Export and Import. Rate of exchange. World market and crises.'[12]

---

[10] Schumpeter, op. cit., p. 47.

[11] M. Dobb, *Political Economy and Capitalism*, London, 1937, p. 58.

[12] Marx, 'Introduction' to *A Contribution to the Critique of Political Economy*, op. cit., p. 214. An interesting insight into the reciprocal relation between the 'problem of

Clearly, the *method* and *object* are organically linked. This helps to explain how those Marxists who have hitherto failed to penetrate the profound originality of Marx's method have also failed to identify the object of his work. In contrast to the dynamic living character of the bourgeois regime of production and exchange as it bursts out from the pages of *Capital*, they have appealed to the 'false mobility' (Marx) of the Hegelian dialectic, the formal conceits of the 'negation of the negation'; they have not seen that the dynamic character of Marx's analysis derives precisely from that *unity of heterogeneous elements* (in which, to repeat, the *objective* factors of production are simultaneously presented as *subjective* agents or social classes).[13] At the same time, led astray by the 'particularized', literary character of the historical narrative of the *Eighteenth Brumaire*, the *Class Struggles in France*, and so on, they have erected a basic distinction between these works and *Capital*, without realizing that since the protagonists of this 'history' are always social *classes*, these writings cannot but be *scientific* historical works, analyses of a *model* situation which – insofar as the development of bourgeois *political* institutions is concerned, and the manner in which the class struggle is articulated at that level – Marx (as is well known) found in French society. There the modern representative state, bureaucratic centralization, and indeed all the political upheavals of bourgeois class society, produced that exemplary or 'classic' phenomenology of which he provided not merely the description, but the socio-historical analysis.[14]

---

history' and the 'theoretical history of the problem' is to be found in Lukács, *History and Class Consciousness* (London, 1971, pp. 33–5). In a discussion of Luxemburg's *Accumulation of Capital*, he considers the major methodological merit of this work to lie in her having linked into a unitary whole both the treatment of the *actual problems* and the *theoretical history* of these problems, i.e. the analysis of the real problems and the analysis of the theoretical interpretations of these problems. '*Capital* and *The Theories of Surplus Value*', he writes, 'are in essence a single work.' However, it is worth noting that Lukács immediately reverts to an idealistic reduction of real history to the history of theory. Instead of seeing in *historia rerum gestarum* a function of the *res gestae*, he reverses the relationship in the Hegelian manner.

[13] Weber, op. cit., p. 107: 'With this work [*Capital*], Marx became not only the discoverer but at the same time the first analyst to see the modern capitalist economy as a gigantic mechanism endowed with its own movement.'

[14] This significance of Marx's historical-political writings was grasped with clarity by Engels in his celebrated preface to the third German edition of the *Eighteenth Brumaire*: 'France is the land where, more than anywhere else, the historical class struggles were each time fought out to a decision, and where, consequently, the changing political forms within which they move and in which their results are summarized have been

'DARWIN AND HEGEL'

In a letter to Kautsky of 26 June 1884, Engels made some critical comments on the latter's *Anti-Rodbertus* manuscript; they provide a conducting thread at least for a preliminary orientation in that complex region, the history of the interpretation of Marx in the period of the Second International.[15] The letter contains this observation: 'As soon as you speak of "means of production" you speak of "society", specifically society co-determined (*mitbestimmte*) by these means of production. Means of production *in themselves*, outside society, without influence upon it, are just as non-existent as is capital *in itself.*' The same point is reiterated and spelled out further in a letter of September 1884, again referring to Rodbertus's method of abstraction and the errors it shared

stamped in the sharpest outlines. The centre of feudalism in the Middle Ages, the model country of unified monarchy resting on estates, since the Renaissance, France demolished feudalism in the Great Revolution and established the unalloyed rule of the bourgeoisie in a classical purity unequalled by any other European land. . . . This was the reason why Marx not only studied the past history of France with particular predilection, but also followed her current history in every detail.' (Marx and Engels, *Selected Works*, Vol. I, pp. 245–6.)

This sociological nature of Marx's historical-political writings and the importance for his analysis of historical or real *models* was also clearly seen by Lenin in *State and Revolution* (*Selected Works in Three Volumes*, Moscow, 1967, pp. 289–90). After posing the question: 'Is it correct to generalize the experience, observations and conclusions of Marx, to apply them to a field that is wider than the history of France during the three years 1848–51 ?' he quotes the passage of Engels cited above. He then continues: 'Let us, however, cast a general glance over the history of the advanced countries at the turn of the century. We shall see that the same process went on more slowly, in more varied forms, in a much wider field: on the one hand, the development of "parliamentary power" both in the republican countries (France, America, Switzerland) and in the monarchies (Britain, Germany to a certain extent, Italy, the Scandinavian countries, etc.); on the other hand, a struggle for power among the various bourgeois and petty-bourgeois parties which distributed and redistributed the "spoils" of office, with the foundations of bourgeois society unchanged; and, lastly, the perfection and consolidation of the "executive power" of its bureaucratic and military apparatus. There is not the slightest doubt that these features are common to the whole of the modern evolution of all capitalist states in general. In the three years 1848–51 France displayed, in a swift, sharp, concentrated form, the very same processes of development which are peculiar to the whole capitalist world.' For the character of *Histoire Raisonnée* in the work of Lenin himself, see the acute observation of Lukács in *History and Class Consciousness* (p. 35); he notes that *State and Revolution* is both a theory of the revolution and at the same time an 'inner history of the European revolutions of the nineteenth century'.

[15] Marx and Engels, *Selected Correspondence*, Moscow, 1965, pp. 376–8.

with that of Kautsky. In both cases, Engels draws our attention to a crucially important theoretical motif: namely, the deformation that the concept of *social relations of production* was then just beginning to suffer at the hands of both the so-called 'orthodox' Marxists (principally Kautsky and Plekhanov) and, later and in the opposite direction, of the Austro-Marxist school.

Later I shall show how each of these tendencies can be traced in turn to the two basic orientations into which bourgeois culture was split in the second half of the nineteenth century. For the moment, however, I shall restrict myself to the 'orthodox' interpretation: for here the basic terms of the divergence can be located precisely in the manner of conceiving the unity of *material* production and production of *ideas*, of production of *things* and production of human *relations*, by which, as we have seen, Marx had succeeded in welding together history and nature.

Production is at once both the unity of distribution, exchange and consumption, and the basis of their entire interrelation. It is the totality of this relation and also what conditions and determines the relation itself. It cannot be regarded as a *prior* determination from which we can *then* pass on to the remaining ones; it is not the skeleton which we subsequently clothe in flesh and blood. The M-C relationship, to repeat, is not only simultaneously a relation between social classes; it already implies a whole series of political and superstructural conditions. To take one example: the relationship between labour-power and the other means of production, i.e. capital, is inconceivable unless we already take into account the juridico-political forms which make the modern labourer a 'free' labourer, that is a labourer free to dispose of his own person, to enter into a *contract*. In other words, unless we already take into account that formal or legal 'equality' which Marx is *obliged* in fact to bring to our attention at the end of the chapter on 'The Transformation of Money into Capital', i.e. just before the section devoted to 'The Production of Absolute Surplus Value' (*Capital*, Vol. I, Chapter 6, p. 176). It is, then, only from *within this* unity of the economic and the political that Marx induces the primary or fundamental role of the economic. This is, to repeat, precisely because it is only by virtue of this unity that the object truly becomes an *object* and hence something *determinate*. The need to consider relations of production and exchange together (and to consider the former as dominant *from within this correlation*) is a necessity inseparable from the one I have already emphasized: namely, that analysis, if it is really to be analysis and hence engage with a determinate object, must always move from *the present*, or, in our case, from the 'present-day capital' which, as Engels wrote, is the 'only really existing capital'. However, the framework we find when we turn to Kautsky and Plekhanov is different. For them, production and social relations, material and ideological relations, are on the contrary disposed in a chronological series, as *before* and *after*. Nature and history are reseparated; the necessary reference to the present moment is lost and consequently we are left with nothing but a *philosophy of history*.

It would not be appropriate here to examine concretely how this new theoretical framework considerably affected even the interpretation of the Marxist theory of crisis, either producing an 'under-consumption' version, which precisely considered consumption *only* insofar as it is a phenomenon external to production; or a version, which goes back to Tugan-Baranowsky,[16] based upon the opposite hypothesis – as Hilferding correctly showed in *Finanzkapital* (second edition, pp. 378–9) – of production alone *in itself* understood as a *purely* economic base. Quite apart from this, it remains true that in Kautsky and Plekhanov the *unity of heterogeneous elements* the axis about which Marx's theoretical forces turned, was transmuted into a series of formally combined but intrinsically disunited 'factors', stratified one on top of the other in a chronological sequence. Here, for example, is how they are presented in *The Fundamental Problems of Marxism*: '1. The state of productive forces; 2. the economic relations conditioned by these forces; 3. the socio-political regime, established upon a given economic "base"; 4. the mentality of men living in society . . . determined in part directly by the economic conditions obtaining, and in part by the entire socio-political system that has arisen on that foundation; 5. the various ideologies reflecting the above mentality.'[17]

It has been noted by one commentator that, in terms of this conception, 'the productive forces develop by themselves, automatically, outside their form of production and independently of the productive relations'; they therefore appear in the guise of an 'abstract premise for the development of all the remaining "factors".'[18]

Some might assume that this refers to an isolated or exceptional case;

[16] M. Tugan-Baranowsky, *Theoretische Grundlagen des Marxismus*, Leipzig, 1905: especially Section III, pp. 209 ff.

[17] G. Plekhanov, *The Fundamental Problems of Marxism*, London, 1969, p. 80.

[18] W. A. Fomina, *Die philosophischen Anschauungen G. W. Plechanows*, Berlin, 1957, p. 303. However, this work, by a Soviet author, is practically useless.

it is worth emphasizing that it is in fact the basic position which emerges from the writings of Plekhanov and Kautsky. 'The production of the means of subsistence and the production of men are two essentially different processes', Kautsky affirms in *Vermehrung und Entwicklung*: 'the relationship between the labourer and things, technique, like that between the consumer and the things he consumes, is clearly something quite different from the relation entered into by men in the labour process, in the economy. Only the latter is social; the former are not.'[19] Hence the unity by virtue of which Marx could affirm in *Capital* that 'the capitalist process of production, considered as a whole, or as a process of reproduction, produces not only commodities, not only surplus value, but produces and reproduces the capitalist relation itself; on one side capital, on the other wage labour', reappears here, dissolved into its abstract, elementary components; on the one side, the *natural* process, on the other the *socio-historical* process.

First nature, *then* society: the relationship is not encapsulated in its only possible concrete form, namely, by thinking the primacy of nature from within the concrete historical condition in which the problem arises, which is clearly a condition in which, besides nature, there is already also man interrogating nature and hence society, and in which the simply natural process has already been surpassed in a *historico*-natural process. Here, however, we are ingenuously transported to the origin of all worlds. We are referred back from the *Wechselwirkung* to a 'third' or 'higher' principle;[20] in effect, to the principle of Monism (in Hegel the Idea and here Matter *as such*), which now appears as the foundation of every historico-deductive process. There is no awareness that this too is to start from an *abstraction*.

Plekhanov writes: 'The characteristics of geographical environment determine the development of productive forces, which, in turn, determines the development of the economic forces and therefore of all other social relations.'[21] Up to a certain point he is thus in complete agreement with Buckle; subsequently, as the categories become increasingly stratified in the course of the chronological succession, the agreement diminishes. Productive activity, which in primitive society is seen to exercise a

[19] K. Kautsky, *Vermehrung und Entwicklung in Natur und Gesellschaft*, Stuttgart, 1910, p. 149 and p. 10.
[20] Plekhanov, 'Zu Hegel's sechzigstem Todestag', in *Die Neue Zeit*, Vol. I, 1891/2, p. 202.
[21] Plekhanov, *The Fundamental Problems of Marxism*, op. cit., p. 51.

direct influence on the world-view, works instead through the mediation of psychology in eighteenth-century France. Like Condillac's statue, history and life are here articulated through successive additions. First we have primitive man; then we make him speak; then pray; and finally write poetry. The category of language is followed by that of religion, the category of religion by that of art, and each corresponds to its historical epoch.[22] The first category to occur in time, in other words, becomes the *foundation* for the whole construction. The book which would provide a 'theoretical justification for historical materialism' would, according to Plekhanov, be a 'resumption of universal history from a materialist point of view'. He continues: 'Such a history could not be written at the present time, either by an individual scholar . . . or by a whole group', since 'a sufficiency of materials does not yet exist, nor will it exist for a long time'.[23] But this long expectation, the source of such bemoanings throughout the Marxism of the Second International – why did Marx not leave to his successors, instead of *Capital*, a reconstruction of the *whole* of history? – was first fulfilled only a few years later in the amorphous commonplaces of the older Kautsky: *Die materialistische Geschichtsauffassung*!

We cannot abandon our analysis here to explore all the implications of this argument. It is enough to emphasize the profound deformations which Marx's analysis underwent both in content and method, through this process. In contemporary Marxist writing the idea is still prevalent (and this is a typical product of the interpretation already affirmed in the Marxism of the Second International), that *Capital* is only an 'example' or 'particular application' of a general conception of the history preceding it. There is a fear that, by emphasizing how the whole of Marxism gravitates and rotates about this work, Marx might be made to appear as a student only of *this particular* phenomenon – and agnostic about all the rest. This reveals a failure to grasp what constitutes the work of *science*; or, more precisely, the (covert) acceptance of an empiricist interpretation of it, in terms of which the traditional separation of levels, between discussion of the totality (or the *philosophical* discourse) and discussion of the parts (or *scientific* discourse) is reproduced within Marxism itself. Take any concept from *Capital*; for example, the concept of labour-power. This involves grasping a very recent phenomenon, peculiar to bourgeois society, that of wage-labour; in other words, it involves understanding

[22] Plekhanov, *The Fundamental Problems of Marxism*, op. cit., pp. 60–1. For the intervention of the psychological factor, see pp. 80–3.   [23] ibid., p. 86.

only a *particular*. Yet we need only follow Marx's analysis to see that the comprehension of this 'particular' is simply the comprehension of the essential differences it presents with regard to all the preceding forms in which the labourer has appeared historically. In bourgeois society, *as opposed to* medieval society in which the direct producer still owned his own means of production, the labourer works in conditions of production which belong to others, as in the case of slavery. But, *as against* slavery, his relation to the owner of the means of production is a purely *contractual* one (the act of surrendering or hiring out work over a short period). The labourer, in other words, is free to choose or change his entrepreneur; moreover, he is not subjected to work or payment obligations *vis-à-vis* his entrepreneur other than those stipulated in the contract. To grasp the 'particular' phenomenon under examination is thus simply to understand all the differences that it presents as compared to other phenomena of its kind. It must, therefore, involve reference to this *kind* but only *negatively*, i.e. in order to seize the *opposition* or essential difference which precisely defines the specific, or fundamental, character of the modern labourer.

In order to differentiate and oppose, it is also necessary to *refer* and make connections. Clearly, the concept of labour-power also in some sense provides the common element in all the historical forms of *concrete* labour, and hence defines labour in *abstract* form, or 'in general'. For indeed, if in order to obtain the common element shared by all types of labour one cannot but ignore the various types of *objects* in terms of which labour has been specified turn and turn about in the course of history, then what remains in common to them all must be precisely the characteristic of the expenditure of labour-power. However, this reference is not an identification or confusion, but an *opposition*. The element common to all part forms is invoked in order to understand the present, but only to be *excluded* from it, i.e. only in order to reveal how the society of today is not any of these other societies but differs essentially from them. Abstract labour is indeed the element common to all types of concrete labour – but precisely insofar as it expresses the novelty, with respect to these types, of the *real* abstraction or separation from the means and object of labour that is achieved *in fact* in bourgeois society: in other words, the modern day or wage worker, i.e. labour power, in its effective separation from the instruments of production. In fact, this is Marx's own procedure in *Capital* (Vol. I, Chapter 7: 'The Labour Process and the Production of Surplus Value'); in order to show the character of productive labour under capitalism, he has to show precisely that it is quite the opposite of what it was in all pre-capitalist societies. It is thus *not* labour aimed at the production of use-values, or values for consumption (as was essentially the case in all earlier forms), but rather labour producing boots, needles, cloth (i.e. use-values) only as *means* (whence the rupture with the earlier forms) of fixing and absorbing labour-power. Clearly, the abstraction 'labour' – abstracted, that is, from the *concrete* form of work (ploughing, weaving and so on) – is here the only possible means of taking into account the specific difference, the real character of labour in *bourgeois* society. In this society the concrete modes of labour are of no consequence; they are not ends but means – precisely, concrete labours as means of expending labour-power, the products of concrete labourers as means of absorbing or fixing this expended energy. Clearly, Marx is not seeking 'general' laws, nonsensical truisms valid for all epochs. Rather, he opens a general perspective on history precisely to the extent that he develops his analysis of the present: i.e. precisely to the extent that he seizes the extreme or essential differences by which the present defines or illuminates, even if indirectly, the past.

The analysis here does not start from the 'genus' and deduce the 'species' from it; it does not start from the simple labour process and deduce from it the process of the production of value. Rather, it proceeds from the analysis of the latter, observing how it presents itself as a labour process, i.e. as formative of use-values, and as a process of valorization, or better, how it is a process of valorization realized *through* the labour process. Thus the general character of labour (conforming, assimilating natural objects to human needs) is here reduced to a mere *instrument* in a process whose aim, far from being the assimilation and adaptation of objects of labour to man, i.e. the satisfaction of needs, is rather the incorporation of living labour-power to their inert objectivity, transforming value into capital, or in other words into *value-creating value*. The 'genus' (the labour process) is treated by Marx not as a premise, but as an articulation or function within the 'species' (the process of valorization). Whence, just as by going thoroughly into the analysis of the latter we can grasp what was rather the general character of production in earlier epochs, understanding this we can also locate the difference between human labour on the one hand and that of animals on the other, as indeed Marx does in Chapter Seven of Volume I of *Capital*:

. . . A spider conducts operations that resemble those of a weaver, and a bee puts to shame many an architect in the construction of her cells. But what distinguishes the worst architect from the best of bees is this, that the architect raises his structure in imagination before he erects it in reality. At the end of every labour-process we get a result that already existed in the imagination of the labourer at its commencement. He not only effects a change of form in the material on which he works, but also realizes a purpose of his own that gives the law to his *modus operandi*, and to which he must subordinate his will. (Op. cit., p. 178.)

The analysis, then, does not start from nature and descend to society; and from society in 'general' to this society in particular. Operations of this type never work for anyone, not even for Hegel. As Marx pointed out: 'There is no bridge by which one can pass from the universal idea of the organism (whether it be vegetable, animal, social, etc.), to the particular idea of the organism of the State or the constitution of the State, nor will there ever be.'[24] Rather, one must begin with the present; as opposed to 'all forms' of society in which 'natural relations still predominate', present reality is dominated by capital; in other words, 'social, historically evolved elements predominate'.[25] Precisely establishing this 'difference', in which the chronological-historical order seems to be inverted, can we then understand how the determinate relationship in other societies was the relationship with nature and, to go further back, how before human societies there was only nature.

It is quite possible that to some this might appear a mere formal reversal. Yet it also represents a reversal in content, producing in one case the type of analysis Marx has given us in *Capital*; in the other that of Kautsky, for example – in other words, a discourse which, in the *Geschichtsauffassung*, moves from 'Mind and Universe' in the first book to 'Human Nature' (instincts, adaptation, sex., etc.) in the second, and only in the third book to 'Human Society'. Even here, note that he begins with 'Race', then turns to 'Human Geography', followed by 'Technique' (natural and artificial organs, etc.) and only after a thousand pages does he finally arrive at a series of impotent, generic definitions concerning history 'in general', classes 'in general', the State 'in general' and so on.[26]

It goes without saying that all this applies mainly to Kautsky the 'philosopher', and that even in this respect there are differences between the 'orthodox' and the later Kautsky. Yet one guiding thread is always

---

[24] Marx: *Critique of Hegel's 'Philosophy of Right'*, trans. J. O'Malley, Cambridge' 1970, p. 14.

[25] Marx, 'Introduction' to *A Contribution to the Critique of Political Economy*, op. cit., p. 213.

[26] K. Kautsky, *Die materialistische Geschichtsauffassung*, Berlin, 1927, 2 volumes.

there, even in the works of the best period: the principle whereby he moves from what all epochs have in common, only later coming to their differences; without realizing that in this way the species or particulars always remain apparent sub-divisions inside the general-generic, hence that it is impossible ever to escape from abstraction. It is true that his writings contain continuous protests against the extrapolation of biological laws into laws of development in general, against Malthusianism, Social Darwinism and so on; just as frequent is his insistence on the specificity of the laws governing each, particular society. However, only a slight knowledge of his work is sufficient to see that Marxism always appears in it as an extension of Darwinism; both are then seen as two particular moments of the genus 'evolution'.[27] There is no grasp in his work of the displacement or reversal by which in history what was once fundamental or specific becomes secondary or generic, and, on the contrary, what was once particular or generic develops into an essential or specific characteristic. Capital, for example, was in the Middle Ages only an articulation of landed property; in bourgeois society it becomes the *basis* of the whole productive process, and land-rent in turn becomes one of its subordinate moments. The same applies to natural conditioning. Climate, the fertility of the soil, and so on, all the natural conditions, operate in human history as functions of social regimes, never vice versa. Now all this may often be 'said' in Kautsky's work; but it is then denied by the ordering and basic construction of his writings. Social life, for example, is for Kautsky a specification of the instinct of self-preservation, a particular form of the struggle for existence. Yet it is never characterized by the *exclusion* of the characteristics of this struggle at other levels, and their replacement by basically new or historical-human characteristics which subordinate the older characteristics to them. Instead, the new elements are *added* to the original ones, which thus remain fundamental. Consequently, his work never moves beyond a 'generalizing framework'; the basis of everything, to use a phrase of Marx, remains 'the immortal discovery that in all conditions men must eat, drink, etc'.[28] It never escapes that generic character to which even Engels at times reduced the meaning

[27] Kautsky, op. cit., Vol. I, pp. 196–8. In his polemic against Woltmann's statement that 'economic materialism grows into *biological materialism* in the sense of Darwin's doctrine of evolution', Kautsky replied: 'The observation is correct, provided that what Woltmann calls Darwin's doctrine of evolution is understood as the doctrine of evolution in general.'

[28] Marx, 'Randglossen zu Adolf Wagners "Lehrbuch der politischen Ökonomie",' *Werke*, Vol. 19, p. 375.

of Marxism: 'Just as Darwin discovered the laws of evolution of organic nature, so Marx discovered the law of the evolution of human history', the law that 'men above all must eat, drink, be housed and clothed', a general law of development for *all* epochs of history!

This is not the place to examine how far this distortion of Marx's thought by Kautsky and Plekhanov (and I have limited my treatment here to episodic references) was already partly prepared, if only in embryo, in some aspects of Engels's work; and how in general the search for most general laws of development in nature and history made these aspects a preconstitution of the contamination with Hegelianism and Darwinism (the latter interpreted mostly according to Haeckel's extrapolation), in which the abstract 'theses' and 'antitheses' of Hegel's dialecticism were forcibly converted into 'heredity' and 'adaptation'. In the preparatory notes for his *Anti-Dühring*, for example, Engels was able to write: 'Haeckel is quite right in considering heredity as essentially the conservative, positive side of the process, and adaptation its revolutionary, negative side.'[29] These extremely generic characters are thereby transposed into the agents of the entire evolutionary process, from the cell to socialism. Nor can we examine fully here the extent to which this substitution of 'simplicity of thought' for the real foundations, and hence of logical-abstract development for concrete-historical development, contributed in turn (via the over-estimation of the work of Morgan) to the emphasis on ethnology in much of the Marxism of the period (particularly of Kautsky and Cunow). Aside from this, in many works of the period we find a formulation, if only approximate and elementary, of the thesis according to which it is precisely Hegel's basic theoretical principle – the idea of 'universal development' – that triumphs with Darwin in the field of natural science. Kuno Fischer's *History of Modern Philosophy* led the way in this respect. At the same time we also witness positivism and idealism combined acting to dissolve the concept of *cause*: on the one hand, because of a typically Hegelian distaste for the distinctions of the intellect and for causal explanation (the famous *Erklären*), and on the other, because of the positivist substitution of scientific abstraction by a mere 'historical' description.

In the same preparatory note, Engels writes:

To science definitions are worthless because always inadequate. The only real definition is the development of the thing itself, but this is no longer a

[29] Engels, *Anti-Dühring*, Moscow, 1959, Appendix, p. 469.

definition. To know and show what life is, we must examine all forms of life and present them in their interconnection.[30]

This is tantamount to admitting that simple historical–chronological succession renders the services of scientific–causal explanation; the evolutionary series of organisms must accordingly hold the key to all the problems of the structure and physiology of organic beings. Ontogenesis, as Haeckel claimed, is nothing but 'a brief and rapid recapitulation of phylogenesis'.[31] The historical dimension is not, as in Marx, welded to the rational or analytical–causal element, creating that fractional reciprocity between reason and matter, the experiment; rather, the former is substituted by the latter. Logical-abstract *continuity* is not fused with the *discontinuity* of the real and the disjunction between species, but replaces them.

We may quote Plekhanov from the *Development of the Monist View of History*:

> What should we now say of a biologist who would attempt to assert that the ultimate explanation of phylogenesis must be sought in ontogenesis? Modern biology acts in exactly the opposite way: it explains the embryological history of the *individual* by the history of the *species*.[32]

And Timirjazev explains in his tenth and final lecture on the *Historical Method in Biology*:

> Darwin and Marx built a bridge between biology and sociology, using the historical method in both cases, as Engels pointed out in his funeral speech on Marx. . . . By studying one by one all the particularities of the organic world and continually finding analogous characteristics but *never a single distinction to break this flow of continuity*, Darwin went as far as moral or mental proprieties.[33]

One sole law governs the homogeneous flow of the ages: whether in the form of the 'negation of the negation', seen as the transformation of liquids into solids, of tadpoles into frogs, and bourgeois society into socialism; or in the great law of 'heredity and adaptation'. Thus Engels asserts in *Anti-Dühring*: 'Political Economy . . . as the science of the conditions and forms under which the various human societies have

[30] Engels, *Anti-Dühring*, op. cit., p. 470.
[31] E. Cassirer, *Storia della filosofia moderna*, Turin, 1958, Vol. IV, pp. 270, 280, 283–92. (The original German text only in typescript.)
[32] G. Plekhanov, *Selected Philosophical Works*, London, 1961, Vol. I, p. 577.
[33] K. A. Timirjazev, 'Die historische Methode in der Biologie' in *Ausgewählte Werke*, Berlin, 1954, Vol. II, p. 481.

produced – political economy in this wider sense has still to be brought into being.' This is to forget what he had, correctly, intuited in his review of Marx's *Contribution to a Critique* . . .: namely, that the scientific method is not the historical-*chronological* method but rather the *logical*-historical method, or rather that the 'reflection of the historical course in abstract and theoretically consistent form' must be continuously 'corrected' and readjusted with respect to the *present*, since each category and each moment is 'to be considered at the point of development of its full maturity, of its classic form', that is, in the light of today. Similarly, Vorländer (to take an example at random), discussing the method used in *Capital* in his *Karl Marx*, regrets that 'the scientific analysis of the forms of human life does not begin, as would have been easier both for the author and for his readers . . . with the history of its effective evolution, but rather "*post festum*" with the final results of the process of development.'[34] Clearly, there is no understanding here that, if science is to be the science of *the real*, it cannot aim at the past other than by way of its *differences* with respect to the *present* (which is the only *existent*) and hence must move from the express categories of the present. Indeed, just as, for example, ground rent *cannot* be understood without capital, while capital, on the contrary, *can* be understood even without ground-rent, so it would as Marx wrote, be 'impractical and erroneous' for science to adopt categories in the order in which they have been determinant in the general course of history. Their order of sequence, according to Marx, is decided rather by their relationship to one another in modern bourgeois society; this order is precisely *the inverse of their natural succession*, as well as of their development in time. It is not, Marx concludes, a question of the place historically occupied by economic relations in the succession of the various societies, even less of their succession in the 'idea' as in the fantastic schemes of Hegel and Proudhon, but rather their *articulation within modern society*.[35]

Hence only from the materiality of the present can scientific abstraction or hypothesis, that is causal-analytical explanation, be derived; just as, inversely, only the real matter of observation, as Engels correctly noted in a passage in his *Dialectics of Nature*,[36] can 'weed out these hypo-

[34] Engels, *Anti-Dühring*, Moscow, 1959, p. 207; Marx and Engels, *Selected Works*, Vol. I, pp. 373–4; K. Vorländer, *Karl Marx, sein Leben und sein Werk*, Leipzig, 1929.

[35] Marx, 'Introduction' to *A Contribution to the Critique of Political Economy*, op. cit., p. 213.

[36] Engels, *Dialectics of Nature*, Moscow, 1966, p. 240.

theses, doing away with some and correcting others, until finally the law is established in a pure form'. To lose sight of materialism is to abandon science; but to abandon the latter, and hence the determinacy or specificity of abstractions, means in turn to lose all reference to reality. That is, the end result is those vague laws, good for any time and any place, the only effect of which is to extrapolate relations valid under *determinate conditions* to all aspects and all levels of reality. Lenin made this point extremely acutely in *The Economic Content of Populism* (1894), with reference precisely to the law of population – treated so differently sixteen years later by Kautsky in *Vermehrung und Entwicklung*. Polemicizing against Lange and Struve, he wrote: 'The conditions for human reproduction are directly dependent on the structure of the different social organisms; that is why the law of population must be studied in relation to each organism separately, and not "abstractly" without regard to the historically different forms of social structure. Lange's explanation that abstraction means to abstract the general from *similar* phenomena turns right against himself: only the conditions of existence of animals and plants can be considered similar, but this is not so with regard to man, because we know he has lived in organizationally different forms of social association.' Lenin continues: 'The thread that runs through the whole of organic nature up to man is not at all broken by Marx's theory'; it does not, in other words, break the *continuity*. 'It merely requires that the "labour problem" – since it only exists as such in capitalist society – be solved not on the basis of "general investigations" into human reproduction, but on the basis of specific investigation of the laws of capitalist relations'. Continuity, that is, must not become the pretext for cancelling out all *differences*; this would result in confusion rather than continuity. And Lenin adds: 'The good Lange has carried his zeal to the point of defending the worker against Marx, proving that the worker is "prompted by want", and that "this ever-growing want [is nothing] but the metamorphosis of the struggle for existence". Such are the discoveries resulting from "general investigations into the existence, reproduction and perfection of the human race!" Do we learn anything at all about the causes of "want", about its political-economic content and course of development if we are told that it is the metamorphosis of the struggle for existence? Why, that can be said about anything you like – about the relation of the worker to the capitalist, the landowner to the factory owner and to the peasant serf, etc., etc. We get nothing but such vapid banalities or naïveties from Lange's attempt to correct Marx.' This only reveals, according to Lenin, 'the impossibility of constructing an abstract law of population, according to the formula about correlation of growth and the means of subsistence, while ignoring historically specific systems of social relations and the stages of their development'.[37]

WEBER AND ASPECTS OF CONTEMPORARY BOURGEOIS SOCIOLOGY

In his introduction to *Die Grenzen der naturwissenschaftlichen Begriffs-bildung*,[38] while taking up a position with respect to the traditional modes of historical reflection, Rickert outlines a brief discussion of Hegel and Comte. His point can be summarized as follows: both idealist and naturalistic philosophies of history have 'discovered', as he puts it, 'meaning' and 'laws' in history, but without ever posing the problem of the theory of knowledge, i.e. without investigating whether this 'meaning' or these 'laws' exist in reality or are at least knowable for the human mind. From this standpoint, he claims, both positions lack a 'gnoseological foundation'; 'however "modern" it may still seem today, Comte's philosophy of history is no less unarmed in the face of the critique of knowledge than that of German idealism'. Both Hegel and Comte, Rickert concludes, theorized about the object without at the same time studying the conditions of the subject–object relation, in other words the conditions of historiographical *judgement*.

This observation is valid within circumscribed limits. For Hegel, discourse on logic, i.e. the subject–object relation *within the subject*, is immediately extended not only into a discourse on *the whole* of reality, but into a real process itself. The reverse is the case for positivist philosophies of history: this naturalism does see that the subject is itself a moment of objectivity, but does not go on to consider that it takes part in it with one of its specific functions, i.e. by *reflecting upon it*, and hence that as well as a *part*, it is at the same time also a *criterion* and selector of reality itself.

The defeat of both positivism and idealism, in other words, lies in their *monistic* approach; they reduce the unity-distinction of thought and being to a mere *identity*, one in the Idea, the other in Matter *as such*. The effective result of this abstract monism is, in both cases, a *de facto dualism*. In Hegel's case, it leads to the celebrated restoration of 'acritical positivism'; for example, he constructs 'a theory of light and colours on the basis of

[37] Lenin, *Collected Works*, Vol. I, pp. 453–60.
[38] H. Rickert, *Die Grenzen der naturwissenschaftlichen Begriffsbildung*, revised third and fourth editions, Tübingen, 1921, pp. 10–12.

pure thought' and this, notes Engels, is 'to fall into the most clumsy empiricism even in the limited experience of the philistines'. For Kautsky, on the other hand, *si parva licet* . . ., the result is the famous restoration of ethical idealism. For instance, after arguing consistently on the basis of animal instinct throughout his *Ethics*, he then postules a *Sollen*, an ethical ideal, which bears no relation whatever to scientific 'determinism',[39] and for which, for precisely this reason, he had to pay a high price when he came to grips with the historical roots of bourgeois 'freedom'.

If we focus on this latter orientation, which basically constituted the object of Rickert's critique to the extent that his argument was directed primarily against naturalism and, through naturalism, against the materialism or historical economism prevalent at that time, the most striking weakness of this approach is its inherent incapacity to account for the moment of *action* or human *intervention* in history. This failure is only a consequence of another: the failure to conceive of production and social relations as a totality, to understand how the *objects* of the economic process are at the same time *subjects* or social classes.

There is no need to cite the extreme case of Lafargue, who reached the point, in *Le Déterminisme économique de K. Marx*, of conceiving modifications of the social environment as changes which react 'directly and mechanically' upon men, *making them function.*[40] By and large, despite efforts in a contrary direction, we may conclude that this was more or less explicitly the position of the 'orthodox' tendency in the Marxism of the period. Plekhanov himself, in the third chapter of his *Role of the Individual in History*, reveals himself incapable of seeing the moment of *conscious* intervention or action except as a factor in a mathematical sum or, more precisely, insofar as it represents a truly individual phenomenon, in terms of mere *accident* revealed at the point of intersection of *necessary* processes.[41]

---

[39] K. Kautsky, *Ethik und Materialistische Geschichtsauffassung*, Stuttgart, 1960, pp. 140–2. This mutual interdependence of economic determinism and Kantian Moralism is, in general, well taken by Lukács in *History and Class Consciousness*, op. cit., p. 38, where he notes, for example, that 'economic fatalism and the reformation of socialism through ethics are intimately connected'. 'It is no accident', he adds, 'that they reappear in similar form in Bernstein, Tugan-Baranowsky and Otto Bauer.'

[40] P. Lafargue, *Le déterminisme économique de K. Marx*, Paris, 1909, p. 40.

[41] In contrast to this position, see Lenin, *Collected Works*, Vol. I, pp. 400–1, where he counterposes objectivism and materialism. See especially: 'The objectivist speaks of "insurmountable historical tendencies"; the materialist speaks of the class which "directs" a given economic order. . . .'

It would be interesting to see how far these positions effectively coincide with certain tendencies within positivism: some of Plekhanov's
formulations, for instance, almost literally recall similar statements by
John Stuart Mill in Book Six of his *System of Logic*, dedicated to the
'logic of the moral sciences'. Also, of course, to see what differences
remain between the two schools of thought. Nevertheless, to cut a long
story short, it is enough here to emphasize that this tendency, despite all
its undeniable internal differences, effectively reduces the moment of
subjectivity to a mere link in an objective chain of *cause and effect*, or,
alternatively, to mere accident. It precludes any possible comprehension
that human practice, including the practice of *knowledge* itself, is inscribed
in objectivity, but also involves a reversed causality, i.e. a *finalism*, a
process characterized (bearing in mind the passage from Marx on human
labour) by the anticipation or *ideal* presence, in the mind, of the result.

There is no conception, in other words, that if subjectivity is a function
of objectivity, and if the relation between man and nature is (fundamentally) a relation within nature, it is also, however, a relation between men,
in which the sensible world – like language in knowledge, and like the
object in labour – is in its turn the *medium* of the vital manifestations of
man. To take an example: insofar as Hegel's philosophy is itself objectively given, a real historical institution and social manifestation, it is clear
that Marx, in revealing that false or incongruous relation set up *within his
philosophy* between thought and being, theory and practice, also lays bare
the false relation *between* this philosophy and the world, between theory
and practice, direction and execution within objectivity, in other words
the false relation between the constituent elements of bourgeois society
itself. In this sense, as I have already argued, the works of Marx's youth,
the so-called 'philosophical' writings, already represent a social enquiry or
sociology. However, if this is true and if philosophy is itself a part, a
manifestation, a real articulation of society, it is no less true that it is
wrong to identify a philosophy immediately with the objects it seeks to
discuss. Indeed, the way in which it testifies to reality derives directly from
the way it preselects aspects of that reality and hence from its nature as a
criterion. To keep to the same example, Marx, in studying Hegel's
Philosophy of Right, was indeed also studying the bourgeois State itself;
yet, at the same time, he was studying Hegel's philosophy as a *method* or
criterion with which to reflect upon this State. The value of its testimony
to reality could not be established except by *verifying* in fact its con-
gruence with reality, in other words, by passing to a *direct* analysis of the

State and of bourgeois society as well. From this latter standpoint, Marx's youthful works are not yet *Capital*: in them, the analysis of real society is articulated only by the amount necessary to sharpen the critique of Hegel's *method* and hence to the establishment of a new methodological perspective – which, however, was only perfected much later in the 1857 Introduction to the *Grundrisse*, i.e. the first extensive rough-draft of *Capital*.

It is impossible, therefore, to exchange social objectivity for any kind of natural objectivity and to ignore the profound distortion undergone, at least by terrestrial nature, with the arrival of man; equally, we cannot exchange biology for sociology. Just as it should also be impossible, on the contrary, to take human practice, let alone *knowledge*, as the *only* objectivity. Yet this was precisely the solution presented by the other theoretical tendency of the Second International: Austro-Marxism.

Max Adler wrote (and one could easily multiply references of this kind): 'Every social causality is only current within a determinate teleological form, imprinted by man's spiritual nature; it is intrinsically finalistic.'[42] 'At the level of spiritual nature', that is to say, of man, '*being* is no longer a material state; rather it is something that can only be considered as a spiritual realization, as thought, will and action'. This implies that '*the it-could-not-be-otherwise* of the necessary, objective course of society is identical to the *choice* and reasoned reflection of the creative consciousness, which alone can pose or produce, through its willed action, this necessary course.'[43] And he concluded: 'Base and superstructure are of the same, identical nature', they form an 'indivisible whole', 'a unitary functional interdependence, in which structure and superstructure have one and the same character, a spiritual character in fact'.[44]

Theory, in other words, is not *one* manifestation of life, but the *only* form of life; reality is no more than the taking place or occurrence of choice; objectivity is nothing but the existence of the *ought*, the product or result of conscious reflection. Reacting against the naturalistic extrapolations of 'economic' determinism, this second tendency did grasp the *Wechselwirkung*, the intrinsic reciprocity of production and social relations. It did grasp, as Hilferding was to point out many years later in his last work on *The Problem of History*,[45] that 'relations of production are relations

---

[42] M. Adler, *Marx als Denker*, Berlin, 1908, p. 35.
[43] Adler, op. cit., p. 38.
[44] M. Adler, *Die Staatsauffassung des Marxismus*, Vienna, 1922, p. 88.
[45] R. Hilferding, *Il Problema Storico*, Rome, 1958.

between men and between men and existing productive forces', hence, 'just as the relation of production is also always simultaneously a legal relation', so 'every economic structure contains a given property relationship, and thus a juridical relationship'. But insofar as this tendency fails to grasp how the *Wechselwirkung* implies, precisely as such, the *distinction* of the two terms and hence the *primacy* of being, it loses this relation, reducing it once again to an *identity*. Hilferding, for example, wrote: 'Relations of production are always the sum of the relations between men; relations they establish and in which they are placed in order to produce what they require to preserve and ameliorate life.' 'The relations of production, the economic structure, is not, therefore, a natural given, but rather a legal and political relation, the content of which is determined by the needs of production.' 'Even the simplest relation of production is by no means something corporeal; it is a human relation, hence it is always spiritually human.' He rejected 'the economic mysticism, according to which economic conditions make history in an autonomous way, so to speak, behind the backs of the consciousness of real men'; he recognized that there is no material production which is not at the same time the production of human relations and hence of ideas. Yet this recognition was granted in such a way that it led to an entirely contrary affirmation; not only can 'interests only become efficacious when they become conscious', but 'only facts of consciousness can determine the will, motivating human action', the force of the state is 'autonomous', politics determines the economy, violence history. The conclusion of all this, since 'violence is blind' and 'its results cannot be foreseen', is that 'this alone is sufficient to limit any conception of historical development governed by laws'. Hilferding concluded that 'we cannot speak of necessity in Marx's sense, but only of *chance*, in the sense of Max Weber'.[46]

On one side, then, a failure to realize that 'conscious, free activity is the specific characteristic of man', that 'man makes his vital activity itself the object of his will and consciousness' and hence that 'conscious, vital activity directly distinguishes human from animal activity' (Marx). On the other side an equal failure to consider that this conscious activity is a property of man insofar as he is an objective natural being – i.e. insofar

---

[46] For the connotation of classes in terms not of their role within production, but of a pure relation of political power, see also Kelsen, *The Communist Theory of Law*, op. cit., pp. 26–9. 'A class may be characterized as "proletarian" to the extent that it is oppressed by another class. . . . A class is "bourgeois" only insofar as it oppresses another class in order to exploit it. As soon as it becomes oppressed, it ceases to be a bourgeoisie.'

as he is part of nature – and hence that reference by man to his own genus or to himself is also, fundamentally, a reference to the *other* beings of nature, a *production* by the criteria of every species. In the first case, in sum, generalizations which take as homogeneous what is not homogeneous, which confuse biology and sociology and, precisely because of their generic or indeterminate nature, cannot but limit the moment of subjective intervention to the role of mere inessential accident. In the second case, on the contrary, a re-evaluation of the subjective or *individual* moment as a moment that excludes generalization, and hence as mere *unrepeatability* that is irreducible to law and hence to truly scientific understanding. Here we have come to the various 'neocriticist' philosophies, and in particular the philosophy of 'values' of Windelband and Rickert, with its separation in principle between nature and history, between *Naturwissenschaften* and *Kulturwissenschaften*, between causality and finalism, between generalizing and individualizing knowledge, between *Erklären* and *Verstehen*, and whose principal objective is not yet that of questioning the possibility of 'sociology' as such (which it accepts, provided that this is strictly understood as a science of *purely* natural regularities), but rather that of rejecting the possibility of any *naturwissenschaftliche Geschichte*,[47] i.e. the possibility of that comprehension of history as a 'historico-natural' process, mentioned precisely in *Capital*, and which as Lenin affirmed had allowed for the first time 'a rigorously scientific approach towards historical and social problems', permitting 'the discovery of repetition and regularity', and placing sociology for the first time 'on a scientific footing, establishing the concept of socio-economic formation as a complex unity of determined relations of production, and (finally) explaining the evolution of such formations as a historical-natural process'.[48]

This is not the place to stop and examine in detail how this separation between generalizing knowledge (in the sense of *generic* generalizations) and individualizing knowledge, at first seen by Rickert only as a 'methodological' distinction between subjective 'viewpoints', inevitably grew thereafter into a separation between 'fields', between objective spheres of research. At this point it is more relevant to show how this dualism of history and nature was subsequently reproduced within historical knowledge itself. In the first place, it determined a reduction of the individual

[47] Rickert, *Die Grenzen*, op. cit., p. 201.
[48] cf. C. Luporini, 'Marxismo e Sociologia: Il Concetto di formazione economico-sociale', in *Filosofia e Sociologia*, by various authors, Bologna, 1954, pp. 195 ff.

object to the mere *category* which defined it; for example, Rickert wrote: 'We do not seek to recover science from the concept of its object, so much as inversely to recover the concept of the object from the concept of the science which discusses it.'[49] Secondly, it produced an insoluble dualism between the historical concept on the one hand, and the individual to which it applied on the other, as for example where, having stated that the individual is *indivisible*,[50] unrepeatable, and hence not accessible to analysis, Rickert goes on to entrust the task of historiography to that 'refugee' from thought[51] – the historian's intuition.

On the one hand, we have a distinction of principle between the social sciences and natural sciences; the former understood as sciences which *construct* or create their own object, the latter as those which deal with *physical* data. On the other hand, within the social sciences a new line is drawn between disciplines that to some extent involve generalization and history, properly speaking; between 'relatively historical' and 'absolutely historical' concepts; or, to introduce Max Weber at last, between 'ideal types' and reality. In the first case, the result is a viewpoint which, to quote Dobb, sees 'the "whole" with which social theories deal [as] concerned with relations that are not definable in terms of common physical properties, but only in *teleological* terms of attitudes which we recognise as similar by analogy with the character of our own minds. Hence from knowledge of our own minds we can derive *a priori* all the general notions which form the subject matter of social theory.' In the case of economics, this reduction of society simply to human relations has as its corollary 'the selection of *the market* as the sole province of economics'; the problem of 'adapting scarce means to given ends' (where 'ends' are defined subjectively in terms of human wishes) becomes 'the aspect of the market upon which economic study is focused'. As regards the second case, while economic theory, as Dobbs puts it, 'at least since Jevons and the Austrians, has increasingly been cast in terms of properties that are common to any type of exchange society . . . institutional, or historico-relative material, while it has not been excluded entirely, has only been introduced into the second storey of the building, being treated in the main as changes in "data" which may influence the value of the relevant variables, but do not alter the main equations themselves by which the governing relationships are defined'. More precisely, 'a line of demarcation is drawn between an autonomous sphere of exchange-relations, possessed of properties and ruled by necessities that are, in the main, independent of any change of

[49] Rickert, op. cit., p. 173.   [50] ibid., pp. 242–3.   [51] ibid., p. 266.

"system", a sphere which is the province of economists; and the sphere of property institutions and class relations which is the territory where sociologists and historians of institutions, with their talk of "systems", can riot to their heart's content.'[52]

We are confronted, then, by a dissociation of nature from history, of economics from politics, of economics from sociology, which only serves to illuminate, by contrast, the greatness of Marx's theoretical achievement. As Schumpeter writes:

There is, however, one thing of fundamental importance for the methodology of economics which he (Marx) actually achieved. Economists always have either themselves done work in economic history or else used the historical work of others. But the facts of economic history were assigned to a separate compartment. They entered theory, if at all, merely in the role of illustrations, or possibly of verifications of results. They mixed with it only mechanically. Now Marx's mixture is a chemical one, that is to say, he introduced them into the very argument that produces results. He was the first economist of top rank to see and to teach systematically how economic theory may be turned into historical analysis and how the historical narrative may be turned into *histoire raisonnée*.[53]

This in turn provides us with the necessary perspective to approach Weber's theory of 'ideal types', that is, the confluence of 'Neocriticist' and 'Marginalist' theory: an attempt, not without subjective greatness, but objectively somewhat desperate, to produce a response from the bourgeois camp; or, better still, a simultaneous refutation and 'capture' of certain basic aspects of Marx's thought.[54]

This is not the place to underline and estimate the extent to which Weber, adopting and updating Rickert's critical insights on Hegel and Comte, was able to make light work of the interpretations of Marx's thought prevalent at that time in Germany. In some cases, he even adopted for the purpose of this polemic his own 'reinterpretation' of certain basic elements of Marx's thought which had for some time escaped the theoretical horizon of the Second International. His observations on the 'will-to-believe of naturalistic monism' (induced by 'the vigorous development of zoologist research on the one hand and the influence of Hegelian panlogism on the other'), which subordinated

---

[52] M. Dobb, *Studies in the Development of Capitalism*, London, 1947, pp. 27–8.

[53] Schumpeter, op. cit., p. 44.

[54] For a profile of Max Weber traced in terms of his criticism of Marx, cf. the introduction by E. Baumgarten to M. Weber, *Soziologie, Weltgeschichtliche Analysen, Politik*, Stuttgart, 1956, pp. xxvii ff.

'everything essential about the object to a scheme of universally valid laws';[55] even his sarcastic references to 'laymen and dilettantes' who 'through the inevitable monistic tendency of every type of thought which is not self-critical . . . content themselves with the most threadbare hypotheses and the most general phrases'; all this certainly points to real weaknesses in the 'orthodox' Marxism of that period – although it is then immediately and too conveniently extended to include the 'so-called "materialist conception of history" with the crude elements of genius of the early form which appeared, for instance, in the *Communist Manifesto*'.[56] The same can be said for some of his acute remarks concerning historical-chronological method, i.e. the substitution of 'priority in time' for general foundation or cause.

A cosmic 'primeval state' which had no individual character or less individual character than the cosmic reality of the present would naturally be a meaningless notion. But is there not some trace of similar ideas in our field in those propositions sometimes derived from natural law and sometimes verified by the observations of 'primitives', concerning an economic-social 'primeval state' free from historical 'accidents', and characterized by phenomena such as 'primitive agrarian communism', sexual 'promiscuity', etc., from which individual historical development emerges by a sort of fall from grace into concreteness?[57]

It is easy to concede the correctness of this observation, as well as the general efficacity, given the historical and cultural context of the period, of the claim that 'for the knowledge of historical phenomena in their concreteness, the most *general* laws, because they are devoid of content, are also the least valuable. The more comprehensive the validity – or *scope* – of a term, the more it *leads us away* from the richness of reality . . .'.[58] However, granted this, it is equally crucial to understand that Weber's response to the various extrapolations of monism never transgresses the limits imposed by his own essentially 'neocriticist' stance, i.e. the renewed proposition of a demarcation of spheres between the natural sciences, oriented to the determination of a system of *laws*, and the cultural sciences, aimed instead at the discovery of 'cultural significance' in human events in all their individuality. Despite the masks and refinements, this is a renewal of the Kantian dualism of *Müssen* and *Sollen*, *knowledge* and *freedom*, natural determinism and ethical life.

At first sight, this would seem to contradict one of the basic characteristics of Weber's thought: the 'ethical neutrality' (*wertfreiheit*) of the social

[55] M. Weber, *The Methodology of the Social Sciences*, Glencoe, 1949, p. 86.
[56] ibid., pp. 68-9.   [57] ibid., pp. 73-4.   [58] ibid., p. 80.

sciences, the independence claimed for scientific historical research from so-called '*value judgements*', that is from 'choices', preferences and so on. We will in due course return to this question. At this point, however, we may note that precisely because of this dualism, the object 'history' undergoes a remarkable reduction at Weber's hands – as it had at Rickert's – to a history of *cultural phenomena alone*. Man is reduced to a purely *cultural being*; economic structure itself is reduced to the mere '*cultural significance* of the economic structure'.[59]

Man appears here only in the form of the *Sinngeber*, the one who extends 'meaning' to reality; while reality is itself reduced until it is *significant* not only insofar as it is exclusively a human product, but insofar as it is a product of the *conscious*, or *cultural*, action of man. For Weber, historical objects *par excellence* arc 'Karl Marx's *Capital*, the Sistine Chapel ceiling, or Rousseau's *Confession*', etc.[60] One could, of course, add exchange, money, or the social phenomenon of prostitution, but *only* to the extent that 'prostitution is a *cultural* phenomenon, on a par with religion or money'.[61] Objectivity only has a bearing as a *vehicle of human communication*; only as a *means* used by men to manifest their ideas and sentiments (in writings, speeches, paintings, acts and gestures, etc.). The reciprocity is never seen; namely, that this exchange of ideas not only takes place between subjects who are also natural beings – and hence cannot fail to produce, with their interconnections, *objective* social relations – but also that these social relations themselves arise, in turn, on the basis of *production*, as an organic exchange within nature, and hence only on the basis of a relation in which man and society appear (in the final analysis) as the vehicle and *means* for a mediation within nature.

History in culture alone; while culture is a 'finite segment of the meaningless infinity of the world process, a segment on which human beings confer meaning and significance'.[62] This means that *industry* is excluded; the relation which, as Marx says, '*objectifies* before us *the essential forces of man*', which provides an '*open book*' of these forces, 'presenting human *psychology* to us in an immediate, concrete form'. All human practice and activity contracts into *consciousness*, i.e. into *intentional* behaviour; it is not what men *do* that counts, but rather the manner in which they *conceive* what they do. From this viewpoint, as Dobb writes: 'Such things as money or capital are not definable in terms of the actual uses to which we find that they are put', but rather 'in terms of the opinions people hold

---

[59] ibid., pp. 77–8.   [60] ibid., p. 144.
[61] ibid., p. 81.   [62] ibid., p. 81.

about them'. This means for Hayek (following Max Weber's line of thought) that the entities which are objects of the social sciences 'are not physical facts', but rather 'wholes' constituted out of 'familiar categories of our own minds'. 'Theories of the social sciences,' he writes, 'do not consist of "laws" in the sense of empirical rules about the behaviour of objects definable in physical terms'; all they provide is 'a technique of reasoning which assists us in connecting individual facts' and can 'never be verified or falsified by reference to facts'. Hayek concludes that 'all we can and must verify is the presence of our assumptions in the particular case. . . . The theory itself . . . can only be tested for consistency.'[63]

The *object* of history consists, then, of men, intentional behaviour, 'world intuitions', 'choices', the goals which have guided their actions, their adoption of positions in favour of certain 'values'. This for Weber constitutes the human-historical *being* or object. Science and knowledge, however, cannot discuss the virtues of values; they cannot counterpose value judgements against value judgements. What they can do is provide a *technical critique* alone, examine within a given teleological action the suitability of the means to the end, determining 'which means for the achievement of a proposed end are appropriate or inappropriate', making it possible to measure their *chances* of success.[64] We can now see why Weber had to accept either a dualism between knowledge and life, between science and reality, or – what is the same thing – irrationalism. For indeed, if objectivity is reduced to mere intentional behaviour, or to 'means-end' relationships, only real and concrete insofar as their 'ends' are effectively *willed*, then it is clear that science must either penetrate this reality, identifying itself with the 'ends' in question, in which case it is no longer *theory* but rather itself a *choice* and life-action, or, alternatively, it does not choose and remains a mere *reflection* upon these ends, but then it loses their concreteness. In the first case, science no longer offers *criteria* for life but is *life* itself; in the second, *reasoning upon* the 'ends', it can never make itself adequate to their effective nature, for they are not objects of theory but objects of *will*.[65]

In the first place, science only refers to the individual historical event or intentional action, and must therefore enclose it in the framework of the

[63] Dobb, op. cit., pp. 27–8, n.

[64] Weber, *The Methodology of the Social Sciences*, op. cit., pp. 52–3.

[65] Interesting insights on the irrationalism of Max Weber may be found in G. Lukács, *Die Zerstörung der Vernunft*, Berlin, 1954, pp. 474 ff., but the general orientation of this analysis is somewhat dubious.

'means-end' *made* relation; since this is only theorized and precisely not 'willed', it must resolve itself into a relation of abstract concepts; the result is precisely 'a conceptual pattern . . . conceived as a formally consistent system', but which 'in content is like a utopia',[66] i.e. has no correlate in reality. (Hence theory cannot grasp the real; abstraction always remains external to life.) In the second place, to the extent that theory really wants to reach reality, it is no longer theory; 'The "interpretation" of intellectual and mental (*geistigen*), aesthetic or ethical creations has . . . the effects of the latter' (that is, it is not strictly *interpretation*, so much as a value choice). Or, as Weber concludes: 'the assertion that "history" in a certain sense is an "art" has in this respect its justifiable "kernel of truth", no less than the designation of the cultural and humanistic sciences as "subjectivizing".'[67]

It is within this framework of alternatives that Weber's theory of 'ideal types' takes shape. In one sense, his 'ideal type' is merely the abstraction of the Marginalists, that is, a purely abstract and *conventional* 'model' which 'can never be empirically traced in reality' but which, like every *utopia*, is formed precisely 'through the one-sided *accentuation* of one or more points of view and by the synthesis of a great many diffuse, discrete, more or less present and occasionally absent, *concrete individual* phenomena . . . arranged . . . in a unified *analytical* construct', which is entirely formal. In this sense, for example, 'abstract economic theory' 'offers an ideal picture of events on the commodity-market under conditions of a society organized on the principles of an exchange economy, free competition and rigorously rational conduct'.[68] Or again, in very much the same way one can work the "idea" of "handicraft" into a utopia by arranging certain traits, actually found in an unclear, confused, state in the industrial enterprises of the most diverse epochs and countries . . .'[69] (Yet Weber had a sufficient knowledge of Marx to know that this meant coming to the defence of all the bourgeois 'Robinsonades': cf. p. 98.) In another sense, however, the 'ideal type' is not a generic abstraction or *utopia* formed by taking the "accentuation' of certain real traits to their extreme limit, *forcing* scientific *simplification* to the point where notions are obtained like 'city economy' or 'country economy', which no longer bear any resemblance to the historical regimes of production to which they refer. Rather they merely express not an abstraction but an *individual*

[66] Weber, *The Methodology of the Social Sciences*, op. cit., p. 90.
[67] ibid., pp. 144-5.
[68] ibid., pp. 90-1.   [69] ibid., pp. 90-1.

value – and not just individual, but unrelated to the whole course of history; the value which, according to Weber, inclusively resumes the 'present-day Christian capitalistic constitutional culture', the only culture we can fully understand, both because it is the only one to which our historical *interest* is oriented, and because this interest in turn is based exclusively upon its values.[70]

It was mentioned earlier on that in his polemic against historical materialism, Max Weber attempted to make use of certain basic elements of Marx's thought, especially those that were at the time beyond the theoretical horizons of the Marxism of the Second International. This is the case, in particular, both with the theory of 'ideal types' – Weber explicitly refers to Marx precisely for the construction of one of the most important examples of an ideal type[71] – and (which amounts to the same thing) with the concept of 'social formation', which he attempted in his fashion to adapt and 'reinterpret', especially in *Über einige Kategorien der verstehenden Soziologie*. Even a superficial comparison is enough to show, not so much the difference between the two approaches, for this is obvious, but rather the unequal possibilities of resolution offered by Weber's 'ideal types' and Marx's 'determinate abstractions'. The achievement represented by the latter appears in Weber only in a dissociated form: on one hand as mere *abstraction*, on the other as mere *individuality* or value, without the two aspects ever being merged or compounded.

Weber, then, was acutely aware that science operates by *simplification*, or, as Hegel put it, by *sharpening* the obtuse multiplicity of the real in order to grasp it in the form of *essential difference*. He understood (against Rickert) that the moment of abstraction, or typification, was also indispensable to the social sciences; that Marx, indeed, was not Comte; that the abstractions of *Capital* were quite different from the vague generalities of the philosophies of history. He grasped, in other words, the *functional* nature of these abstractions. However, the *present* from which he moved was not the material organization of *this* society, but only the 'values' *present* to his own consciousness as a bourgeois intellectual. His abstractions, therefore, lacked that 'material of observation' which, precisely because it is *material*, can 'weed out . . . hypotheses, doing away with some and correcting others until finally the law is established in a pure form' (Engels). Hence in Weber the functional character of scientific abstractions degenerated into a mere *conventionalism*, i.e. into the im-

[70] ibid., pp. 155-7. [71] ibid., p. 103.

possibility of evading the plurality of causes by experimental verification. The scientific concept became a *utopia*, an indeterminate notion; this notion was extended to link together the most disparate phenomena, regardless of the specificities of socio-historical regimes (as in Weber's concepts of bureaucracy, the state, etc.), calmly assimilating elements specific to the present and to the past. This indeterminacy can be seen, for example, in the fact that Weber recognized his *'idea' of capitalist culture* in only one of a great many utopias of this kind, which could be worked out, 'of which *none* is like another and *none* of which can be observed in empirical reality'.[72] The content of theoretical generalization could not, in other words, engage with reality. Analytical-causal explanation, which in its dissolution had, with positivism, taken the path of mere historical *descriptivism*, has now been dispersed into the multiplicity of causes and hence into a mere *probability calculation*.

Inversely, having lost the possibility of seeing that scientific abstraction is not a vacuous generalization, but the simplest characterization of a concrete object of study, and hence a real aspect of the object itself, Weber could reformulate the instance of the *present* only on the ground of the irrationalism of the philosophy of values, not only as *value* (rather than *fact*) but as an incommunicable, 'non-relative' value. The comprehension of the present had now to be presented only in the aspects in which it *excludes* the past; the latter only had a bearing as a means 'to delimit certain concepts with which we operate in the study of *European* cultural history, from the quite different cultural traits'[73] of other previous cultures. He failed to see that the differences *between* past and present also divide the past *from today*, and are hence ways of throwing light on the relativity and transitory character of the present. Science, which Weber had earlier understood only as a technical critique or logico-formal construction, neutral and external to real content (or 'values' to employ Weber's terminology), now had itself to be turned into a *value* or *choice*, as gratuitous and unquestionable as any other. Science is thereby demoted to the level of a form of human conduct, as individual and arbitrary as any other subjective belief. At most, it represents no more than a means of 'intuitively understanding life and reality' in one out of many epochs – specifically the bourgeois, capitalist epoch.

Weber sought the essence of capitalism, not in its economic anatomy and physiology but in that variety of mental attitudes and forms of human behaviour that he summed up in the notion of 'the spirit of capitalism',

[72] ibid., p. 91.   [73] ibid., p. 156.

i.e. in that still generic notion 'calculability', charactcristic of the running of the capitalist enterprise, and hence in the attitude of 'rational and systematic pursuit of profit'. Capitalism, therefore, came for him to be more or less identified with the rational simplification of science and technique. Thus, inversely, the latter could only appear to Weber now as no more than a subjective belief, and precisely one of the 'values' or goals, irrational like the ideals of all other epochs, produced by a particular civilization in response to the 'challenge' presented to it by the world.[74]

Having started from the point of departure that historical reality is a reality consisting only of *intentional* conduct, we now discover that the same is true of *reflection* on this reality, i.e. science. Not only social relations are ideological relations – the science of society itself is ideology. Here we can already discern the further development (and impoverishment) of Weber's work by Mannheim. Social reality for Mannheim is nothing more than the totality of the 'meanings' attributed to the world by members of society; these meanings, however, contain nothing objective, they only have a 'certain psychological-sociological function, namely to fix the attention of those men who wish to do something in common upon a certain "definition of the situation".'[75] I.e. concepts now represent only 'taboos against other possible sources of meaning', mere 'myths' or pragmatic instruments which allow a 'simplifying and unifying of the manifoldness of life for the sake of action'. Not only is all reality 'ideologies', but the *Wissensoziologie* that discusses them, the ideology of ideology, too, is an ideology.[76] Once knowledge is considered *merely* as a manifestation of human life, rather than also as a testimony and *reflection* upon reality, it has nothing to manifest but the collective 'unconscious' or 'psyche'. Thus sociology becomes a *psychoanalysis* of society, i.e. a way of 'discovering' that every form of knowledge is merely a vehicle and mask for psychological interests, while, inversely, the revelation of this state of affairs is a 'catharthis', a purifying form of knowledge. The connection with Weber is still evident. Only – as Lukács correctly observes[77] – Rickert's neo-Kantianism has now been replaced by 'a sociologized form of existential philosophy *à la* Jaspers-Heidegger'; that is, by an even more contrived and disordered irrationalism, if that were possible.

---

[74] Merleau-Ponty takes up some of these themes, banalizing them, in *Les Aventures de la Dialectique*, Paris, 1955; for example, p. 36.

[75] K. Mannheim, *Ideology and Utopia*, London, 1960, p. 19.

[76] ibid., pp. 20, 69.

[77] Lukács, *Die Zerstörung der Vernunft*, op. cit., p. 501.

Bernstein and the Marxism of the Second International

In the introduction he wrote for the first reprinting of *The Class Struggles in France*, in March 1895 – only a few months before his death – Engels observes that the chief error made by Marx and himself at the time of the 1848 revolution was that they had treated the European situation as ripe for socialist transformation:

History has proved us, and all those who thought like us, wrong. It has made clear that the state of èconomic development on the continent at that time was not by a long way ripe for the elimination of capitalist production; it has proved this by the economic revolution, which, since 1848, has seized the whole of the continent . . . and has made Germany positively an industrial country of the first rank. . . .[1]

According to Engels, this error of judgement concerning the real level of capitalist development in 1848 was to a considerable extent matched by a mistaken *political* conception that he and Marx had derived from preceding revolutionary experience, and particularly that of France: the idea of revolution as the action of a *minority*. 'It was . . . natural and unavoidable that our conceptions of the nature and course of the "social" revolution proclaimed in Paris in February 1848, of the revolution of the proletariat, should be strongly coloured by memories of the prototypes of 1789 and 1830.' While 'all revolutions up to the present day have resulted in the displacement of one definite class rule by another', 'all ruling classes up to now have been only small minorities in relation to the ruled mass of the people'; hence, 'the common form of all these revolutions was that they were minority revolutions. Even when the majority took part, it did so – whether wittingly or not – only in the service of the minority; but

---

[1] Marx and Engels, *Selected Works* in one volume, London, 1968, p. 656. All the following quotations are from Engels's introduction (pp. 651–68), dated London, 6 March 1895.

because of this, or simply because of the passive, unresisting attitude of the majority, this minority acquired the appearance of being the representative of the whole people.'

The undue extension of this character of preceding revolutions to 'the struggle of the proletariat for its emancipation' had now been sharply contradicted by history. History 'has done even more: it has not merely dispelled the erroneous notions we then held; it has also completely transformed the conditions under which the proletariat has to fight. The mode of struggle of 1848 is today obsolete in every respect, and this is a point which deserves closer examination on the present occasion.'

The conclusion Engels drew from this analysis was that, given the scale of modern standing armies (besides, of course, the character of socialist transformation itself), 'the time of surprise attacks, of revolutions carried out by small conscious minorities at the head of the unconscious masses', is irrevocably past. 'Where it is a question of a complete transformation of the social organisation, the masses themselves must also be in it, must themselves already have grasped what is at stake, what they are going in for, body and soul. The history of the last fifty years has taught us that. But in order that the masses may understand what is to be done, long persistent work is required and it is just this work which we are now pursuing and with a success which drives the enemy to despair.'

The necessity for this long, patient work, – 'slow propaganda work and parliamentary activity' – is recognized as 'the immediate task of the party' not only in Germany but also in France and other 'Latin countries', where, 'it is realized more and more that the old tactics must be revised'. But, 'whatever may happen in other countries', this was the path that German Social Democracy, as the vanguard of the international movement, must continue to pursue.

The two million voters whom it sends to the ballot box, together with the young men and women who stand behind them as non-voters, form the most numerous, most compact mass, the decisive 'shock force' of the international proletarian army. This mass already supplies over a fourth of the votes cast; and as by-elections to the *Reichstag*, the Diet elections in individual states, the municipal council and trades court elections demonstrate, it increases incessantly. Its growth proceeds as spontaneously, as steadily, as irresistibly, and at the same time as tranquilly as a natural process. All government intervention has proved powerless against it. We can count even today on two and a quarter million voters. If it continues in this fashion, by the end of the century we shall conquer the greater part of the middle strata of society, petty bourgeois and small peasants, and grow into the decisive power in the land, before which all other powers will have to bow, whether they like it or not. To keep this growth going without interruption until it of itself gets beyond the control of the prevailing governmental system, that is our main task.

This confident vision of the direction of events and the rapidity with which the goal could be attained ('by the end of the century' or within five years if the process were not interrupted by tactical errors), enabled Engels to re-emphasize the central theme of his text: namely, the necessity and timeliness of the 'turn' which German Social Democracy had made and which was now on the agenda in other countries as well. This 're-vision' of the old tactics was now essential, since today 'there is only one means by which the steady rise of the socialist fighting forces in Germany could be temporarily halted, and even thrown back for some time: a clash on a big scale with the military, a blood-letting like that of 1871 in Paris'. This too would be overcome in the long run, but, it could not but 'impede' the 'normal development'.

On the other hand, the new tactics alone could further and ensure the progressive and irresistible development towards socialism which capital-ist development itself, now at the peak of its maturity, demanded: the tactics of the 'intelligent utilization' the German workers had been able to make of universal suffrage, and to which they owed the astonishing growth of the party, documented by the statistics of its electoral support, which Engels quoted:

Thanks to the intelligent use which the German workers made of the univer-sal suffrage . . . the astonishing growth of the party is made plain to all the world by incontestable figures: 1871, 102,000; 1874, 352,000; 1877, 493,000 Social-Democratic votes. Then came recognition of this advance by high authority in the shape of the Anti-Socialist Law; the party was temporarily broken up, the number of votes dropped to 312,000 in 1881. But that was quickly overcome, and then . . . rapid expansion really began: 1884, 550,000; 1887, 763,000; 1890, 1,427,000 votes. Thereupon the hand of the State was paralysed. The Anti-Socialist Law disappeared; socialist votes rose to 1,787,000, over a quarter of all the votes cast. The government and the ruling classes had exhausted all their expedients – uselessly, purposelessly, unsuccessfully. . . . The state was at the end of its tether, the workers only at the beginning of theirs.

By this use of the franchise, the German workers had not only built 'the strongest, most disciplined and rapidly growing Socialist Party'. They had also supplied 'their comrades in all countries with a new weapon, and one of the sharpest' in showing them how to use universal suffrage. The franchise had been 'in the words of the French Marxist programme, *transformé, de moyen de duperie qu'il a été jusqu'ici, en instrument d'émancipation* – transformed by them from a means of deception, which it was before, into an instrument of emancipation'. It was precisely this 'successful utilization of universal suffrage' that constituted the 'new method of struggle' already adopted, which the proletariat should seek to use also in the future. It was already crystal-clear that the '*bourgeoisie* and the Government' had come to be 'much more afraid of the legal than the illegal action of the workers' party, of the results of elections than those of rebellions'.

Engels concluded:

The irony of world history turns everything upside down. We the 'revolutionists', the 'overthrowers', we are thriving far better on legal methods than on illegal methods and overthrow. The parties of order, as they call themselves, are perishing under the legal conditions created by themselves. They cry despairingly with Odilon Barrot: *la légalité nous tue*, legality is the death of us; whereas we, under this legality, get firm muscles and rosy cheeks and look like life eternal.

THE SUBSTANCE OF BERNSTEIN'S CRITIQUE

This text of Engels, which became, through his subsequent death, a political testament, dated from 1895. A year later, Bernstein began to publish the series of articles in *Die Neue Zeit* called *Problems of Socialism*. These were interrupted and begun afresh several times between 1896 and 1898 in response to the polemical reactions they raised; they finally appeared in March 1899, recast and amplified by the author, under the title: *The Premises of Socialism and the Tasks of Social Democracy*.[2] Bernstein's approach to his theme immediately recalls the questions Engels had raised in his 'Introduction': the erroneous judgement of Marx and himself concerning the temporality of social and political developments; the mistaken conception of revolution as a 'revolution of the minority',

---

[2] E. Bernstein, *Die Voraussetzungen des Sozialismus und die Aufgaben der Sozialdemokratie*, Stuttgart, 1899, published in English under the title *Evolutionary Socialism*. The major rejoinders to Bernstein's book were those of Kautsky, *Bernstein und das sozialdemokratische Programm*, Stuttgart, 1899, and Rosa Luxemburg, *Sozialreform oder Revolution?*, Leipzig, 1899, published in English as *Social Reform or Revolution?* London, 1966. Cf. also the articles Plekhanov wrote in criticism of *Problems of Socialism* and in response to Conrad Schmidt's reply in defence of Bernstein, in the Russian edition of his *Works*, Vol. XI.

the need to 'revise' outdated insurrectionist tactics in favour of new tactics based on utilization of the franchise, already adopted by the German Social Democrats.

Engels had written of a revision of *tactics*; Bernstein objected that this tactical revision necessarily implied a revision of *strategy*, a revision of the premises of theoretical Marxism. The errors denounced by Engels were not merely a result of contingent factors; they derived from essential points of doctrine and until the latter were revised it would be impossible to avoid making these errors. Bernstein was not disputing the new tactics. The political practice of the party was correct. But in order to proceed unhesitatingly and without contradictions along the path indicated by the new tactics, it was, he claimed, essential to free the party from the utopian and insurrectionist phraseology cultivated by the old theory. 'The practice of the German party has frequently, indeed almost always, been opportunist in character.' Despite this, or precisely because of this, 'its policy has in every case proved more correct than its phraseology. Hence I have no wish to reform the actual policy of the party . . .; what I am striving for, and as a theoretician must strive for, is a unity between theory and reality, between phraseology and action.'[3] This statement is from a letter to Bebel, written in October 1898. In February 1899, Bernstein wrote to Victor Adler as follows: 'The doctrine [i.e. Marxism] is not sufficiently realistic for me; it has, so to speak, lagged behind the practical development of the movement. It may possibly still be all right for Russia . . . but in Germany we have outgrown its old form.'[4]

There was then, according to Bernstein, a contradiction between the theoretical premises of socialism and the practice of Social Democracy – hence the title of his book. The task he proposed was that of examining the theory, now outdated and utopian, and bringing it into line with the practical politics of the party. In short, the aim was to contest the necessary relation between Marxism and the workers' movement. Socialism must liberate itself from the encumbrance of the old theory. 'The defect of Marxism' lay in its 'excessive abstraction' and the 'theoretical phraseology' which resulted. 'Do not forget,' he wrote to Bebel, 'that *Capital*, with all its scientificity, was in the last analysis a tendentious work and remained incomplete; it did so, in my opinion, precisely because the conflict between scientificity and tendency made Marx's task more and

[3] V. Adler, *Briefwechsel mit August Bebel und Karl Kautsky*, Vienna, 1954, p. 259. Bernstein's letter to Bebel is dated 20 October 1898.

[4] ibid., p. 289.

more difficult. Seen from this standpoint, the destiny of this great work is almost symbolic and constitutes, in any event, an eloquent warning.'[5]

The errors denounced by Engels were not, therefore, accidental but sprang from the theory itself. The incorrect estimation of the temporality of capitalist development resulted from a dialectical apriorism of the Hegelian type, from the fatalism and determinism of the materialist conception of history. It was, in short, the error of the 'theory of breakdown' (*Zusammenbruchstheorie*), the constant expectation of the inevitable and imminent 'catastrophe', to which, according to Marxism, the capitalist system was condemned by its very nature. The incorrect notion in 1848 of a seizure of power by 'revolution' or through a 'political catastrophe' and hence the overthrow of the state, also arose from an aprioristic and tendentious cast in Marx's argument, an argument shared in this case, in Bernstein's view, completely with Blanquism.

In short, an apriorism deriving from the conception of historical development in terms of dialectical antithesis, and a tendentious spirit or, as one might put it today, an 'ideological' intention, induced Marx to do violence to the evidence of scientific analysis. To this basic error Bernstein ascribed the theory of the polarization of society into two classes: the idea of the growing immiseration and proletarianization of the middle strata; and finally, the concept of the progressive worsening of economic crises and the consequent growth of revolutionary tension.

The proof of the apriori character of all these theses lay, according to Bernstein, in the fact that they had been invalidated by the course of history. Things had not proceeded in the way Marx had hoped and predicted. There was no concentration of production and no elimination of small- by large-scale enterprises; while this concentration had taken place extremely slowly in commerce and industry, in agriculture the elimination of small units had not merely failed to occur – the opposite was the case. No worsening and intensification of crises; not only had these become more rare and less acute, but with the formation of cartels and trusts capitalism now had at its disposal more means of self-regulation. Finally, no polarization of society into two extreme classes; on the contrary, the absence of any *proletarianization* of the middle strata and the improvement of living conditions of the working classes had attenuated, rather than exacerbated, the class struggle. 'The aggravation of social relations,' Bernstein wrote, 'has not occurred in the manner described in the *Manifesto*. To attempt to conceal this fact is not only useless but mad. The

[5] ibid., p. 261.

number of property owners has grown, not diminished. The enormous growth in social wealth has not been accompanied by an ever-narrowing circle of great capitalist magnates, but by an ever-growing number of capitalists at every level. The character of the middle strata has changed, but they have not vanished from the social hierarchy.' Finally, he added: 'from a political point of view, in all the advanced countries, we observe the privileges of the capitalist *bourgeoisie* steadily giving way to democratic institutions. Under the influence of this, and driven by the ever more powerful pressure of the workers' movement, there has been a reaction of society against the exploitative tendencies of capital, which, even if it is still uncertain and hesitant, is there nonetheless, and invests wider and wider sectors of economic life.' In short, 'factory legislation', the 'demo-cratization of communal administration', and 'universal suffrage' tend to erode the very basis of class struggle. This only confirms and proves once more that where parliamentary democracy is dominant, the state can no longer be seen as an organ of class rule. 'The more the political institutions of modern nations become democratized, the more the occasions and necessity for great political crises are removed.' Hence the working class should not strive to seize power by revolution, but should rather seek to reform the State, remodelling it in a more and more democratic mould. To conclude: there is a contradiction between political democracy and capitalist exploitation. The development of the former, that is of political equality, must necessarily gradually reduce and overcome economic in-equalities and hence class differences.

Obviously, in his last text, Engels had not intended to say anything like this. Besides, Bernstein himself, while underlining the importance of the 'political testament', recognized that Engels himself could scarcely have been expected to undertake this 'necessary revision of the theory'. Nevertheless, at the moment when he began his series of articles in *Die Neue Zeit*, Bernstein enjoyed considerable prestige within German Social Democracy, not only because of his direction of the Party organ at Zurich for several years during the period of the exceptional laws; and not only because of his collaboration with Kautsky in the preparation of the Erfurt programme;[6] but also and above all because he had lived for years in England close to Engels as both his disciple and friend. Kautsky recalled later: 'From 1883 Engels considered Bernstein and myself as the most trusted representatives of Marxist theory.'[7] When Engels died in August

---

[6] K. Kautsky, *Das Erfurter Programm*, Stuttgart, 1892, p. viii.

[7] F. Engels, *Briefwechsel mit Karl Kautsky*, Vienna, 1955, p. 90.

1895 it seems that of the two Bernstein was especially favoured; it was to him as executor that Engels entrusted the 'literary legacy' of Marx and himself.

Clearly, it would be futile to attempt to construe these elements as implying Engels and Bernstein had a common outlook. Though Bernstein insinuated on occasion that his 'internal struggle' and 'new viewpoint' were no secret to Engels, it cannot be doubted, as Kautsky wrote, that 'if Engels had suspected the change in Ede's [Bernstein's] outlook . . . he would certainly not have entrusted him with his literary legacy'.[8] However, even if we lay aside these secondary considerations, their close relationship at least serves, in my view, to underline two important facts: not only that 'revisionism' was born in the heart of the Marxism of the Second International, and advanced from there, but also that Bernstein's polemic is incomprehensible if we fail to grasp the particular character of *that* Marxism from which it originated and in relation to which it always remained, in a real sense, complementary.

THE 'BREAKDOWN THEORY'

The pivot upon which the whole of Bernstein's argument turns is his critique of the 'theory of breakdown'. In his book, *Bernstein and the Social-Democratic Programme*, which appeared in the same year, 1899, Kautsky correctly pointed out that 'Marx and Engels never produced a special "theory of breakdown" and that this term originates from Bernstein himself, just as the term "theory of immiseration" owes its existence to the adversaries of Marxism'.[9] But what Bernstein understood by this theory was in substance nothing other than the content of the famous paragraph in *Capital* on the 'historical tendency of capitalist accumulation'.

In Marx's account, the imperative laws of competition determine the progressive expropriation of smaller capitalists by larger and hence an ever more accentuated 'centralization of capital'. This process, periodically accelerated by economic crisis, reveals the inherent limit of the capitalist regime: the contradiction between the social character of production and the private form of appropriation. On the one hand, these 'develop, on an ever-extending scale, the cooperative form of the labour process . . . the transformation of the instruments of labour into instru-

---

[8] Letter from Kautsky to V. Adler, 21 March 1899, in Adler, op. cit., p. 303.
[9] Kautsky, *Bernstein und das sozialdemokratische Programm*, op. cit., p. 42.

ments of labour only usable in common, the economizing of all means of production by their use as the means of production of combined, socialized labour'. On the other hand, 'along with the constantly diminishing number of the magnates of capital, who usurp and monopolize all advantages of this process of transformation, grow the mass of misery, oppression, slavery, degradation, exploitation; but with this too grows the revolt of the working class, a class always increasing in numbers, and disciplined, united, organized by the very mechanism of the process of capitalist production itself'.

Marx concludes:

The monopoly of capital itself becomes a fetter upon the mode of production, which has sprung up and flourished along with, and under it. Centralization of the means of production and socialization of labour at last reach a point where they become incompatible with their capitalist integument. This integument is burst asunder. *The knell of capitalist private property sounds. The expropriators are expropriated.*[10]

It is true that Bernstein did not accept this account of the 'historical tendency of capitalist accumulation', which he regarded as a 'purely speculative anticipation'. Not by chance is the major thrust of his book directed at denying or strictly circumscribing what is today regarded, even by non-Marxist economists, as the most verified of all Marx's predictions; the capitalist concentration and centralization he forecast. Here we need refer only to the judgement of the eminent American economist, W. Leontiev, who rejects many aspects of Marx's theory. Discussing Marx's 'brilliant analysis of the long-run tendencies of the capitalist system', he observes:

The record is indeed impressive: increasing concentration of wealth, rapid elimination of small and medium-sized enterprises, progressive limitation of competition, incessant technological progress accompanied by the ever-growing importance of fixed capital, and, last but not least, the undiminishing amplitude of recurrent business cycles – an unsurpassed series of prognostications fulfilled, against which modern economic theory with all its refinements has little to show indeed.[11]

In this sense, Rosa Luxemburg was right to point out that 'what Bernstein questions is not the rapidity of the development of capitalist society, but

[10] Marx, *Capital*, Vol. I, p. 763.

[11] Proceedings of the Fiftieth Annual Meeting of the American Economic Association, 1937 (*American Economic Review Supplement*, March 1938, pp. 5, 9).

the march of this development itself and consequently, the very possibility of a change to socialism'. He 'not merely rejects a certain form of the collapse. He rejects the very possibility of collapse'.[12] Or, better still, he denied not only the 'breakdown' (which we shall see, is not one of Marx's ideas), but also – quite apart from any notion of automatic 'breakdown', such as Luxemburg's own thesis that the system 'moves towards a point where it will be unbalanced when it will simply become impossible'[13] – the vital nucleus of Marxism itself: namely, the idea that the capitalist order is a *historical* phenomenon, a *transitory* and non-natural order, which, through its own internal and objective contradictions inevitably nurtures within itself the forces that impel it towards a different organization of society.

There is no doubt that Bernstein expressly rejected all this. The best proof, if proof were needed, is his concern to demonstrate the possibility of the 'self-regulation' of capitalism. Cartels, credit, the improved system of communications, the rise of the working class, insofar as they act to eliminate or at least mitigate the internal contradictions of the capitalist economy, hindering their development and aggravation, ensure for the system the possibility of unlimited survival. In other words, for Marx's basic conception according to which the advent of socialism has its *preconditions* and *objective* roots within the process of capitalist production itself, Bernstein substituted a socialism based upon an *ethical ideal*, the goal of a civilized humanity free to choose its own future in conformity with the highest principles of morality and justice. As Rosa Luxemburg acidly commented: 'What we are offered here is an exposition of the socialist programme based upon "pure reason". We have here, in simpler language, an idealist exposition of socialism. The objective necessity of socialism, as the result of the material development of society, falls to the ground.'[14]

However, granted this, it is also necessary to point out that the way in which Marx's own theory was expounded by the Marxism of that period transformed what Marx himself had declared a *historical tendency* into an 'inevitable *law of nature*'. A violent crisis would sooner or later produce conditions of acute poverty which would turn people's minds against the system, convincing them of the impossibility of continuing under the existing order. This extreme and fateful economic crisis would then

[12] Luxemburg, *Social Reform or Revolution?*, op. cit., pp. 10–11.

[13] ibid., p. 10. This thesis was later developed by Luxemburg in *The Accumulation of Capital*.   [14] ibid., p. 12.

expand into a generalized crisis of society, only concluded by the advent to power of the proletariat. Such, according to Bernstein, was the dominant conception within Social Democracy. The conviction had become deeply rooted, he wrote, that 'this path of development was an *inevitable natural law* and that a generalized economic crisis was the necessary crucible for the emergence of a socialist society'.

The attribution to German Social Democracy of this thesis of an imminent and inevitable 'breakdown' (*Zusammenbruch*) of bourgeois society under the fatal impact of 'purely economic causes' was energetically attacked by Kautsky in his thorough reply to *The Premises of Socialism and the Tasks of Social Democracy*. He wrote: 'In the official declarations of German Social Democracy, Bernstein will seek in vain any affirmation that could be construed in the sense of the "theory of breakdown" he imputes to it. In the passage of the Erfurt Programme dealing with crises, there is no mention of "breakdown".'[15] Yet Bernstein's accusation was not altogether wide of the mark: this can be shown not only by some of the reactions it aroused in Marxist circles (Cunow for example), reaffirming that Marx and Engels did indeed believe in a catastrophic breakdown of capitalism,[16] but also by the Erfurt Programme itself, drawn up by Kautsky in 1891–2. In the Erfurt Programme, the conversion or transformation of the 'historical tendency' Marx had discussed into the terms of a *naturalistic* and fatal necessity is quite evident.

Kautsky wrote in his commentary to the programme:

We consider the breakdown (*Zusammenbruch*) of existing society as inevitable, since we know that economic development creates with a natural necessity conditions which force the exploited to strive against private property; that it increases the number and power of the exploited while it reduces the number and power of the exploiters, whose interest is to maintain the existing order; that it leads, finally, to unbearable conditions for the mass of the population, which leave it only a choice between passive degeneration and the active overthrow of the existing system of ownership.

And he added:

Capitalist society has failed; its dissolution is only a question of time; irresistible economic development leads with natural necessity to the bankruptcy of the

[15] Kautsky, *Bernstein und das sozialdemokratische Programm*, op. cit., p. 43.
[16] For a reconstruction of the 'breakdown controversy' see P. M Sweezy, *The Theory of Capitalist Development*, New York, 1968, pp. 190 ff.

capitalist mode of production. The erection of a new form of society in place of the existing one is no longer something merely *desirable*; it has become something *inevitable*.[17]

This theme of the approaching breakdown of capitalism and the imminent passage to socialism constitutes an essential guide-line in the *Bernstein-Debatte*. This was not only for the theoretical or doctrinaire reasons already mentioned, to which we shall have occasion to return; but also because, in the various forms this *theme* assumed around the turn of the century, we can trace the reverberation of a real historical process, which must at least be mentioned at this point.

THE 'GREAT DEPRESSION'

For economists, the last quarter of the nineteenth century has for some time now come to assume the significance of a crucial phase in the history of capitalism. The period is marked by a long-drawn-out economic crisis, which has become known as the 'Great Depression', lasting from 1873 to 1895, though punctuated by two moments of recovery.[18] During this crisis, which began with a violent slump but soon adopted a milder, but exhaustingly lengthy movement (which helped many contemporaries to fail to identify it as a real crisis in the classical sense of the term), all the fundamental categories of Marx's analysis came fully into play: the tendency for the rate of profit to fall due to the increased 'organic composition' of capital; stagnation and partial saturation of outlets for investment; unimpeded action of competition, which, apart from affecting profit margins, resulted in a spectacular fall in prices.

In his edition of the third volume of *Capital*, Engels inserted a lengthy note into Marx's discussion of joint-stock companies, in which he referred to the Depression then taking place in the following terms:

The daily growing speed with which production may be enlarged in all fields of large-scale industry today, is offset by the ever-greater slowness with which the market for these increased products expands. What the former turns out in months, can scarcely be absorbed by the latter in years. . . . The results are a general chronic over-production, depressed prices, falling and even wholly

[17] Kautsky, *Das Erfurter Programm*, op. cit., pp. 106, 136.
[18] M. Dobb, *Studies in the Development of Capitalism*, London, 1947, pp. 300 ff. For bibliographical references and quantitative information (arranged by topics: employment, investment, prices, etc.) see S. G. E. Lythe, *British Economic History since 1760*, London, 1950.

disappearing profits; in short, the old boasted freedom of competition has reached the end of its tether and must itself announce its obvious, scandalous bankruptcy.[19]

The insistence in this text on the 'ever-greater slowness' with which the market expands refers in particular to an essential feature of this period, to which Engels frequently drew attention: the end of the British industrial monopoly of the world and the beginning of international struggle for markets – not, of course, for the export of commodities, but for the export of capital. It was indeed precisely during the Great Depression period that German and American industry, which embarked on the process of centralization earlier and more fully than British industry, began to contest British economic world supremacy.[20]

This end to the 'British industrial monopoly' acquired great significance in Engels's thinking in his last years. He refers to it in his Preface of 1892 to the *Condition of the Working Class in England*: the breakdown of this monopoly, he wrote, must entail the loss of the 'privileged position' of the British working class and hence 'there will be socialism again' in Britain. It would seem that the effects of the depression and the 'bankruptcy' of free competition reinforced to some extent in Engels – and even more clearly in the case of his disciples – the sensation that the system was rapidly moving towards the final settlement of accounts.

Kautsky later recalled:

At the time of my third stay in London (1885), Engels unceasingly affirmed that the British workers' rejection of socialism was connected with the monopoly position of British industry over the world market, which allowed the capitalists to concede extraordinary favours to the Trade Unions. But now, with the rise of powerful industries in other countries, this monopoly would end; with its demise the opposition between organized labour and capital would become more acute even in Britain.

[19] Marx, *Capital*, Vol. III, p. 428.
[20] G. M. Trevelyan, *English Social History*, London, 1946, p. 557. 'The Franco-Prussian war of 1870 was the first shock. And during the three following decades America and Germany rose as manufacturing powers rival to our own. The immensely greater natural resources of America, the scientific and technical education provided by the far-sighted governments in Germany, told more and more every year. To meet this new situation, our island liberty, Free Trade and individualist self-help might not alone be enough. Some sense of this led to improved technical education over here. It led, also, to greater interest in our own 'lands beyond the sea', the Imperialist movement of the nineties; and it induced a more friendly and respectful attitude to America . . . and "the Colonies", as Canada and Australasia were still called.'

And Kautsky added:

Indeed, we expected much more from the crisis at that time. . . . Not only the revival of the socialist movement in Britain, but the breakdown (*Zusammenbruch*) of capitalism throughout the world. This hope proved illusory. Capitalism survived the crisis, despite its considerable extension in space and time and its inordinate intensity. A new phase of capitalist prosperity ensued. But what emerged was an entirely altered capitalism. The older form of capitalism had been eclipsed.[21]

This is perhaps the crucial point. The long crisis passed and capitalism survived. Indeed it overcame the crisis by transforming itself. Learning from the drastic effects of competition on prices and profit margins, capitalism reacted by decisively adopting the path of monopolistic development.[22] Capitalism entered the Great Depression in the classical nineteenth-century form of a competitive economy; it emerged at the end of the century with a radically altered physiognomy. The old banner of *laisser-faire* was rolled up. Unlimited competition was restricted; faith in the providential self-regulating virtues of the system gave way to agreements on prices and production quotas. Until the 1870s free competition went almost uncontested; by the end of the century, cartels had already become one of the bases of economic life. The great business upswing after 1895 and the new crisis of 1900–3 took place, for the first time, at least in the mining and iron-and-steel industries, entirely under the sign of monopolistic cartelization.

Free trade gave way steadily to protectionism: but with the difference that, while the initial task of protectionism had been that of safeguarding growing national industries from the unequal competition of more advanced industrial countries, its function was now altered, indeed inverted. It was transformed, 'from a means of defence against the conquest of the home market by foreign industry' into 'a means of conquering overseas markets on behalf of home industries; . . . from a defensive weapon of the weak' into 'an offensive weapon of the strong'.[23]

Similarly profound mutations occurred in the field of colonial policy.

[21] *F. Engels' Briefwechsel mit K. Kautsky*, op. cit., pp. 174–5. Kautsky's Commentary on the letters dates from 1935.

[22] W. W. Rostow, 'Investment and the Great Depression' in *Economic History Review*, May 1938, p. 158 (cited by Dobb, op. cit., p. 312), observes that capitalists 'began to search for an escape (from narrower profit-margins) in the ensured foreign markets of positive imperialism, in tariffs, monopolies, employers' associations'.

[23] R. Hilferding, *Das Finanzkapital*, Berlin, 1955, p. 460.

In the classic period of free trade, the colonial system had fallen into such discredit that, as Lenin remarked, even after 1860 'the leading British bourgeois politicians were *opposed* to colonial policy and were of the opinion that the liberation of the colonies, their complete separation from Britain, was inevitable and desirable'.[24] From 1880 onwards, on the contrary, a new feeling awakened for the economic value of colonies. Hobson in his book on imperialism marks out the period from 1884 to 1900 as that of the maximum territorial expansion of the major European powers. Africa, only a tenth of whose total area had been annexed by 1876, was by 1900 nine-tenths under foreign rule.

The effects of this deep and substantial change in capitalist development were a decisive factor in the 'crisis of Marxism' which erupted at the turn of the century. The system, which seemed to have entered a period of prolonged coma since the 1870s, beyond which – imminent and palpable – seemed to be visible the collapse of bourgeois society and the advent of socialism, now enjoyed a sudden upswing; the result was a profound shift in the European and world picture, destroying the expectations of an imminent 'breakdown' of the old society which had seemed to rest upon unbreakable and inevitable 'natural necessity'. As Labriola wrote, on the outbreak of the *Bernstein-Debatte*:

Behind all the din of battle, in fact, there lies a deep and crucial question. The ardent, energetic and precocious hopes of several years ago – the prediction of the details, the over-precise itineraries – have now come up against the more complex resistance of economic relations and the ingenuity of political contrivances.[25]

A new epoch of capitalist prosperity began. Capitalism sprang from its ashes, its physiognomy profoundly altered. And even if the Great Depression came to be characterized by later economists as 'forming a watershed between two stages of capitalism: the earlier vigorous, prosperous and flushed with adventurous optimism; the latter more troubled, more hesitant, and some would say, already bearing the marks of senility and decay,'[26] the dominant impression for many contemporaries was that of entering into a *new* epoch, governed by only partially explored mechanisms, bristling with unforeseen problems.

[24] Lenin, *Imperialism, the Highest Stage of Capitalism* in *Selected Works*, op. cit., Vol. I, p. 737.
[25] Letter from Labriola to Lagardelle, 15 April 1899, in Antonio Labriola, *Saggi sul Materialismo storico*, Rome, 1964, p. 302.
[26] Dobb, op. cit., p. 300.

Labriola was not alone in sensing this. In the issue of *Die Neue Zeit* in which, for the first time, he stated explicitly his disagreement with Bernstein, Kautsky observed that the political and economic changes of the past twenty years had revealed characteristics which were still hidden at the time of the *Manifesto* and *Capital*. 'A re-examination, a revision of our positions had therefore become necessary.' Even if he did not share the method, or results, which had hitherto emerged from Bernstein's articles, at least he granted them the merit of having posed the problem.[27]

The state of unease and uncertainty in the face of the newly emerging situation was all the more acute for the incautious, credulous optimism of several years before. For the older generation it was complicated by the disarray caused by the recent loss of Engels's guidance. 'All this is only part of the difficulties which have burdened us through the death of Engels', Adler wrote to Bebel: 'the Old Man would also have made the "revision" easier, to the extent that it is needed'.[28] Shortly after, in a letter to Kautsky, he added: 'You [Bernstein and Kautsky himself] should both have done this work, which was or rather still is needed, to bring the party up from the 1847 viewpoint to that of 1900.'[29]

In the course of a few years, then, the economic and social situation emerged in a new light; what had shortly before seemed the immediate prelude to the 'final crisis' now unexpectedly assumed the profile of a new epoch. As always, at moments of crossing a critical watershed, minor differences between closely related positions are enough to reveal globally different outlooks. In 1895, in the Introduction to the new edition of *The Class Struggles in France*, Engels optimistically saw capitalism moving ineluctably towards its rapid decline 'by the end of the century', while the rise of Social Democracy to power seemed to proceed 'as spontaneously, as steadily, as irresistibly and at the same time as tranquilly as a natural process'. Everything, in short, seemed to conspire towards the

---

[27] cf. L. Amodio in Rosa Luxemburg, *Scritti scelti*, Milan, 1963, p. 137. This feeling explains the favourable, even sympathetic reception accorded to Bernstein's articles in *Die Neue Zeit*. Even in November 1898, after the Stockholm Congress in which Bernstein's theses were rejected by the German Social Democratic Party, Labriola, for example, showed a sympathetic consideration for them (cf. G. Procacci, 'Antonio Labriola e la revisione del marxismo attraverso l'epistolario con Bernstein e con Kautsky' in *Annali dell' Instituto G. G. Feltrinelli*, 1960, Milan, 1961, p. 268). Besides, as V. Gerratana has shown in his introduction to Labriola, *Dal Materialismo storico*, Rome, 1964, p. 11, n. 1, even Lenin at first did not realize the significance of Bernstein's articles (cf. Lenin, *Collected Works*, Vol. 34, pp. 35–6).

[28] V. Adler, op. cit., p. 268.   [29] ibid., p. 352.

imminent ruin of the existing order, even the 'legality' the *bourgeoisie* had provided for itself. In 1896, on the other hand, we are confronted by Bernstein's doubts, 'disappointment' and confusion; by now he could only see the 'tactics', the everyday routine of the 'movement', and no longer saw the meaning of the 'final goal' (*das Endziel*).

Both perceived the same phenomena, both recorded the birth of cartels and trusts. But in their arguments, these same phenomena acquired radically opposed significances. In the long note, already discussed, which Engels inserted in Marx's treatment of joint-stock companies in the third volume of *Capital*, he wrote of 'new forms of industrial enterprises . . . representing the second and third degree of stock companies'. In each country, he wrote, 'the big industrialists of a certain branch [join] together in a cartel for the regulation of production. A committee fixes the quantity to be produced by each establishment and is the final authority for distributing the incoming orders. Occasionally, even international cartels were established, as between English and German iron industries.'[30] For Engels this monopolistic cartelization and resultant 'regulation' of production was the final process of involution, the imminent extinction of the system, the 'bankruptcy' of free competition as the basic principle of the capitalist system. Bernstein, on the contrary, as Kautsky acutely observed,[31] overlooked cartels when they spoke in confirmation of the real occurrence of capitalist concentration, and hence 'to Marx's advantage', only referring to them where they could serve as evidence 'against' Marx. In his view, cartels and the slight degree of 'regulation' of production they allowed signified the opposite: the advent of a *new*, so to speak, regenerated capitalism which had learned to correct its old faults (anarchy) by 'regulating itself' and hence was capable of indefinite survival.

This difference of viewpoints stems essentially from a different perception of the historical moment. In this respect, in his awareness that times were changing, it must be conceded that Bernstein was in advance of Engels, Kautsky and all the rest. His advantage and strength lay in his consciousness that he was facing a new historical situation. His actual attempt to cast light on the phenomena of the most recent capitalist development was irrelevant from a scientific standpoint, but this foresight explains why it is that, despite the archaism of so much of his argument, he nonetheless appears in some respects – in his prompt intuition of the new course of development, obviously, rather than in the

[30] Marx, *Capital*, Vol. III, p. 428.
[31] Kautsky, *Bernstein und das sozialdemokratische Programm*, op. cit., p. 80.

interpretation he gave of it – nearer to the generation of a Lenin and a Hilferding than to that of a Kautsky and a Plekhanov. Stock companies, the development of cartels and trusts, the separation of 'ownership' and 'control', the growing 'socialization of production', the 'democratization of capital', etc., all themes which are central to Bernstein's argument, are also the themes of Hilferding's *Finance Capital* and Lenin's *Imperialism*. That is why the most effective answers to Bernstein can be found in these texts.

TELEOLOGY AND CAUSATION

However, the experience of the Great Depression and the consequent 'turn' in capitalist development were not the only factors underlying the 'breakdown' controversy. It is also essential, even for a summary reconstruction of the historical moment when Bernstein's book was published, to include another crucial component: the character of the Marxism of the Second International; the way it received and interpreted Marx's work; the influence exercised by Engels's writings;[32] the contamination and subordination of this Marxism *vis-à-vis* the dominant cultural developments of the period.

[32] As far as I know, an exhaustive investigation of the influence of Engels's writings on the formation of the principal exponents of Marxism in the Second International still remains to be carried out. It will suffice here to note that the complete identification of Marx's thought with that of Engels (in the uncritical form in which they are still received) begins to take shape precisely in this period (it was later made peremptory and absolute by Lenin and Russian Marxism). Engels's influence, as confirmed by all direct testimony, seems to have been due to several factors. Firstly, most of Engels's theoretical texts (written either in the last years of Marx's life or after his death) coincided with the formation of Kautsky's and Plekhanov's generation with whom Engels had common cultural interests (Darwinism, ethnological discoveries – in short, the whole cultural atmosphere of the period). Secondly, this influence (which was reinforced by close personal relations), quite apart from the wider diffusion and greater simplicity and expository clarity of Engels's writings – often emphasized by Kautsky, Plekhanov and all the others, cf. K. Kautsky, *F. Engels: Sein Leben, Sein Werken, seine Schriften*, Berlin, 1908, p. 27 – seems to be linked to the place given in Engels's work to philosophical-cosmological developments, 'the philosophy of nature', in other words, the 'extension' of historical materialism into 'dialectical materialism': as is well known, the latter term owes its origin to Engels himself. This aspect of Engels's work had a determinant weight also for the succeeding generation: Max Adler, for example, claimed (*Engels als Denker*, Berlin, 1925, pp. 65 ff.) that Engels's merit lay precisely in having liberated Marxism from the 'special economic-social form' it assumes in Marx's own detailed work, broadening its scope to the dimensions of *eine Weltauffassung*.

Bernstein's view on this question was that the theory of 'breakdown' descended directly from the 'fatalism' and 'determinism' of the materialist conception of history. The expectation of an imminent and inevitable catastrophe of *bourgeois* society, brought about by 'purely *economic*' causes, reproduced, according to Bernstein, the inherent limits of any materialist explanation, in which matter and the movements of matter were the cause of everything. 'To be a materialist means, first and foremost, to reduce every event to the necessary movements of matter.' Secondly, 'the movement of matter takes place, according to the materialist doctrine, in a necessary sequence like a mechanical process'. Since this movement is also that which must determine 'the formation of ideas and the orientation of the will', it follows that the historical and human world is represented as a chain of predetermined and inevitable events; in this sense the materialist, Bernstein concluded, is 'a Calvinist without God'.

It is, of course, true that the Marxists of the period sharply denied the accusation of 'fatalism'. Kautsky replied that historical materialism had, on the contrary, never dreamed of forgetting the essential importance of human intervention in history. The overthrow of capitalist society was never entrusted by Marx solely to the effect of 'purely economic' causes. In the very paragraph on 'the historical tendency of capitalist accumulation', besides the aggravation of economic contradictions, Marx had also underlined another factor: the 'maturity' and education of the working class, the high level of consciousness attained, its capacity for organization and discipline.[33] Plekhanov's response, as we shall see, did not greatly differ from Kautsky's, though it was philosophically more systematic, and notably more virulent in its polemic; besides, Plekhanov had himself published, in 1898, *The Role of the Individual in History*. However, the anti-Bernstein positions of that period (as, indeed, much of present-day Marxism, which would blush even to imagine itself 'determinist') were characterized by a presupposition they shared with Bernstein himself: a vulgar[34] and naïve conception of the 'economy'.

Here, too, Bernstein's argument rests upon yet another famous 'self-criticism' by Engels, dating from 1890:

[33] Kautsky, *Bernstein und das sozialdemokratische programm*, op. cit., p. 46.

[34] For documentary evidence of this 'vulgarity' see the initial chapters of O. Lange, *Political Economy*, Warsaw, 1963, which refer, moreover, to Marxist authors and texts of the Second International.

According to the materialist conception of history, the *ultimately* determining element in history is the production and reproduction of real life. More than this neither Marx nor I have ever asserted. Hence if somebody twists this into saying that the economic element is the *only* determining one, he transforms that proposition into a meaningless, abstract, senseless phrase.[35]

Engels continued:

Marx and I are ourselves partly to blame for the fact that the younger people sometimes lay more stress on the economic side than is due to it. We had to emphasize the main principle *vis-à-vis* our adversaries, who denied it, and we had not always the time, the place or the opportunity to give their due to the other elements involved in the interaction.[36]

These self-critical observations of Engels were regarded by Bernstein as a substantial innovation compared to the original 'determinism' of the materialist conception of history, as formulated by Marx in the 'Preface' to *A Contribution to the Critique of Political Economy* of 1859. It is notable that a similar judgement (though without the critical reference to the 1859 text) has for some time been prevalent in contemporary Marxism. There is the same emphasis on the value of Engels's solution to the problem – for example in his letter to Starkenburg of 1894:

Political, religious, juridical, philosophical, literary, artistic, etc. development is based on economic development. But all these react upon one another and also upon the economic basis. It is not that the economic situation is *cause, solely active*, while everything else is only passive effect. There is, rather, inter-action on the basis of economic necessity, which ultimately always asserts itself.[37]

Bernstein's comment on this passage by Engels emphasized that it did more harm than good to historical materialism arrogantly to reject as eclecticism the decisive accentuation of 'other factors' which are not

[35] Letter from Engels to J. Bloch, 21 September 1890, in Marx and Engels, *Selected Correspondence*, Moscow, 1963, p. 498.

[36] ibid., p. 500. It should be pointed out that these 'self-critical' statements by Engels (which, incidentally, seriously perplexed writers as diverse as Plekhanov and Max Adler) are not easy to interpret. Taken literally, they would seem to signify that there is, in Marx's work, an over-emphasis on the 'economic factor'. But Engels himself, later in the letter, excludes this interpretation ('But when it came to presenting a section of history, that is to making a practical application, it was a different matter and there no error was possible'). The fault to which he refers would seem then to apply to general pronouncements on historical materialism. Yet it is notable how rare such pronouncements are in Marx's work and how they (in *Theses on Feuerbach*, Part One of *The German Ideology*, etc.), except perhaps in one case (cf. note 38), are unscathed by this type of criticism. [37] ibid., p. 549.

'purely economic', and to restrict the field to production techniques (*Produktionstechnik*). Eclecticism, he added in polemic against Plekhanov's *Monism*, is often precisely a natural reaction against the doctrinaire impulse to deduce everything from one sole principle.

Nonetheless, despite their differences, what Bernstein shared with Plekhanov, and what Engels's 'self-criticism' could not correct but only confirm, was the profound adulteration of the concept of the 'economy' or, better still, of 'social relations of production', precisely the core and foundation of Marx's entire work. The so-called 'economic sphere' – which in Marx had embraced both the production of *things* and the production (objectification) of *ideas*; production and intersubjective communication; material production and the production of social relations (for Marx, the relation between man and nature was also a relationship between man and man, and vice versa) – was now seen as *one isolated factor*, separated from the other 'moments' and thereby emptied of any effective *socio-historical* content, representing, on the contrary, an antecedent sphere, prior to any human mediation.[38] *Social* production is thus transformed into 'production *techniques*'; the object of political economy becomes the object of technology. Since this 'technique', which is 'material production' in the strict sense of the term, is separated from that other simultaneous production achieved by men, the production of their *relations* (without which, for Marx, the former would not exist), the *materialist* conception of history tends to become a *technological* conception of history. If so those critics of Marxism, like Professor Robbins, for

---

[38] This, in my view, is the danger that arises from the theory of 'factors', suggested by Engels in his letters. Precisely to the extent that he emphasizes the decisive role, not only of the 'economic base' but also of the 'superstructure', his account encourages the interpretation of the 'economic base' as a 'purely material' or '*technical*-economic' domain, not including social relations and hence inter-subjective communication. Even though one should be cautious on this point, it is notable in this connection that Woltmann, for example, believes he has located a difference between the social concept of the 'economy' characteristic of Marx and the naturalistic concept of Engels, Kautsky and Cunow (cf. Kautsky, *Bernstein und das sozialdemokratische Programm*, op. cit., p. 47). The distinction between 'structure' and 'superstructure' rarely occurs in Marx and is little more than a metaphor for him; in later Marxism it has acquired an inordinate importance. On the other hand, it is also true that at least part of the blame for these later developments must fall to Marx's famous 'Preface' to *A Contribution to the Critique of Political Economy* (1859), in which formulations like: 'The mode of production of material life conditions the social, political and intellectual life process in general' – would suggest, if taken literally, a 'material production' which is not at the same time a 'social process'.

whom historical materialism signifies the idea that 'the material technique of production conditions the form of all social institutions and that all changes in social institutions are the result of changes in productive techniques' – the idea, in short, that 'History is the epiphenomenon of technical change' – are right.[39]

The main consequence of this 'factorial' approach, which runs more or less openly through all the Marxism of the period as the common basis for arguments as diverse as those of Bernstein and Plekhanov, is the divorce of 'production' and 'society', of *materialism* and *history*, the separation of man's relation with nature from the simultaneous relations between men. In short, the result is an incapacity to see that without human or social mediation, the very existence of labour and productive activity is inconceivable. Marx had written:

In production, men not only act on nature but also on one another. They produce only by co-operation in a certain way and by mutually exchanging their activities. In order to produce, they enter into definite relations with one another and only within these relations does their action on nature, does production, take place.[40]

The intertwining of these two processes is the key to *historical* materialism. Traditional materialism, which sees men as products of their environment, forgets, according to Marx,[41] that men in turn change their circumstances and that 'it is essential to educate the educator himself'. It forgets that it is not enough to consider practical-material circumstances as the *cause* and man as their *effect* – the inverse must also be taken into account. Just as man, the effect, is also the cause of his cause, so the latter is also the effect of its own effect.

In other words, as a product of objective material causation, man is also and simultaneously the beginning of a new causal process, opposite to the first, in which the point of departure is no longer the natural environment but the concept, the *idea of man*, his mental project. This second process – whose *prius* is the *idea* and in which therefore the cause is not an object but a *concept*, the object being the goal or point of arrival – is the so-called *final causality*, the finalism or teleological process as opposed to the *efficient causality* or material causality in the case of the first process. 'An

[39] L. Robbins, *An Essay on the Nature and Significance of Economic Science*, London, 1948, p. 43.
[40] *Wage Labour and Capital*, in Marx and Engels, *Selected Works*, op. cit., p. 81.
[41] Third Thesis on Feuerbach.

end,' according to Kant, 'is the object of a concept so far as this concept is regarded as the cause of the object (the real ground of its possibility); and the causality of a concept in respect of its object is finality (*forma finalis*).'[42] Finalism, therefore, inverts the sequence of efficient causality. In the latter case, the cause precedes and determines the effect; in the former, the effect is an *end*, an intentional goal, and therefore it determines the efficient cause, which in turn becomes simply a *means* to accomplish it.

Now the simultaneity of these two processes, each of which is the inversion of the other, but which together form the *umwälzende* or *revolutionäre Praxis* referred to in the *Theses on Feuerbach*, is the secret of and key to *historical materialism* in its double aspect, of causation (materialism) and finality (history). But it also permits an explanation of that sensitive point in Marx's work: his concept of 'production' or 'labour' as at once production of *things* and production (objectification) of *ideas*, as production and intersubjective communication, as material production and production of social relations.

In a celebrated passage in *Capital* Marx writes:

A spider conducts operations that resemble those of a weaver, and a bee puts to shame many an architect in the construction of her cells. But what distinguishes the worst architect from the best of bees is this, that the architect raises his structure in imagination before he erects it in reality. At the end of every labour-process we get a result that already existed in the imagination of the labourer at its commencement. He not only effects a change of form in the material on which he works, but also realizes a purpose of his own that gives the law to his *modus operandi*, and to which he must subordinate his will.[43]

The product of labour, then, is the objectification or externalization of the *idea* of the labourer: it is the *external*, real becoming of the concept or programme with which the labourer sets about his task. This means that labour is a *finalistic* activity; that production is not only a relation between man and nature but also a relation between men, that is a *language*[44] or manifestation of man to man. On the other hand, insofar as it is necessary for the *realization* of the idea or labour project that it takes into account the specific nature of the materials employed, the labour process reveals as well as finalism, *efficient causation*. Indeed, to objectify the idea, 'the

[42] I. Kant, *The Critique of Judgement*, trans. J. C. Meredith, Oxford, 1952, Part I, p. 61.

[43] Marx, *Capital*, Vol. I, p. 178.

[44] In *The German Ideology* (London, 1965, p. 37), production is defined as 'The language of real life'.

ideal motive which is the inherent stimulus and precondition of production', in the product, and thereby to transform nature according to
our plans and designs, it is necessary that the idea both determines the
object and is determined by it. According to Bacon's celebrated aphor-
ism, to command nature we must also obey her; to make the object
conform to us, it is indispensable that we conform ourselves to it. 'Production,' says Marx, 'accordingly produces not only an object for the
subject, but also a subject for the object.' The 'ideal impulse' which acts
as 'an internal image, a need, a motive, a purpose' is not only cause but
effect; for indeed, 'It is itself as an impulse mediated by the object. The
need felt for the object is induced by the perception of the object.'[45]

This is not the place to examine how this relation finality/causation
is the same as the relation deduction/induction and how the Marxist concept of the 'social relations of production' therefore implicitly contains a
logic of scientific enquiry. It is more appropriate here, returning to
Bernstein and the controversy he raised over the 'determinism' of the
materialist conception of history, to show instead how all the Marxist
tendencies within the Second International came up against the difficulty
of grasping the reciprocal interrelation of finality and causation outlined
above.

'Man's activity,' Plekhanov wrote in one of his articles against Bernstein and his critique of materialism, 'can be considered from two different
standpoints.' Firstly, 'it appears as the *cause* of a given social phenomenon', insofar as man himself knows he is such a cause, 'insofar as he
supposes that *it depends on him* to provoke such social phenomena.'
Secondly, 'the man who appears to be the cause of a given social phenomenon can and must in turn be considered a *consequence* of those social
phenomena which have contributed to the formation of his character and
the direction of his will. Considered *as a consequence*, social man can no
longer be considered a *free* agent; the circumstances which have determined his actions do not depend upon his will. Hence his activity now
appears as an activity *subordinated to the law of necessity*.'[46]

The argument could not be clearer: man, who in his own *consciousness*
imagines himself to be the cause, is *in reality* the effect and nothing but
the effect. Plekhanov, in other words, fails to link together finalism and

---

[45] Marx, '1857 Introduction' to *A Contribution to the Critique of Political Economy*,
op. cit., p. 197.
[46] G. Plekhanov, *Works* (Russian edition), Vol. XI, p. 77. 'Cant against Kant, or Mr.
Bernstein's spiritual testament'.

causation. The concept of *umwälzende Praxis*, that is of productive activity which subverts and subordinates to itself the conditions from which it stems, or that of the 'educator who must himself be educated', remain undecipherable formulae for Plekhanov. Hence the only way he can combine the two elements is by recognizing only necessity or material causation as *real*, and assigning to freedom or finalism only the role of registering necessary and inevitable order. Freedom, for Plekhanov, repeating Engels and through Engels Hegel, is the 'recognition of necessity'.[47] Freedom, in other words, is the consciousness of being determined.

We have not the space here to show how this reference to Hegel concerning the relation between necessity and freedom, like all the other Hegelian propositions shared by the 'dialectical materialism' of Engels and Plekhanov, is based on a somewhat arbitrary 'reading' of the texts of the great German philosopher.[48] The identity of freedom and necessity or, which is the same thing, the *identity* of thought and being,[49] are recurring *motifs* only in Engels's later philosophical works; they are absolutely foreign to the thought of Marx. Moreover, the real paternity of this identification is made all too transparent, somewhat ingenuously, by Plekhanov himself, when he appeals in support of the identity of freedom and necessity not only to Hegel, but to the end of the fourth section of Schelling's *System of Transcendental Idealism*.[50] However, it is more relevant to underline here the gulf of principle that separated the 'orthodox' Marxism of the Second International from Marx's original problematic.

Man is considered as a mere link in the material, objective chain, a

[47] G. Plekhanov, *Essais sur l'histoire du matérialisme*, Paris, 1957, p. 123.

[48] For this relation to Hegel, see especially Plekhanov's article 'Zu Hegel's sechzigstem Todestag' in *Die Neue Zeit*, 1891-2, Vol. I, pp. 198 ff., 236 ff., 273 ff.

[49] Plekhanov, *The Fundamental Problems of Marxism*, op. cit., p. 95.

[50] F. W. J. Schelling, *System des transzendentalen Idealismus*, Tübingen, 1800. This reference to Schelling recurs in almost all of Plekhanov's philosophical works. The passages on which Plekhanov modelled his own thought on the subject are particularly the following: 'The intelligence is only free as an internal appearance, and we therefore are and always believe inwardly, that we are free, although the appearance of our freedom, or our freedom, insofar as it is transferred to the objective world, is subject to the laws of nature, like anything else' (p. 438). 'Every action, whether it is the action of an individual, or the action of the whole species, as action must be thought of as free, but as objective achievement it must be thought of as subject to the laws of nature. Hence subjectively, to internal appearances, we act, but objectively we never act, another acts as if through us' (p. 442).

being whose action is 'determined' by a superior, transcendent force –
Plekhanov called it 'Matter' but he could also have called it the 'Absolute'
or the 'ruse of Reason' – which acts through human action itself, insofar
as the intentions men might consciously (and hence deludedly) pursue
give rise to different results. The novelty and specificity of the historico-
human world – contained in the complex Marxist concept of 'production'
as both production of human *relations* and production of *things*, as production of the self and reproduction of the 'other' – is, therefore, totally
lost and forgotten. As a result, the conception obtained can only be a
rather ingenuous metaphysics and evolutionary-historical cosmology, a
philosophy of providence, which can quite justly be accused of fatalism.

Plekhanov wrote:

> Several writers, Stammler for instance, claim that if the triumph of Socialism is
> a historical necessity, then the practical activity of the Social Democrats is com-
> pletely superfluous. After all, why work for a phenomenon to occur which must
> take place in any case? But this is nothing but a ridiculous, shabby sophism.
> Social Democracy considers historical development from the standpoint of
> necessity, and its own activity as a *necessary link* in the chain of those *necessary
> conditions* which, combined, make the triumph of socialism inevitable. A *neces-
> sary* link cannot be *superfluous*. If it were suppressed, it would shatter the whole
> chain of events.[51]

The primary result of this outlook is precisely to submerge, or better
surpass, the specific level of historical-materialist analysis, Marx's socio-
economic problematic, in a cosmology and cosmogony which is called
'materialist' but is nothing but a philosophical fiction. Everything becomes the dialectical evolution of Matter. And this evolution is realized,
at every level, by generic, omnipresent 'laws' which govern not only
mechanical movement and natural development, but also human society
and thought.[52] Marx's 'economic base' thus becomes Matter. This matter
is not specified or determinate; it is simultaneously everything and
nothing, a mere metaphysical hypostasis and hence anti-materialist by
its very nature. It reveals its theological credentials when, in Plekhanov's
ingenuous prose, it emerges as the latest version of the *deus absconditus*:
'In the life of peoples there exists a something, an X, an unknown quantity, to which the peoples' "energy", and that of the different social
classes existing within them, owes its *origin, direction* and *transformations*.

[51] Plekhanov, *Works*, op. cit., Vol. XI, p. 88 n.
[52] Engels, *Anti-Dühring*, op. cit., pp. 166–67, and *Dialectics of Nature*, op. cit., p. 67.

In other words, something clearly underlies this "energy" itself; it is our task to determine the nature of this unknown factor.'[53]

Attention is resolutely directed away from history, from the analysis of socio-economic formations, to be concentrated instead upon the study of its chosen object, namely, the primeval Matter from which everything is descended, the great *fictio* of this popular religiosity. 'It is an eternal cycle in which matter moves . . . wherein nothing is eternal but eternally changing, eternally moving matter and the laws according to which it moves and changes.' And, since everything changes and nothing dies, 'we have the certainty that matter remains eternally the same in all its transformations, that none of its attributes can ever be lost, and, therefore, also that with the same iron necessity that it will exterminate on the earth its highest creation, the thinking mind, it must somewhere else and at another time again produce it.'[54]

The identity of thought and being is thus transferred into the heart of Matter itself. There is no longer a theory of thought as the thought of the natural being 'man' – of his social character – and hence, no longer a theory of thought in its unity-distinction with *language* and that practical-experimental activity, production and labour. The theory of thought by-passes man altogether; the treatment of thought is once again the treatment of the Absolute as the primitive identity of thought and being. Epistemology and gnoseology are annulled by a simplistic recourse to 'evolution': 'the products of the human mind', Engels writes, 'are themselves products of nature in the last analysis; they do not constitute a break in the preceding natural chain, but correspond to it.' A Hegel in 'popular format' takes Marx's place. And behind Hegel appears Schelling; and behind Schelling, Spinoza. Plekhanov, who encouraged the most vulgar forms of materialism, repeating in all tranquillity that thought is a secretion of the brain;[55] Plekhanov, who thought that materialist gnoseology was already fully present in Helvétius and Holbach; Plekhanov was one of those who regarded Marx as a mere extension and explication of Spinoza:

I am fully convinced that Marx and Engels, after the *materialist* turn in their development, never abandoned the standpoint of Spinoza. This conviction of mine is based in part on the personal testimony of Engels. In 1889, while I was in Paris for the International Exhibition, I took the opportunity of going to

[53] Plekhanov, *Essais sur l'histoire du matérialisme*, op. cit., p. 138.
[54] Engels, *Dialectics of Nature*, op. cit., p. 39.
[55] Plekhanov, *Works*, op. cit., Vol. XVIII, p. 310.

London to meet Engels in person. I had the pleasure of spending almost a week in long discussions with him on various practical and theoretical subjects. At one point our discussion turned to philosophy. Engels strongly criticized what Stern rather imprecisely calls the 'materialism in the philosophy of nature'. 'So for you,' I asked him, 'old Spinoza was right when he said that thought and extension were nothing but two attributes of one and the same substance?' 'Of course,' Engels replied, 'old Spinoza was absolutely right.'[56]

JUDGEMENTS OF FACT AND JUDGEMENTS OF VALUE

While Plekhanov reduced Marx to Spinoza, Kautsky reduced him to Darwin. According to Kautsky, man lives in two worlds, the world of the past and the world of the future.[57] The former is the world of experience, scientific knowledge, determinism and necessity; the latter, that of freedom and action. The opposition between these two worlds is removed with the removal of the distinction between 'nature' and 'society'. Whatever its specificity, the historical human world is only a 'moment' in an evolutionary series. The world of freedom and moral law is only one fragment (*Stückchen*) of the world of the senses.[58]

Kautsky wanted to guarantee the distinction between freedom and necessity, while at the same time avoiding dualism. He even understood the difficulty of enlightenment, empiricism and sensualism, which, in reducing moral life to simple instinct, failed to account for the peculiarity of the 'will'; for, unlike instinct, the latter implies choice, deliberation and hence responsibility. Nonetheless, Kautsky could not avoid the conclusion of compressing the historical-social world into the framework of cosmic-natural evolution, to such an extent that they were no longer distinguishable. Moral choice itself was reduced in the process to a mere instinct (*ein tierischer Trieb*) and the 'ethical law' to a natural impulse equivalent to the instinct of procreation.[59]

[56] G. Plekhanov, *Bernstein and Materialism, Works*, op. cit., Vol. XI, p. 21. See also *The Fundamental Problems of Marxism*, op. cit., p. 30, where, after asserting that Feuerbach represented 'Spinozism disencumbered of its theological setting', Plekhanov goes on: 'it was the viewpoint of this kind of Spinozism . . . that Marx and Engels adopted when they broke with idealism'.

[57] Kautsky, *Ethik und materialistische Geschichtsauffassung*, op. cit., p. 36.

[58] ibid., p. 39.

[59] ibid., pp. 63 and 67. For a critique of this Neo-Kantian work of Kautsky's from a Neo-Kantian position, cf. O. Bauer, 'Marxismus und Ethik', in *Die Neue Zeit*, 1906, Vol. II, pp. 485–99. For Kautsky's rejoinder see 'Leben, Wissenschaft und Ethik', *Die Neue Zeit*, 1906, Vol. II, pp. 516–29.

The naïvely monist and metaphysical nature of these 'orthodox' Marxist constructions of the Second International allows us in turn to understand the kind of antitheses to which they gave rise, and which were their natural and complementary counterpart. Like Plekhanov, Bernstein proceeded from a naturalistic concept of the 'economy'. He referred to the economy as an 'instinct' or natural force (*ökonomische Naturkraft*) analogous to the physical forces. However, for Plekhanov this world of objective causal concatenation was all-embracing; for Bernstein, above and beyond it lay the 'moral ideal', Kant's 'ought' now entrusted with the realization of socialism.[60] The society of the future was no longer the inevitable result of objective evolution but rather an ideal goal freely chosen by the human will.

Iron necessity thus evokes its abstract opposite, Freedom; determinism absolute indeterminacy; the closed chain of 'being' the open and indefinite perspective of the 'ought to be'. Since each of these opposed principles has the power to destroy the other, while depending on it for its own existence, both positions constantly reproduced each other, even within the work of the same theorist. For example, in *Ethics and the Materialist Conception of History*, Kautsky imperiously denounces the ethical socialism of the neo-Kantians and reduces moral decisions to simple 'instinct', and then unexpectedly concludes by appealing to a 'moral ideal' which even the class struggle cannot do without, and which, through its opposition to all that exists in present society, and hence also through the *negativity* of its content, is nothing but the *formalism* of the will invoked by the neo-Kantians.

Even Social Democracy as the organization of the proletariat in its *class struggle* cannot do without the ethical ideal, without ethical indignation against exploitation and class rule. But this ideal has nothing to do with *scientific* socialism, which is the scientific study of the laws of the evolution and motion of the social organism. . . . It is, of course, true that in socialism the investigator is always also a militant and man cannot be artificially cut into two parts with nothing to do with each other. Even in a Marx the influence of a moral ideal sometimes breaks through in his scientific research. But he rightly sought to avoid this as far as possible. For in science the moral ideal is a source of error. Science is always only concerned with the knowledge of the necessary.[61]

[60] For this integration of historical materialism with Kantian ethics, see also K. Vorländer, *Marx und Kant*, Vienna, 1904. The ideas expressed in this lecture were taken up again and developed further by Vorländer in *K. Marx, sein Leben und sein Werk*, Leipzig, 1929.

[61] Kautsky, op. cit., p. 141.

The counterposing of causality and finalism reappears here in the form of an opposition between *factual and value judgements*, between science and ideology.[62] Science 'observes'; it has no options to suggest for human action. Between the objective and impartial factual observations of science and the finalities of the will, there is a radical distinction. From the *indicative* premises of science one cannot draw conclusions which are determinant of, and binding for, action.

Hilferding wrote in the preface to *Finance Capital*:

It has been said that politics is a normative doctrine ultimately determined by value judgements; since such value judgements do not belong within the sphere of science, the discussion of politics falls outside the limits of scientific treatment. Clearly, it is not possible here to go into the epistemological debate about the relation between the science of norms and the science of laws, between teleology and causality. . . . Suffice it to say that for Marxism the object of political investigation can only be the discovery of causal connections. . . . According to the Marxist viewpoint, the task of a scientific politics is to discover the determination of the will of classes; hence a politics is scientific when it describes causal connections. As in the case of theory, Marxist politics is exempt from 'value judgements'.

And he concluded:

It is therefore incorrect, though widely diffused both *intra* and *extra muros*, simply to identify Marxism and socialism. Considered logically, as a scientific system alone, apart, that is, from the viewpoint of its historical affectivity, Marxism is only a theory of the laws of motion of society. . . . To recognize the validity of Marxism (which implies the recognition of the necessity of socialism) is by no means a task for value judgements, let alone a pointer to a practical line of conduct. It is one thing to recognize a necessity, but quite another to place oneself at the service of that necessity.[63]

The divorce between science and revolution, between knowledge and transformation of the world could not be more complete. In this divorce, moreover, lay the subordinate nature of the Marxism of the Second International, divided between positivist scientism and neo-Kantianism, and yet internally consistent within this opposition. Deterministic objectivisms could not include the ideological moment, the revolutionary political

---

[62] For a brilliant reconstruction of these alternatives in the Marxism of the Second International, see the essay by L. Goldmann, 'Y a-t-il une sociologie marxiste?' in *Les Temps Modernes*, No. 140, October 1957.

[63] Hilferding, op. cit. Cf. E. Thier, 'Etappen der Marxinterpretation', in *Marxismus-studien*, Tübingen, 1954, pp. 15 ff.

programme.[64] On the other hand, excluded from science, ideology was readmitted in a world of 'ethical freedom', alongside the world of 'natural necessity', thereby reproducing the Kantian dualism of *Müssen* and *Sollen*, 'is' and 'ought'.

It is true that in Hilferding, as in Max Adler and the Austro-Marxist school in general, this line of thought was developed with a subtlety of argument that one would seek in vain in the philosophical writings of Kautsky and Plekhanov. And yet the conviction that there can be a body of scientific knowledge acquired independently of any *evaluation*, clearly reveals the naïve positivism underlying this line of thought and its inability to recognize that the role of finalism in scientific research is, at least, *in one aspect*, the very role of *deduction*. Finalism, in Kant's definition, is the causality of a concept in relation to its object; it is the process whose *a priori* is an idea. Now the impossibility of eliminating this process from scientific enquiry is the impossibility for science to do away with ideal *anticipation* and hypothesis. Theory must be *a priori*, for without ideas there can be no observation; we only see what our preconceived ideas prepare us or predispose us to see. As Myrdal has observed: 'Theory . . . must always be *a priori* to the empirical observations of the facts', since, 'facts come to mean something only as ascertained and organized in the frame of a theory.'[65] 'We need to pose questions before responses can be obtained. And the questions are expressions of our own interest in the world; they are ultimately evaluations.'[66] This is equivalent to Kant's observation that 'when Galileo experimented with balls of a definite weight on the inclined plane, when Torricelli . . . [etc.] and Stahl . . . [etc.], they learned that reason only perceives that which it produces after its own design; that it must not be content to follow, as it were, in the leading-strings of nature but must

---

[64] In a marginal note to *The German Ideology*, op. cit., p. 52, Marx noted that 'so-called *objective* historiography just consists in treating the historical conditions independent of activity. Reactionary character.'

[65] G. Myrdal, *Economic Theory and Underdeveloped Regions*, London, 1963, p. 160; see the short but important chapter 12 entitled 'The Logical Crux of All Science'.

[66] G. Myrdal, *The Political Element in the Development of Economic Theory*, London, 1953, p. VII, with the important self-criticism of the initial assumption on which the book was originally based: 'Throughout the book there lurks the idea that when all metaphysical elements are radically cut away, a healthy body of positive economic theory will remain, which is altogether independent of valuations [. . .]. This implicit belief in the existence of a body of scientific knowledge acquired independently of all valuations is, as I now see it, naïve empiricism' (p. 101).

proceed in advance . . . and compel nature to reply to its questions'.[67] This implies that what at first appears to be simple observation, a *statement of fact*, is in effect deduction, the objectification of our ideas, i.e. a projection into the world of our evaluations and pre-conceptions.

On the other hand – and here finalism in turn is reconverted into causality, deduction into induction – the inevitable preconceptions of science are distinguished from the prejudgements of metaphysics (the hypotheses of the former from the hypostases of the latter) in that 'if theory is *a priori* it is on the other hand a first principle of science that the facts are sovereign'. This means that 'when observations of facts do not agree with a theory, i.e. when they do not make sense in the frame of the theory utilized in carrying out the research, the theory has to be discarded and replaced by a better one, which promises a better fit'. In other words, to be truthful, theory must acquire its *source* and *origin* in and from reality, it must be accompanied by 'basic empirical research' which must be 'prior to the construction of the abstract theory' and is 'needed for assuring it realism and relevance'.[68]

To summarize: value judgements are inevitably present in scientific research itself, but as judgements whose ultimate significance depends on the degree to which they stand up to historical-practical verification or experiment, and hence on their capacity to be converted ultimately into factual judgements. This is precisely the link between science and politics, between knowledge and transformation of the world, that Marx accomplished in the historical-moral field. ('Marx', it has been observed '*inextricably* united in his work statements of fact and value judgements'.)[69] This in turn allows us to understand that what Bernstein and so many others saw as a defect or weakness of *Capital* – the co-presence within it of science and ideology – on the contrary represents its most profound originality and its strongest element.

THE LABOUR THEORY OF VALUE

The inadequacy and simplification of the concept of 'economy', which, as we have seen, is an element more or less common to all the tendencies of Marxism in the Second International, helps to explain the foundation, during the same period, of an interpretation of the *labour theory of value* from which even later Marxism has been unable to free itself. This

---

[67] I. Kant, *Critique of Pure Reason*, London, 1964, p. 10.
[68] Myrdal, op. cit., pp. 160–3.   [69] Goldmann, op. cit.

interpretation consisted in the reduction of Marx's theory of value to that of Ricardo, or even to the theory of value which developed in the course of the 'dissolution of the Ricardian school'. Its hallmark is the inability to grasp, or even to suspect, that Marx's theory of value is identical to his *theory of fetishism* and that it is precisely by virtue of this element (in which the crucial importance of the relation with Hegel is intuitively evident) that Marx's theory differs in principle from the whole of classical political economy.

'Political economy has indeed analysed, however incompletely, value and its magnitude and has discovered what lies beneath these forms. But it has never once asked the question why labour is represented by the *value* of its product and labour-time by the *magnitude of that value*.'[70]

The achievement and the limitation of classical political economy are indicated here with extraordinary clarity. First, the achievement: political economy, in spite of its incompleteness and its various inconsistencies, understood that the *value* of commodities is determined by the *labour* incorporated in them, or, in other words, that what appears as the 'value' of 'things' is in reality (here is 'the content hidden in the form') the 'human labour' necessary for their production. Second, the limitation: it never posed the problem of why that content assumes this particular form, why human labour takes on the form of *value of things*, or, in short, on the basis of what historical-social conditions the product of labour takes the form of a *commodity*. This problem could not be posed by political economy, since, Marx goes on to explain, the economists could not see that 'the value-form of the product of labour is not only the most abstract but is also the most universal form taken by the product in bourgeois production'. They wrongly held instead that the production of commodities, far from being a *historical* phenomenon, was a 'self-evident necessity imposed by nature'.[71] They believed, in other words, that there could be no production in society without this production being *production of commodities*, that in all societies the product of human labour must necessarily assume this form.[72]

The main consequence of this different approach is as follows. Classical political economy, taking the existence of the *commodity* as a 'natural'

---

[70] Marx, *Capital*, Vol. I, p. 80.   [71] ibid., p. 81 and n.

[72] This identification is already present in the first pages of *The Wealth of Nations*, where Smith identifies the 'division of labour' with 'exchange'. For this question, see Sweezy, op. cit., pp. 23–4, and Rosa Luxemburg, *Einführung in die Nationalökonomie*, in *Ausgewählte Reden und Schriften*, Vol. I, Berlin, 1951, p. 675.

and hence non-problematical fact, restricted itself to investigating the proportions in which commodities exchange for one another, concentrating their analysis on *exchange value* rather than *value* in the strict sense: 'The analysis of the magnitude of value almost completely absorbs the attention of Smith and Ricardo,' Marx wrote.[73] For Marx, on the contrary, the essential problem, prior to that of exchange rates of commodities is to explain *why* the product of labour takes the form of the *commodity*, why 'human labour' appears as a 'value' of 'things'. Hence the decisive importance for him of his analysis of 'fetishism', 'alienation' or 'reification' (*Verdinglichung*): the process whereby, while *subjective* human or social labour is represented in the form of a quality intrinsic in *things*, these things themselves, endowed with their own *subjective, social* qualities, appear 'personified' or 'animated', as if they were independent subjects. Marx writes:

Where labour is in common, relations between men in their social production are not represented as 'value' of 'things'. Exchanges of products as commodities is a certain method of exchanging labour, and of the dependence of the labour of each upon the labour of the others, a certain mode of social labour or social production. In the first part of my work I have explained that it is characteristic of labour based on private exchange that the social character of the labour is 'represented' as a 'property' of the things; and inversely, that a social relation appears as a relation of one thing to another (of products, values in use, commodities).[74]

Marx explained the operation of this exchange of the subjective with the objective and vice versa – in which the fetishism of commodities consists – with his celebrated concept of *'abstract labour'* or *'average human labour'*. Abstract labour is what is equal and common to all concrete human labouring activities (carpentry, weaving, spinning, etc.) when their activities are considered apart from the real objects (or use-values) to which they are applied and in terms of which they are diversified. If

[73] Marx, *Theories of Surplus Value*, Part II, London, 1969, p. 172: Ricardo 'does not even examine the form of value – the particular form which labour assumes as the substance of value. He only examines the magnitude of value'; in consequence, 'Ricardo is rather to be reproached for very often losing sight of this "real" or "absolute value" and only retaining "relative" and "comparative value".' And in Part III (Marx-Engels, *Werke*, Vol. 26.3, p. 28): 'The error Ricardo makes is that he is only concerned with the *magnitude of value* . . .' Cf. also p. 135. Schumpeter, too (*History of Economic Analysis*, New York, 1954, pp. 596–7) sees this as the most important distinction between Ricardo's theory of value and Marx's theory of value.

[74] Marx, *Theories of Surplus Value*, Part III (op. cit., p. 127).

one abstracts from the material to which labour is applied, one also abstracts, according to Marx, from the determination of productive activity, that is from the concrete character that differentiates the various forms of useful labour. Once this *abstraction* is made, all that remains of all the various sorts of labour is the fact that they are all *expenditures of human labour power.* 'Tailoring and weaving, though qualitatively different productive activities, are each a productive expenditure of human brains, nerves and muscles, and in this sense are human labour.'[75] It is this equal or *abstract* human labour – labour considered as the expenditure and objectification of undifferentiated human labour-power, independently of the concrete forms of activity in which it is realized – that produces *value.* Value is 'a mere congelation of homogeneous human labour, of labour-power expended without regard to the form of its expenditure'. As products of *abstract labour*, all the products of concrete forms of labour lose their perceptible or real qualities and now represent only the fact that 'human labour-power has been expended in their production, that human labour is embodied in them; . . . as crystals of this social substance, common to them all, they are – Values.'[76]

The point to be emphasized here is that not only Marx's critics, but indeed his own disciples and followers – and not only those of the Second International but also more recent ones, to this very day – have all shown themselves incapable of understanding or realizing fully the significance of this concept. 'Abstract labour' seems at least to be a perfectly straightforward and clear notion. And yet neither Kautsky in his *Economic Doctrines of K. Marx*[77] nor Hilferding in his important reply to Böhm-Bawerk,[78] nor Luxemburg in her ample *Introduction to Political Economy*,[79] nor Lenin and *tutti quanti*, have ever really confronted this 'key' to the entire theory of value. Sweezy, who has gone further than most, writes: 'Abstract labour is abstract only in the quite straightforward sense that all special characteristics which differentiate one kind of labour from another are ignored. Abstract labour, in short, is, as Marx's usage quite clearly attests, equivalent to "labour in general"; it is what is common to all productive human activity.'[80]

[75] Marx, *Capital*, Vol. I, p. 44.
[76] ibid., p. 38.
[77] K. Kautsky, *Karl Marx's ökonomische Lehren*, Jena, 1887.
[78] R. Hilferding, *Böhm-Bawerks Marx-Kritik* (Offprint from *Marx Studien*, Vol. I), Vienna, 1904.
[79] Luxemburg, *Einführung in die Nationalökonomie*, op. cit., pp. 41 a 73[?]
[80] P. Sweezy, op. cit., p. 30.

The meaning of this argument is clear. 'Abstract labour' is an abstraction, in the sense that it is a mental *generalization* of the multiplicity of useful, concrete kinds of labour: it is the general, *common* element of all these kinds of labour. This generalization, moreover, as Sweezy goes on to point out, corresponds to capitalist reality, in that in this kind of society labour is shifted or diverted according to the direction of capital investments; hence a determinate portion of human labour is, in accordance with variations of demand, at one time supplied in one form, at another time in another form. This proves the secondary importance in this regime of the various specific kinds of labour, as against labour in general or in and for itself. In spite of Sweezy's plea that 'the reduction of all labour to a common denominator . . . is not an arbitrary abstraction, dictated in some way by the whim of the investigator' but 'rather, as Lukács correctly observes, an abstraction "which belongs to the essence of Capitalism",'[81] despite this, in the absence of what seems to me the decisive point, 'abstract labour' remains, in the last analysis, essentially a *mental generalization*.

The defect of this interpretation of 'abstract labour' lies not only in the fact that – if abstract labour is a mental generalization – it is not clear why what this labour is supposed to produce is something real – *value*; but also in the fact that this opens the door to the transformation of value itself into an abstract generality or *idea* as well. For, in the sense that here only useful and concrete kinds of labour are regarded as real, whereas 'abstract' labour is seen as a merely *mental* fact, so too only the products of useful kinds of labour or *use-values* are real, whereas *value*, the merely general element *common* to them, is abstract.

The interpretation that Bernstein adopted was precisely this one. 'Value' is *ein Gedankenbild*, a mere thought-construct: it is in Marx's work a formal principle which serves to bring system and order to the complexity of the analysis, but itself has no real existence. 'Insofar as we take into consideration the individual commodity', Bernstein comments, 'value loses any concrete content and becomes a mere mental construction'. Hence it is clear that 'the moment that labour-value is only valid as a mental formula (*gedankliche Formel*) or scientific hypothesis, surplus value also becomes a pure formula, a formula based on a hypothesis'.[82]

This interpretation had, of course, already been advanced before Bernstein by Werner Sombart and Conrad Schmidt, in time for Engels to confront it in his *Supplement* to Volume III of *Capital*.[83] Value, according

[81] ibid., p. 31.   [82] op. cit., p. 22.   [83] Marx, *Capital*, Vol. III, pp. 871 ff.

to Sombart, is 'not an empirical, but a mental, a logical fact' while for Schmidt the law of value within the capitalist mode of production is a 'pure, although theoretically necessary fiction'.

It is striking that even at this point, decisive for the genesis of 'revisionism', Engels's response is both uncertain and substantially erroneous. Even if he makes some reservations towards Sombart and Schmidt, he ends up by accepting their essential thesis (that is, the unreal nature of the law of value when commodities are produced under *capitalist conditions*), and hence falls back to the position of Smith (already criticized in its time by Marx)[84] which had relegated the action of the law of value to *precapitalist* historical conditions.

In other words, 'abstract labour' and 'value' – the point on which everything hangs – are understood simply as mental generalizations introduced by the scientist, in this case by Marx; ignoring the fact that, if this were effectively so, in introducing these generalizations Marx would have been committing a 'clumsy error' and the whole of Böhm-Bawerk's critique would indeed be correct. The central argument of Böhm-Bawerk's critique – already present in *Geschichte und Kritik der Kapitalzinstheorien* (pp. 435ff.) and restated in 1896 in *Zum Abschluss des Marxchen Systems* (a text which may have influenced Bernstein) – was that if 'value' is the generalization of 'use-values', it is then *use-value* 'in general' and not, as Marx had argued, a qualitatively distinct entity. Marx's error, according to Böhm-Bawerk, was the error of those who 'confuse abstraction from the *circumstance in general* (*von einem Umstande überhaupt*), and abstraction from the *specific forms* in which this circumstance manifests itself';[85] the error of those who believe that to abstract from the *differences* between one use-value and another is to abstract from use-values *in general*; for the real value is *use-value*, the true theory of value a theory of *value-utility*. According to Böhm-Bawerk, this 'wrong idea' he attributes to Marx means that instead of seeing in 'exchange value' a relation or a mere quantitative proportion between use-values, and hence, like any

---

[84] For this critique of Smith by Marx, see *Theories of Surplus Value*, Part I, London n.d., pp. 71–2.

[85] E. Böhm-Bawerk, *Zum Abschluss des Marxschen Systems* (in a volume of writings in honour of Karl Knies), Vienna, 1896; English translation by Paul Sweezy: *Karl Marx and the Close of his System*, New York, 1949, pp. 73–4. Hilferding's reply to Böhm-Bawerk, which is the best Marxist critique of the theory of marginal utility, is nonetheless deficient on this question – cf. Hilferding, op. cit., p. 127: 'We have in fact nothing more than a disregard by Marx of the specific forms in which use-value manifests itself.'

relation, an unreal value outside the entities related together, Marx invoked the existence behind exchange-value of an objective being 'value', without seeing that this 'entity' was only a 'scholastic-theological' product, a hypostasis arising from his defective logic.[86]

The response that has traditionally been given to these objections by Marxists is well known. It consists, at most, in an appeal to the original conception of Ricardo who had, as can be seen from his last incomplete memoir, already before Marx distinguished between *Absolute Value and Exchangeable Value*. However, apart from Marx's remarks on the tendency of Ricardo's analysis to dwell more on 'exchange-value' than on 'value' itself, this response is further weakened by the fact that, confronted by the non-coincidence of 'values' and 'costs of production', this interpretation has continuously been forced to fall back on to Sombart-Schmidt positions or even Bernstein positions. For once it is accepted that value is not identified with the concrete exchange-values or competitive prices at which the capitalistically produced commodities are in fact sold, this interpretation retreats to a position of attributing to 'value' the significance, essentially, of an abstraction. Dobb's case is typical. After stating that 'value [is] only an abstract approximation to concrete exchange-values', that this 'has generally been held to be fatal to the theory, and was the *onus* of Böhm-Bawerk's criticism of Marx', he limits himself to concluding that 'all abstractions remain only approximations to reality . . . it is no criticism of a theory of value merely to say that this is so'.[87]

THE THEORY OF VALUE AND FETISHISM

The decisive point which, I believe, remains misunderstood in all these interpretations is, as already indicated, the concept of 'abstract labour'; i.e. (a) how this abstraction of labour is produced, and (b) what it really means.

The first part of the question is relatively straightforward. According to Marx, the products of labour take the form of *commodities* when they are produced for *exchange*. And they are produced for exchange when they are products of autonomous, *private* labours carried out independently of one another. Like Robinson Crusoe, the producer of com-

[86] E. Böhm-Bawerk, op. cit., pp. 68–9. The same critique is to be found in E. Calogero, *Il metodo dell' economia e il marxismo*, Bari, 1967, pp. 37 ff.

[87] M. Dobb, *Political Economy and Capitalism*, London, 1960, pp. 14–15.

modities decides by himself how much and what to produce. But unlike Robinson Crusoe he lives in society and hence within a *social division of labour* in which his labour depends on that of others and vice versa. It follows that while Crusoe carried out *all* his indispensable labour *by himself* and relied only on his own labour for the satisfaction of his needs, the producer of commodities carries out only *one* determinate form of labour, the products of which are destined for others, just as the products of the other producers' different forms of labour go to him.

If this social division of labour were a conscious and planned distribution to all its members on the part of society of the various necessary types of labour and quantities to be produced, the products of individual labour would not take the form of *commodities*. For example, in a patriarchal peasant family there is a distribution of the work which the members themselves must carry out, but the products of this labour do not become commodities, nor do the members of the family nucleus buy or sell their products to each other.[88] On the other hand, in conditions of commodity production, the work of individual producers is not labour carried out at the command or on behalf of society: rather it is *private, autonomous* labour, carried out by each producer independently of the next. Hence, lacking any conscious assignment or distribution on the part of society, individual labour is not *immediately* an articulation of social labour; it acquires its character as a part or *aliquot* of aggregate labour only through the *mediation* of exchange relations or the market.

Now Marx's essential thesis is that in order to *exchange* their products, men must *equalize them*, i.e. abstract from the physical-natural or use-value aspect in which one product differs from another (corn from iron, iron from glass, etc.). In abstracting from the object or concrete material of their labour they also abstract *ipso facto* from that which serves to differentiate their labours. 'Along with the useful qualities of the products themselves, we put out of sight both the useful character of the various kinds of labour embodied in them and the concrete forms of that labour; there is nothing left but what is common to them all . . . human labour in the abstract.'[89]

Hence in abstracting from the natural, sensory *objectivity* of their products, men also and simultaneously abstract from what differentiates their various *subjective* activities. 'The Labour . . . that forms the substance of value is homogeneous labour-power, expenditure of one uniform labour-power. The total labour-power of society which is embodied in

[88] cf. *Capital*, Vol. I, pp. 77–8.　　　　　　[89] ibid., p. 38.

the sum total of the values of all commodities produced by that society counts here as one homogeneous mass of human labour-power, composed though it be of innumerable individual units. Each of these units is the same as any other, so far as it has the character of the average labour-power of society and takes effect as such.'[90]

By now it should be clear that the process whereby 'abstract labour' is obtained, far from being a mere *mental* abstraction of the investigator's, is one which takes place daily in the *reality of exchange itself*. ('When we bring the products of our labour into relation with each other as values, it is not because we see in these articles the *material receptacles* of homogeneous human labour. Quite the contrary: whenever by an exchange we equate *as values* our *different products*, by that very act we also equate, as human labour, the different kinds of labour expended upon them. We are not aware of this, nevertheless we do it.')[91]

It remains to deal with the second aspect of the problem, the real significance of this abstraction. The crucial point here is again quite simple. Unlike those interpreters who think it is obvious and non-problematical that in commodity production each individual labour-power is considered as a 'human labour-power identical to all others' or as 'average social labour power', and hence have never asked themselves what this equalization of labour signifies – unlike them, I believe that this is precisely where the significance of 'abstract labour' and the entire theory of value is to be found. For while the working capacities or labour-power of the various producers are in fact different and unequal, just as are the individuals to whom they belong and who *'would not be different individuals if they were not unequal'*,[92] in the reality of the world of commodities, on the other hand, individual labour powers are equalized precisely because they are treated as abstract or *separate* from the real empirical individuals to whom they belong. In other words, precisely insofar as they are regarded as a 'force' or entity 'in itself', i.e. separated from the individuals whose powers they are. 'Abstract labour', in short, is *alienated* labour, labour separated or estranged with respect to man himself.

'The labour-time expressed in exchange value is the labour-time of an individual', Marx wrote, 'but of an individual in no way differing from the next individual and from all other individuals insofar as they perform equal labour. . . . It is the labour time of an individual, *his* labour-time,

---

90 ibid., p. 39.   91 ibid., p. 74.

92 Marx, 'Critique of the Gotha Programme', in Marx and Engels, *Selected Works*, op. cit., p. 324.

but only as labour-time common to all; consequently it is quite immaterial whose individual labour-time it is.'[93] Hence labour is considered here precisely as a process in itself, independent of the man who carries it out. We are not concerned with the particular man who performs the labour, nor with the particular labour he accomplishes, but with the labour-power thus expended, leaving aside *which* particular individual it belongs to and to what particular labour it has been applied. In short, we are concerned here with human energy *as such*, labour power and nothing more, outside and independently of the man who expended it, as if the *real subject* indeed were not the man but labour-power itself, nothing being left to the man but to serve as a mere function or vehicle for the manifestations of the latter.[94] Labour-power, in other words, which is a

[93] Marx, *Contribution to the Critique of Political Economy*, op. cit., p. 32.

[94] Some clarifications may help the reader to follow more easily the argument presented here. Where labour is in common (the simplest example is the primitive community) *social* labour is simply the sum of individual, concrete labours: it is their totality and does not exist separately from its parts. In commodity production, where social labour appears instead in the form of *equal* or *abstract* labour, it is not only calculated apart from the individual concrete labours, but acquires a distinct and independent existence. An individual labour of, say, ten hours may as social labour be worth five. For example: 'The introduction of power-looms into England' meant that 'the handloom weavers, as a matter of fact, continued to require the same time as before; but for all that, the product of one hour of their labour represented after the change only half an hour's social labour and consequently fell to one-half its former value' (cf. *Capital*, Vol. I, p. 39). This *self-abstraction* of labour from the concrete labouring subject, this acquisition by it of independence from man, culminates in the form of the modern wage-labourer. The inversion whereby labour no longer appears as a manifestation of man but man as a manifestation of labour assumes here a real and palpable existence. The wage-earner is *owner* of his working capacity, his labour-power, i.e. of his physical and intellectual energies. These energies, which are in reality inseparable from the living personality, are *abstracted* (or separated) from man to such an extent that they become *commodities*, i.e. as a 'value' which has the man as its 'body' (or 'use-value'). The wage carner is merely the vehicle, the support of the commodity labour-power. The subject is this commodity, this private property; the man is the predicate. It is not that labour-power is a possession of the man's but rather that the man becomes a property or mode of being of 'private property'. 'For the man who is nothing more than a *labourer*', Marx writes, 'his human qualities exist, to the extent that he is a labourer, only insofar as they are for him *foreign* capital.' Indeed, insofar as it manages to realize itself on the market as a commodity (in purchase and sale), labour power becomes part of capital. This is the part that Marx defined as 'variable capital', as we know. The inversion to which we referred reappears here in a more precise form: as the 'value' of labour-power, which, in that as a 'value' it is itself part of capital, annexes the *use* of a working capacity, that is the labourer himself. In his labour, the man does not belong to himself, but to whoever has purchased his labour-power. His energies are no longer 'his own' but

property, a determinant or an attribute of man, becomes an independent subject, by representing itself as the 'value' of 'things'. The human individuals, on the other hand, who are the real subjects become determinations of their determination, i.e. articulations or appendages of their common, reified labour-power, 'Labour, thus measured by time, does not seem, indeed, to be the labour of different persons, but on the contrary the different working individuals seem to be mere organs *of this labour*.'[95] In short: 'men are effaced by their labour . . . the pendulum of the clock has become as accurate a measure of the relative activity of two workers as it is of the speed of two locomotives.' Hence 'we should not say that one man's hour is worth another man's hour, but rather that one man during an hour is worth just as much as another man during an hour. Time is everything, man is nothing; he is at the most time's carcass.'[96]

An analogy may be of help here. Hegel separated human thought from man, turning it into an 'independent subject' called 'the Idea'; for him it was no longer the thinking individual who thinks but the Idea or Logos which thinks itself through man. In this case, as Feuerbach pointed out, 'abstraction means placing man's essence outside himself, the essence of thought outside the act of thinking'. Hence 'speculative philosophy has theoretically fixed the separation of the essential qualities of man from man himself and thus ends by turning abstract qualities into divinities as if they were self-sufficient essences'.[97] The effect of the world of commodities on real men has been similar. It has factually separated or *abstracted* from man his 'subjectivity', i.e. his 'physical and mental ener-

---

'someone else's'. The productive capacity of his labour becomes the *'productive power of capital'*. This 'self-estrangement', or acquisition by labour of independence from man, culminates in modern industry, where it is not the labourer who 'applies the conditions of labour, but inversely, the conditions of labour which apply the labourer' (cf. also *Capital*, Vol. I, p. 422: 'In the factory we have a lifeless mechanism independent of the workman who becomes its mere living appendage.'); modern industry, which, for Marx, represents 'the essence of capitalist production or, if you will, wage labour; labour alienated from itself which confronts the wealth it creates as the wealth of a stranger, its own productivity as the productivity of its product, its own enrichment as self-impoverishment, its social power as the power of society over it' (*Theorien über den Mehrwert*, Part III, op. cit., p. 255).

[95] Marx, *Contribution to the Critique of Political Economy*, op. cit., p. 30.

[96] Marx, *The Poverty of Philosophy*, New York, 1969, p. 54.

[97] L. Feuerbach, *Grundsätze der Philosophie der Zukunft* (Principles of the Philosophy of the Future), in *Sämtliche Werke*, ed. W. Bolin and F. Jodl, Stuttgart, 1959, Vol. II, pp. 227 and 243.

gies', his 'capacity' for work, and has transformed it into a separate essence. It has fixed human energy *as such* in the 'crystal' or 'congelation' of labour which is *value*, turning it into a distinct entity, an entity which is not only independent of man, but also dominates him.

As Marx writes:

There is a definite social relation between men, that assumes in their eyes the fantastic form of a relation between things. In order, therefore, to find an analogy we must have recourse to the mist-enveloped regions of the religious world. In that world the productions of the human brain appear as independent things endowed with life, and entering into relation both with one another and the human race. So it is in the world of commodities with the products of men's hands. This I call the Fetishism which attaches itself to the products of labour, so soon as they are produced as commodities, and which is therefore inseparable from the production of commodities.[98]

To conclude, 'abstract labour' is not only that which is 'common' to all human productive activities, it is not only a mental generalization; rather, it is in itself a real activity, if of a kind opposed to all concrete, useful kinds of labour. More precisely, unlike all the others, it is an activity which does not represent an *appropriation* of the objective, natural world so much as an *expropriation* of *human subjectivity*, a separation of labour 'capacity' or 'power' conceived as the totality of physical and intellectual attitudes, from man himself. This in turn implies that in a society in which individual activities have a *private* character, and in which therefore the interests of individuals are divided and counterposed, or, as we say, *in competition* with one another, the moment of *social unity* can only be realized in the form of an *abstract equalization*, ignoring the individuals themselves; hence, in this case, as a reification of labour-power – a labour-power which is said to be *equal* or *social*, not because it genuinely belongs to *everyone* and hence mediates between the individuals, but because it belongs to *nobody* and is obtained by ignoring the real inequalities between the individuals. This is precisely what Marx is expressing when he writes that abstract labour is 'labour in which the individual characteristics of the workers are obliterated'; or that, when buyer and seller exchange their products and hence *equalize* their labour in the act of exchange, both 'enter into it only insofar as their individual labour is negated, that is to say, turned into money as *non*-individual labour';[99] or, finally where he defines capital as an 'independent *social force*' which,

[98] Marx, *Capital*, Vol. I, p. 72.
[99] Marx, *Contribution to the Critique of Political Economy*, op. cit., pp. 29, 95.

because it has acquired its own autonomous existence, has become 'the power *of a portion of society*' over the rest – a power, therefore, maintaining and multiplying itself '*by means of its exchange for direct, living labour power*'.[100]

I cannot stop here to show how this conception of the theory of value constitutes the element of deepest continuity between the works of the young Marx and those of his maturity. Even in *The German Ideology*, Marx underlines the fact that, under modern conditions, the productive forces 'appear as a world for themselves, quite independent of and divorced from the individuals, alongside the individuals'. As a result, on the one hand 'we have a totality of productive forces, which have, as it were, taken on a material (objective) form and are for the individuals no longer the forces of the individuals, but of private property and hence of the individuals only insofar as they are owners of private property themselves'. On the other hand, 'standing over against these productive forces we have the majority of the individuals from whom these forces have been wrested away and who, robbed thus of all real life-content, have become abstract individuals'.

Nor can we deal here with the fact that our own interpretation of the theory of value which assimilates 'value' to Hegel's hypostasization processes, also links together the *equalization* which is the precondition of 'abstract labour' and the *purely* political equality realized in the modern representative state. (The collective interest, according to Marx in *The German Ideology*, 'takes an independent form as the *State*, divorced from the real interests of the individual and community', insofar as 'just because individuals seek *only* their particular interest which for them does not coincide with their communal interest – in fact the general is the illusory form of communal life – the latter will be imposed on them as an interest "alien" to them and "independent" of them, as in its turn a particular, peculiar "general" interest.' Hence 'the social power' transformed into the power of the state 'appears to these individuals . . . not as their own united power, but as an alien force existing outside them, of the origin and goal of which they are ignorant.')[101] We can, however, deal with one other point here: this confluence of the theory of value and the theory of fetishism or alienation in Marx represents not only his main difference of principle with the classical political economists, for whom the theory of alienation is absolutely inconceivable; it also constitutes the

---

[100] Marx, *Wage Labour and Capital*, in *Selected Works*, op. cit., p. 82.
[101] Marx and Engels, *The German Ideology*, London, 1965, pp. 82, 45–6.

viewpoint from which he explained the birth and destiny of political economy as a science. Firstly, its *birth*: the precondition for the emergence of economic reflection lay for Marx in the process whereby social relations became obscured and objectified in the eyes of men as a consequence of the *generalization*, with the emergence of modern bourgeois society, of the production of commodities and the fetishism inherent in it. ('The ancient social organisms of production are far more simple and transparent than the bourgeois organism'; even though commodity production occurs within them, it emerges as a secondary or marginal branch among kinds of production based on a natural economy – based, that is, on the immediate consumption of products rather than their sale on the market.) Secondly, its later *destiny*: the task of political economy as a science consisted for Marx essentially – if we can accept a neologism – in the de-fetishization of the world of commodities, in the progressive comprehension that what represents itself as the 'value' of 'things' is in reality not a property of these things themselves, but reified human labour. This theme, according to Marx, runs through the entire history of economic theory from mercantilism to Smith: the gradual rediscovery, beneath the mask of fetishized objectivity, of the alienated human subject. In the 'Introduction' of 1857, he wrote: 'The Monetary system, for example, still regards wealth quite objectively as a thing existing independently in the shape of money. Compared with this standpoint, it was a substantial advance when the Manufacturing Mercantile System transferred the source of wealth from the object to the subjective activity – mercantile or industrial labour – but it still considered that only this circumscribed activity itself produced money.' He continues: 'In contrast to this system, the Physiocrats assume that a specific form of labour – agriculture – creates wealth, and they see the object no longer in the guise of money, but as a product in general, as the universal result of labour. In accordance with the still circumscribed activity, the product remains a naturally developed product, an agricultural product, a product of the land *par excellence*.' Finally, a tremendous step forwards was achieved by Smith in rejecting 'all restrictions with regard to the activity that produces wealth – for him it was labour as such, neither manufacturing, nor commercial, nor agricultural labour, but all types of labour.'[102]

We have already seen how, despite its real merits, classical political economy as well as *Vulgärökonomie*, remained in the end a prisoner of

[102] Marx, '1857 Introduction' to *A Contribution to the Critique of Political Economy*, op. cit., p. 209.

fetishism,[103] because of its inability to pose the problem of why the product of labour takes the form of the commodity and hence why human labour is presented as the 'value' of 'things'. This gives us the chance to raise a crucial point, which today has been entirely forgotten. Marx considered that with the end of commodity production, the *political economy* born with it would *also come to an end*. It is in this sense that his work is a *critique* of political economy itself, rather than the work of an economist in the strict sense.[104] Hence the subtitle of *Capital*, the title of the *Contribution to the Critique* of 1859, not to mention the vast *brouillon* of 1858 which goes by the name of *Grundrisse der Kritik der politischen Ökonomie*.

'Value' is the product of human labour. 'Surplus value', which is produced by human wage labour, is subdivided into profit and rent (besides, of course, the restitution of the wage). To *political economy*, which fails to coordinate or reduce these categories to a unity, rent appears as the product of land as such, as some *rudis indigestaque moles*; profit appears as a product of the notorious 'productivity of capital', that is of machines and raw materials as such; the wage appears as the product of labour. Physical, natural categories (land, means of production) and economic–social categories (profit, rent, etc.) – i.e. magnitudes which cannot be compared with one another – are fetishistically confused and muddled together, as Marx points out in his famous chapter on 'The Trinity Formula'.[105] In Marx's own *critique* of political economy, on the

[103] *Theorien über den Mehrwert*, Part III, op. cit., p. 255. 'In proportion as political economy developed – and this development, at least in its basic principles, found its highest expression in Ricardo – it represented labour as the only element of value. . . . But to the extent that labour is conceived as the *only* source of exchange-value, . . . 'capital' is conceived by the same economists and especially Ricardo (but even more by Torrens, Malthus, Bailey, etc., after him) as the regulator of production, the source of wealth and the goal of all production. . . . In this contradiction, political economy merely expressed the essence of capitalist production, or if you like of wage labour: labour alienated from itself, to which the wealth it creates is counterposed as the wealth of a stranger, its own productivity as the productivity of its product, its own enrichment as self-impoverishment, its social power as the power of society over it.'

[104] This theme of the end of political economy was taken up by Hilferding, *Böhm-Bawerk's Criticism of Marx*, op. cit., pp. 133–4; by Luxemburg, *Einführung*, op. cit., p. 491; and finally was central to the work of the Russian economist and member of the Trotskyist opposition, E. Preobrazhensky, *The New Economics*, Oxford, 1966. An extremely interesting discussion of these problems can be found in Karl Korsch, *Karl Marx*, London, 1938.

[105] Marx, *Capital*, Vol. III, chapter 48.

other hand, the whole picture is decisively altered. The mysterious trinity of Capital, Land and Labour is swept away. Since 'value' is now considered as the objectification of human labour-power, the critical-scientific or anti-fetishistic discourse of *Capital* comes to coincide with the *self-consciousness of the working class* (a further proof of the unity of science and ideology). For just as wage labour, by recognizing the essence of 'value' and 'capital', sees that essence as an objectification of 'itself' (and hence reaches self-consciousness through this knowledge), the working class, by becoming conscious of itself, achieves – for profit and rent are forms derived from surplus value – the knowledge of the origin and basis of other classes and hence of society as a whole.[106]

This point serves to indicate the profound difference between Marx and his Marxist but (more or less consciously) Ricardian interpreters. They failed to grasp the organic unity between the *theory of value* and the *theory of fetishism* and therefore could not avoid confusing two totally distinct things. On the one hand, in dividing its total labour force between different employments, society must take account of the *labour-time* involved in each of these employments.[107] On the other hand, we have the specific way in which this law operates *under capitalism* where, in the absence of a conscious or planned division of social labour, the labour-time required by the various productive activities is presented as an *intrinsic quality* in the products themselves, as the 'value' of a 'thing'. This confusion between the law of labour-time (which applies to all societies) and its fetishized realization in the world of capital and of commodities, or between the *principles of planning and the law of value* (to bring the confusion up to date), is the root of modern revisionism, as is all too evident

[106] This point was developed by Lukács in *History and Class Consciousness*, op, cit.

[107] Marx, *Grundrisse der Kritik der politischen Ökonomie*, Berlin, 1953, p. 98: 'In conditions of communal production the determination of time obviously remains essential. The less time it takes society to produce corn, cattle, etc., the more time it gains for other forms of production, material or spiritual. As in the case of a single individual, the universality of his development, of his pleasures, of his activity, depends upon the way he economizes his time. The economy of time, ultimately all economy is reduced to this. Society must distribute its time functionally so as to obtain a production in accordance with all its needs; so the individual must also divide his time correctly to acquire knowledge in the right proportions and to fulfil the various demands on his activity. In conditions of production in common the first economic law remains, there-fore, the economy of time, the planned distribution of labour-time between the different branches of production. This law becomes even more important under these conditions. But all this is quite distinct from the measurement of exchange values (labours or labour products) by "labour-time".'

in the present economic debates in the Soviet Union. In Italy, it is the basis for the recent theoretical positions, which I cannot accept, of two theorists, Galvano della Volpe and Giulio Pietranera, to whom in other respects I am much indebted. First, in the case of della Volpe: to Sweezy's wholly correct statement that 'value and planning are as opposed to each other, and for the same reasons, as capitalism and socialism', della Volpe objects that 'between value and planning there is only a difference of *degree*, that is of *development*: there is nothing negatively "opposed" or "contrary" in the two terms'.[108] As for Pietranera, he follows Oscar Lange in referring to the 'market' and 'profit' in socialist society, not as survivals of bourgeois institutions that are inevitable in what is *par excellence* a *transitional* society but as 'rational criteria and indices of economic efficiency, and hence something *positive*, to be maintained in a planned socialist economy' – in other words as institutions *socialist* by their very nature.[109] This brings to mind a further, more recent error of Della Volpe. The latter presents (in the most recent edition of *Rousseau e Marx*) the state under socialism – the state, mark you, i.e. the hypostasis of the 'general interest', which (as Marx says) has become independent and 'alien' from the generality of interests that compose it – not as a *survival*, but as a state which is wholly new, socialist in its inner structure. (Compare Lenin's conception of the state in *State and Revolution*: the presence in socialism of 'bourgeois right in regard to the distribution of consumption goods inevitably presupposes the existence of the *bourgeois state*, for right is nothing without an apparatus capable of *enforcing* the observance of the standards of right'. It follows that 'there remains for a time not only bourgeois right but even the bourgeois state without the bourgeoisie!')[110]

EQUIVALENCE AND SURPLUS VALUE

If we now turn to Bernstein, we can see that the first and most important consequence of his interpretation of 'value' as a mere 'mental construction' is that – since he is quite incapable of explaining value, and *a fortiori* surplus value as a result of capitalist *production* – he is obliged to transfer its point of origin from the sphere of production to the sphere of circulation and exchange, as though surplus value originated, in other

---

[108] G. della Volpe, *Chiave della dialettica storica*, Rome, 1964, p. 32 n.
[109] G. Pietranera, *Capitalismo ed economia*, Turin, 1966, p. 236.
[110] Lenin, *Selected Works*, op. cit., Vol. II, pp. 342–3.

words, in a violation of *commutative* justice, i.e. in a violation of the law of exchange on the basis of equivalents. He thus reinstated the old mercantilist conception of 'profit upon alienation', i.e. of the origin of profit in the difference between selling and buying prices (indeed, this is why 'consumer cooperatives' assume such importance in Bernstein's thought). This viewpoint, which restores the schema of 'utopian socialism', and in this case Proudhon's account of exploitation as *theft* and hence of the *contradiction* between exploitation and legality, constitutes the essential core of 'revisionism'. For Marx modern *social inequality* or capitalist exploitation occurs simultaneously with the fullest development of *juridical-political equality*; here, on the contrary, juridical-political equality – and hence the modern representative State – becomes the instrument for the progressive elimination and dissolution of real inequalities, which seem arbitrarily produced rather than an organic consequence of the system as such.

The importance of this connection between equality and inequality in Marx's thought deserves emphasis here; besides its repercussions in political philosophy, which we shall examine, it also contained one of Marx's most important scientific achievements, his solution of the so-called 'paradox' of the law of value.

The law of value, according to Smith, is the law of the exchange of equivalents. It presupposes, besides the equal value of the commodities exchanged, the equality, as Marx pointed out, of the contracting parties in the act of exchange. In exchange the owners of commodities 'mutually recognize in each other the rights of *private proprietors*' establishing '*a juridical relation* which thus expresses itself in a contract, whether such contract be part of a developed legal system or not'.[111] Now the 'paradox' is that the production of commodities (production for exchange) becomes dominant for the first time only under purely capitalist conditions; yet just when the law of value should find its fullest application it seems to be contradicted by the existence of surplus value and exploitation, in other words, the emergence of an *unequal* exchange.

Smith, of course, reacted to this 'paradox' by turning away from a labour theory of value *contained*, to a theory of value based on *command* of labour, thus relegating the validity of the law of value to precapitalist conditions. Ricardo, while he showed the difference between equal exchange of commodities for commodities, and the inequality characterizing the exchange of commodities for labour power (specifically capitalist

[111] Marx, *Capital*, Vol. I, p. 84.

exchange), failed to explain 'how this *exception* could be in accordance with the law of value'.[112] Marx's theory explains the phenomenon of expropriation or of modern inequality precisely through the generalization of *property rights* or purely *juridical* equality.

Capitalism for Marx is the *generalization of* exchange; under capitalism all important social relations become exchange relations, starting with the productive relations themselves, which presuppose the buying and selling of labour-power. With this generalization of exchange a sphere of *juridical equality* is created, extended for the first time to all. The modern labourer is a holder of rights, a *free* person, and therefore is capable of entering into a contract, just as much as the employer of labour. 'Wage labour on a national scale, and hence also the capitalist mode of production, is not possible unless the labourer is personally free. It is based on the personal freedom of the labourer'.[113] Both the seller and buyer of labour-power are juridically equal persons because they are *private-proprietors*, owners of commodities.

However, according to Marx, what makes this relation of equality *formal* and conceals the real inequality is the fact that the property at the disposal of the worker (his own labouring *capacity*) is only property in *appearance*. In reality, it is the opposite, a state of need, so that 'if his capacity for labour remains unsold, the labourer derives no benefit from it, but rather he will feel it to be a cruel, nature-imposed necessity that this capacity has cost for its production a definite amount of the means of subsistence and that it will continue to do so for its reproduction'.[114]

In short, 'in the concept of the *free labourer*, it is already implicit', Marx writes, 'that he is a *pauper*, or virtually a pauper. According to his economic conditions he is *pure living working capacity*', which, since it is endowed with living requirements yet deprived of the means to satisfy them, is in itself not a *good* or form of *property*, but 'indigence from all points of view'.[115]

Hence the *generalization* of exchange – the typical phenomenon of modern capitalism – not only for the first time extends to all the sphere of juridical equality, making even the modern labourer into a *free person*; it achieves this liberation in a dual way, since the extension of contractual relations to production through the buying and selling of labour power means on the one hand that the labourer is free in the sense that he is 'a

[112] Marx, *Theorin über den Mehrwert*, Part III, op. cit., p. 170.
[113] ibid., p. 424.
[114] Marx, *Capital*, Vol. I, p. 173.   [115] Marx, *Grundrisse*, op. cit., p. 497.

free owner of his own working capacity and of his own person' and on the other that he is free in the sense of *expropriated* from the means of production, i.e. 'deprived of *everything* necessary for the realization of his labour-power'.[116]

Now the application of equal rights or property rights to two persons, of whom only one is really a property owner, explains why this formal equality of rights is in reality the *law of the stronger*. This is Marx's point when he writes that 'the bourgeois economists have merely in view that production proceeds more smoothly with modern police than, e.g. under club law. They forget, however . . . that the law of the stronger, only in a different form, still survives even in their "constitutional State".'[117]

In conclusion: the law of value which is indeed a law of exchange of *equivalents*, as soon as it is realized and becomes *dominant*, reveals its true nature as the law of *surplus value* and capitalist appropriation.

The exchange of equivalents, the original operation with which we started, has now become turned round in such a way that there is only an *apparent* exchange. This is owing to the fact, first, that the capital which is exchanged for labour power is itself but a portion of *the product of others' labour appropriated without an equivalent*; and secondly, that this capital must not only be replaced by its producer but replaced together with an *added surplus*. . . . At first the rights of property seemed to us to be based on a man's own labour. At least, some such assumption was necessary since only commodity owners with equal rights confronted each other, and the sole means by which a man could become possessed of the commodities of others was by alienating his own commodities; and these could be replaced by labour alone. Now, however, property turns out to be *the right* on the part of the capitalist to appropriate *the unpaid labour of others* or its product and to be the impossibility on the part of the labourer of appropriating his own product. The *separation of property from labour* has become the necessary consequence of a law that apparently originated in their identity.[118]

Hence Marx's opposition to 'utopian socialism' or 'revisionism' *ante litteram*, which, he claimed, 'especially in its French version' (Proudhon) saw socialism 'as the realization of the ideas of *bourgeois* society enunciated by the French Revolution'; as though the full realization of the 'rights of man', the principles of 1789 – or, as we would now say, the republican Constitution – could dissolve the modern *social* inequalities which these

---

[116] Marx, *Capital*, Vol. I, p. 169.
[117] Marx, 'Introduction' to *A Contribution to the Critique of Political Economy*, op. cit., p. 193.   [118] Marx, *Capital*, Vol. I, pp. 583–4.

legal and constitutional principles have claimed were the precondition for
their own appearance, and which they have reinforced ever since. These
socialists

affirm that exchange, exchange-value, etc. *originally* (in time) or in their *concept*
(in their adequate form) are a system of liberty and equality for all, but have
since been adulterated by money, capital, etc. . . . The answer to them is that
exchange value, or more precisely the monetary system, is in fact the system of
equality and liberty, and that what seems to them to distort the subsequent
development of the system is distortions immanent to that system itself, precisely the realization of the *equality* and freedom which reveal themselves as
inequality and despotism. . . . To want exchange-value not to develop into
capital, or the labour, which produces exchange-value, not to become wage-
labour, is as pious as it is stupid. What distinguishes these gentlemen from the
bourgeois apologists is, firstly, their awareness of the contradictions contained in
the system; but secondly, the utopianism which prevents them from discerning
the necessary distinction between the real and ideal forms of bourgeois society,
and hence makes them want to undertake the vain task of trying to re-realize
the ideal expression itself, while in fact this is only a reflected image of existing
reality.[119]

Legal reforms cannot, therefore, grasp or transform the fundamental
mechanisms of the system. This is so because, as Rosa Luxemburg
acutely pointed out in the polemic against Bernstein, what distinguishes
bourgeois society from preceding class societies, ancient or feudal, is the
fact that class domination does not rest on 'inherited' or *unequal* rights as
previously, but on real economic relations mediated by *equality* of rights.

No law obliges the proletariat to submit itself to the yoke of capitalism.
Poverty, the lack of means of production, obliges the proletariat to submit itself
to capital. . . . And no law in the world can give to the proletariat the means of
production while it remains in the framework of bourgeois society, for no laws,
but economic development, has torn the means of production from the producers. . . . Neither is the exploitation *inside* the system of wage labour based on
laws. The level of wages is not fixed by legislation but by economic factors. The
phenomenon of capitalist exploitation does not rest on a legal disposition. . . .
In short, the fundamental relation of domination of the capitalist class cannot
be transformed by means of legislative reforms, on the basis of capitalist society,
because these relations have not been introduced by bourgeois laws, nor have
they received the form of such laws.

In our legislative system, as Rosa Luxemburg points out, not one legal
formulation of the present class domination can be found. 'How then

[119] Marx, *Grundrisse*, op. cit., p. 160.

can one overcome wage slavery gradually, by legal means, when this has never been expressed in legislation?' That, she continues, is

> why people who pronounce themselves in favour of the method of legislative reform *in place of* and *in contradistinction to* the conquest of political power and social revolution, do not really choose a more tranquil, calmer and slower road to the *same goal*, but a *different goal*. Instead of taking a stand for the establishment of a new society, they stand for surface modifications of the old society. If we follow the political conceptions of revisionism, we arrive at the same conclusion that is reached when we follow the economic theories. They aim not towards the realization of *socialism*, but the reform of *capitalism*, not the suppression of the system of wage labour but the 'diminution' of exploitation, that is the suppression of the *abuses* of capitalism instead of the suppression of capitalism itself.[120]

'SOCIAL CAPITAL'

The insistence with which I have underlined the limits of the theoretical comprehension of Bernstein and the Marxism of the Second International should not allow us to forget, however, that these limits, and the regression in relation to Marx typical of so much of late nineteenth-century Marxism, only acquired their decisive importance in the context and under the impact of a new and complex historical situation, in which a series of phenomena – occasionally anticipated by Marx, but only now macroscopically developed – fundamentally transformed the traditional features of capitalist society.

The period of the transition of capitalism to the monopoly phase marked a colossal leap forward in the process of *socialization* of production, introducing the great modern 'masses' into production and social life, where formerly they were dispersed in occupations surviving from previous modes of production. This *'socialization' process*, accelerated by the formation of 'joint-stock companies', meant not only an enormous growth in the scale of production and enterprise which could not have been achieved with individual capitals; it also meant the birth of the modern so-called 'social enterprise', insofar as it gave rise to the complex phenomenon of the dissolution of *private* capitalist industry on the basis of the capitalist system itself.

The capital, which in itself rests on a social mode of production and presupposes a social concentration of means of production and labour-power, is

120 Rosa Luxemburg, *Social Reform or Revolution?*, op. cit., pp. 50–2.

here [in the case of the joint-stock company] directly endowed with the form of social capital (capital of directly associated individuals) as distinct from private capital, and its undertakings assume the form of social undertakings as distinct from private undertakings. It is the abolition of capital as private property within the framework of capitalist production itself.[121]

The main consequences of this phenomenon (beginning with the 'separation of ownership and control') were already grasped in their essential features by Marx himself, even though they were still in their initial phase when *Capital* was written. The development of *social capital*, he wrote, implies the

transformation of the actually functioning capitalist into a mere manager, administrator of other people's capital, and of the owner of capital into a mere owner, a mere money-capitalist. Even when the dividends which they receive include the interest and the profit of enterprise, i.e. the total profit . . . this total profit is henceforth received only in the form of interest, i.e. as mere compensation for owning capital that now is entirely divorced from the function in the actual process of production, just as . . . the manager is divorced from ownership of capital.[122]

This in turn had two effects, which Marx did not fail to point out. Firstly, big capital exerted an action of 'peaceful expropriation' towards small capitals, whether already formed or in the process of formation, through the credit system and in particular through the joint-stock company. This created a situation in which the great majority of shareholders were deprived of control over their property in favour of a small minority of owners who came to wield a power that went far beyond the limits of their own actual property. Secondly, the progressive *depersonalization* of property, brought about by the development of the great modern 'limited liability' company, implied the emergence as *a subject* of *the object* of property itself, i.e. the complete emancipation of property from man himself, with the result that the firm seemed to acquire an independent life of its own as though it were nobody's property, transforming itself into an entity in itself with similar characteristics to those of the State.

This spread of joint-stock companies, of course, as Marx pointed out, encouraged speculation and adventurers, 'a new financial aristocracy, a new variety of parasites in the shape of promoters, speculators and simply nominal directors; a whole system of swindling and cheating by means of

[121] Marx, *Capital*, Vol. III, p. 427.   [122] ibid., p. 427.

corporation promotion, stock issuance, and stock speculation'. And yet this process was the chief support for Bernstein's thesis of a progressive 'democratization of capitalism'. In his view, modern *industrial concentration* is not accompanied, as Marx claimed, by a similar concentration of *property*; rather it leads, through joint-stock companies, to a *diffusion* of property, a multiplication of the number of capitalists, a growth in the number of those who share in the benefits of the modern 'social enterprise'. Since the number of capitalists increases rather than diminishes, Marx's discussion of concentration and accumulation of wealth at one pole of society is contradicted and invalidated.

This theme has, of course, been taken up again relatively recently, thanks to two American neo-liberals, Berle and Means.[123] Their thesis is that the large firms represent only a *technical*-industrial concentration, which does not imply a concentration of property, but rather its diffusion and decentralization. Hence joint-stock companies or corporations signify the 'end of capitalism', provided that (a) control of these 'quasi-public' enterprises is entrusted to disinterested technicians (Berle and Means look forward to the appearance of an 'impartial technocracy'); and (b) that share ownership is progressively extended to all layers of society.

However, this is not the place to do more than note this development. To return to Bernstein, the scientific ingenuity behind his thesis of the multiplication of capitalists is revealed by two criticisms levelled at him by Rosa Luxemburg. Firstly, 'by "capitalist" Bernstein does not mean a category of production but the right to property. To him, "capitalist" is not an economic but a fiscal unit. And "capital" for him is not a factor of production but simply a certain quantity of money.' Hence, she concludes, 'he moves the question of socialism from the domain of production into the domain of relations of fortune . . . between rich and poor'. Secondly, Bernstein's thesis of the progressive dissolution of big capital into myriads of small capitals, and more generally his propensity to emphasize counter-tendencies to concentration, besides being based on utopian fantasy is essentially *reactionary*. If true, it would lead to 'an arrested development of the capitalist system of production', its regression or involution to a pre-natal phase.[124]

The same could be said for Bernstein's arguments about the persistence and increase in the number of small and medium enterprises. The

[123] A. Berle and G. Means, *The Modern Corporation and Private Property*, New York, 1934.
[124] Rosa Luxemburg, op. cit., pp. 31, 37.

'almost unshakeable phalanx' of medium-sized firms is a sign for him that the development of big industry does not resolve itself into giant concentrations as Marx had prophesied. Schumpeter's judgement is conclusive enough on this point: 'Bernstein was an admirable man but he was no profound thinker and especially no theorist. In some points, especially as regards . . . the concentration of economic power, his argument was distinctly shallow.'[125] Rosa Luxemburg's comment, however, is also pertinent: 'To see the progressive disappearance of the middle-sized firms as a necessary result of the development of large industry is to misunderstand sadly the nature of this process.' In relation to big industry the small firms 'initiate new methods of production in well-established branches of industry; they are also instrumental in the creation of new branches of production not yet exploited by big capital. . . . The struggle of the middle-sized enterprise against big capital cannot be conceived as a regularly proceeding battle in which the troops of the weaker side continue to melt away directly and quantitatively. It should be regarded as a periodic mowing down of the small enterprises, which rapidly grow up again, only to be mowed down once more by big industry.' This process does not necessarily mean 'an absolute diminution in the number of middle-sized enterprises . . . [but rather], first a progressive increase in the minimum amount of capital necessary for the functioning of enterprises in the older branches of production; second, the constant diminution of the interval of time during which the small capitalists conserve the opportunity to exploit the new branches of production'.[126]

Besides, Bernstein's 'ingenuous' marshalling of statistical material to support his argument, both as regards the diffusion of small and medium firms and variations in the flow of income, is exhaustively documented in Kautsky's reply to Bernstein. (Little reference has been made here to this book, though – especially in the central chapters – it is one of Kautsky's best works, along with the *Agrarfrage*.) As for Bernstein's argument in support of the 'new middle classes' thesis, the best answer is to be found in Kautsky's book and in Hilferding's *Finance Capital*. Here we can only touch on the problem, important though it is in the period of imperialism, developing as a result of the abnormal growth of the distribution sector provoked by monopoly, besides the mushrooming of the bureaucratic-military apparatus characteristic of the modern State.

[125] J. Schumpeter, *History of Economic Analysis*, London, 1967, p. 883.
[126] Rosa Luxemburg, op. cit., pp. 18–19.

Here it only remains to turn to a consideration of the so-called theory of the 'absolute immiseration' or long-term impoverishment of the masses, which, since Bernstein, has been often attributed to Marx by a variety of commentators: notably, until a few years ago, by the most primitive exponents of 'dialectical materialism' in the Soviet Union.

Not only is such a theory absent in Marx, but it would have been *impossible* for him to have produced it, as is proved simply by one thing (among others): that Marx introduces an explicitly *historical-moral* component into the determination of the 'price of labour' (thus distinguishing himself from Ricardo). In determining the 'sum of means of subsistence' necessary for the maintenance of a worker 'in his normal state as a labouring individual', it is not enough, Marx argues, to consider only 'natural wants such as food, clothing, fuel and housing, 'which "vary according to the climatic and other physical conditions of his country".' It is also necessary to consider that the *'number and extent of so-called necessary wants,* as also the modes of satisfying them, are themselves *the product of historical development* and depend therefore to a great extent on the degree of civilization of a country, more particularly on the conditions under which, and consequently on the habits and degree of comfort in which, the class of free labourers has been formed'.[127] This *historically relative* character of the determination of the 'price of labour' is explicitly stated: 'In contradistinction . . . to the case of other commodities, there enters into the determination of the value of labour-power a historical and moral element.' If we reflect on this we can understand that for Marx, above all others, it is impossible in principle to speak of a *long-term immiseration* of the workers, a worsening in *absolute* terms of their living standards in the centuries of capitalist development.

It is true that in the *Manifesto* and many other writings, Marx refers to a pauperization of the working class, its growing dependence for its subsistence on the will of others, that is of the capitalists; he writes of the 'immiseration', 'degeneration' and 'enslavement' of the workers and refers to the growing precariousness and insecurity of their labour: 'To the extent that capital is accumulated, the situation of the worker *whatever his retribution,* high or low, can only worsen' (my italics). But this conviction, to which Marx remained faithful all his life, can only mean one thing: capitalist development, contrary to illusions of 'betterment' nourished by reformists, is not destined to transform everyone into capitalists and property owners; nor will it abolish, by gradual reforms,

[127] Marx, *Capital*, Vol. I, p. 171.

the basic social *inequality* between capital and labour but quite to the contrary tends constantly to reproduce it, and to reproduce it in an aggravated form. This is a theory, in other words, of *relative* immiseration or an increase in the imbalance or inequality of the workers' conditions *in relation* to the conditions of the class that owns the means of production.[128]

As Marx wrote in 1849:

A noticeable increase in wages presupposes a rapid growth of productive capital . . . [which] brings about an equally rapid growth of wealth, luxury, social wants, social enjoyments. Thus, although the enjoyments of the worker have risen, the social satisfaction that they give has fallen in comparison with the increased enjoyments of the capitalist, which are inaccessible to the worker in comparison with the state of development of society in general. Our desires and pleasures spring from society; we measure them, therefore, by society and not by the objects that serve for their satisfaction, because they are of a social nature, they are of a relative nature.[129]

Hence not only does Marx's theory not exclude increases in real wages, but this increase, whatever Bernstein and Joan Robinson may think, proves absolutely nothing which contradicts Marx's thought. Indeed, the theory of increasing exploitation holds good even in the case where wages have risen. And not only because the increase of the workers' enjoyment does not exclude that the 'social satisfaction' he obtains from it diminishes *proportionately*, but because we measure our needs and enjoyments not only by 'the material means for their satisfaction', but according to a social scale or social 'relation'. 'Just as little as better clothing, food and treatment and a larger peculium, do away with the exploitation of a slave, so little do they set aside that of the wage-worker.'[130] This is, in fact, the decisive point in the entire Marxist theory of exploitation – a point on which our own reading of the theory of value as a theory of alienation can help to throw light. It is the *dependence* which ties the workers to the will of the capitalist class, and not their absolute poverty, that represents 'the *differentia specifica* of capitalist production'.[131] In other words, capitalist appropriation is not exclusively or primarily an appropriation of *things*, but rather an appropriation of subjectivity, of working energy itself, of the physical and intellectual powers of man.

[128] J. Gillman, *The Falling Rate of Profit*, London, 1957, pp. 145 ff.
[129] Marx, *Wage Labour and Capital*, in *Selected Works*, op. cit., pp. 84–5.
[130] Marx, *Capital*, Vol. I, p. 618.
[131] ibid.

CAPITALISM AND THE CONSTITUTION

When Bernstein's book is considered as a whole, it can be seen that the point to which his argument constantly returns and from which all his theses stem is, on the one hand, the 'contradiction' between *political equality* and *social inequality*; and, on the other, the capacity of the parliamentary government or modern representative state progressively to iron out the tensions and conflicts arising from class differences, to the point where their very source is removed.

The appeal to the inalienable 'rights of man' proclaimed by the French Revolution; the emphasis on natural law underlying Bernstein's 'ethical' socialism; his exaltation of 'liberalism', which he sees as the soul of modern democracy, to the extent of reducing the latter to the 'political form' of liberalism (*die Demokratie ist nur die politische Form des Liberalismus*) – all this does not require comment, given the eloquent clarity with which it is expressed. If time and space allowed, it would be obligatory to compare it with that remarkable document of ethico-political reflection, Marx's early text on *The Jewish Question.*

But to bring back our argument to the initial point, I shall rather emphasize that the development of this interclassist conception of the state in German Social Democracy was a gradual one, almost a slow historical accretion, interlinked with the practical political vicissitudes of the party. In 1890, with the fall of Bismarck, the anti-socialist law came to an end. The introduction of this law, which forced on German Social Democracy a quasi-illegal existence for twelve years, was not un-connected with difficulties consequent on the economic depression discussed above. According to Mehring, 'with the anti-socialist law, big industry, under the impact of the crash, made common cause with the reactionary classes. It obtained its industrial tariffs, while the bankrupt Junkers were artificially kept alive by agrarian tariffs and subsidies. These tariffs freed military absolutism from parliamentary control, still inconvenient in spite of the feebleness of the bourgeois parties in the *Reichstag.*'[132]

From this difficult period, however, which it had confronted with courage and determination, German Social Democracy emerged enormously strengthened. When the anti-socialist laws were passed, the party had 437,000 votes and the trade unions had 50,000 members; by the

---

[132] F. Mehring, *Geschichte der deutschen Sozialdemokratie*, 8th and 9th editions, Stuttgart, 1919, Part II, Vol. 4, p. 338.

time they came to an end, the party could boast 1,427,000 votes and the unions 200,000 members. 'In twelve years of struggle the Party had not only become larger and more powerful, but was also considerably enriched in its innermost essence. It had not only resisted and hit back, but also worked, learned; it had given proof not only of its strength but also of its spirit.'[133]

This quantitative growth and the return to legality, even in the limited terms allowed by German conditions, created a series of qualitatively new problems. Having reached the point of its fullest development, the party now had to confront the difficult and complex transition from a phase of simple propaganda to one of concrete political choices and constant co-ordinated and practical action. So long as the party was proscribed, it had no choice but to use parliament as a propaganda tribune for socialism. But now that Bismarck had been dismissed and there was a prospect of rapid and steady electoral growth, with a general climate which seemed favourable to social reforms, should this purely negative attitude be abandoned? Should the parliamentary delegates of the party become spokesmen for the demands of the trade-union movement, favour the adoption of those measures that seemed feasible and in some way insert themselves positively in the *Reichstag* debates, passing from non-cooperation to a constructive policy?[134]

This turn posed serious tactical and strategic problems. Was it right to seek collaboration or alliance with other political forces or was this not to run the risk that the party, still young and moreover swollen with recent recruits, would thereby lose its independence and identity? Then there was the question of the *Reich*, founded in 1870: should it be regarded as an enemy to fight, or accepted as a fact within which it was possible to work to obtain in the meanwhile the bourgeois-democratic reforms from which the German state was still so far removed?

At the Erfurt Congress (October 1891) the prevailing attitude seemed largely inspired by confidence and optimism. The party suffered, it is true, a minor rupture on the left, but this only underlined the firm determination of the majority to struggle forward in legality. The period which was now opening would see the party and the trade-union movement grow with gradual but irresistible force. In a reasonable period of time, the Social Democrats would conquer the majority of seats in the

133 ibid., p. 326.
134 For this section in general, see G. D. H. Cole, *A History of Socialist Thought*, Vol. III, *The Second International*, Part I, London, 1963, pp. 249 ff.

Reichstag – a majority that no government soldiery could ever disperse. At that point, backed by the maturity and consciousness attained by the masses, the party would undertake the socialist transformation of society, using parliament itself to this end. The fact that the party did not yet have this decisive influence in the *Reichstag* should not induce it to condemn the system outright. 'Parliament', said old Wilhelm Liebknecht at the Congress, 'is nothing more than representative of the people. If we have not yet achieved results in parliament, this is not because of a defect in the system but simply because we have not yet got the necessary backing in the country and among the people.'[135] 'The other road' which some urged, the 'shorter' or 'violent' road, was merely that of anarchy.

The passage from Engels cited at the beginning of this essay essentially reflects this strategic perspective. The right to vote is considered as a weapon which can, in a short space of time, carry the proletariat to power; the Paris Commune is regarded as a blood-letting not to be repeated. It must be made clear that this strategic vision is by no means yet 'revisionism'. But if it is not 'revisionism' it is nonetheless its unconscious preamble and preparation.

German Social Democracy chose the 'parliamentary road' at Erfurt, not because it had already abandoned the class conception of the State, but because its 'fatalistic' and 'providential' faith in the automatic progress of *economic evolution* gave it the certainty that its eventual rise to power would come about 'in a spontaneous, constant, and irresistible way, quite tranquilly, like a natural process'. On the other hand, the naturalistic objectivism which is the counterpart to this concept of 'economic evolution' had its counterpart in the dissolution of the Marxist theory of the State.

Let us examine this question more closely. The theory of the State in the Marxism of the Second International was the theory in Engels's *Origins of the Family, Private Property and the State* (1884). This text, like all the Marxist discussions of the State which followed, is characterized by a transposition of the *specific* features of the modern representative State to the State *in general*, whatever the historical epoch or economic-social regime underlying it. Marx's well-known statement that in bourgeois society 'particular' or class interests take the illusory form of 'universal' or 'general' interests – which is the very pivot of his entire analysis of the above-discussed modern relation between *political equality* and *social inequality* – is represented by Engels as a characteristic of *all*

135 Cited by Cole, op. cit., pp. 253 ff.

types of class domination. As a result, it is impossible to relate this process of objective 'abstraction' or 'sublimation' to specifically *capitalist* economic-social conditions, and hence to explain it as an organic product of this *particular* type of society; it is seen instead as a *conscious* 'disguise' or fraud by the ruling classes, in much the same way as Voltaire imagined that religion owed its origin to the cunning of priests.

Two consequences flow from this inability really to relate the modern State to its specific economic foundation. Firstly, a *voluntarist* conception which sees the State, or at least the form it assumes, as an intentional product of the ruling class, an invention *ad hoc*. Secondly, insofar as the form of the State is seen as *indifferent* to the type of social relations over which it presides, a conception which tends both to frantic subjectivism and to interclassism (following a route which has recently been traversed again). In the first case, the rise to power of a particular political personnel, rather than a modification of the roots on which the power structure rests, is seen as decisive and essential for socialism (hence regimes of the Rakosi type). In the second case, since power is understood as an identical instrument that can serve different, opposed interests according to the context, it is automatically voided of any class content (as in recent theories of the so-called 'State of the whole people').

As Lenin pointed out in *The State and Revolution*: 'Marx . . . taught that the proletariat cannot simply conquer State power *in the sense that the old apparatus passes into new hands* (our italics), but must smash, break this apparatus and replace it by a new one',[136] i.e. by a State which begins slowly to 'wither away', making room for ever more extensive forms of direct *democracy*. This is a debatable position, of course, but one which has deep roots in Marx's thought. It seems to me, however, that it is a position already coming into crisis in Engels's 'political testament'. For here, just as 'legality' seems to revolt against the social and political forces which originally gave rise to it, the old State apparatus seems destined to welcome its inheritors to its breast, provided they know how 'to keep this [electoral] growth going, until it of itself gets beyond the control of the governmental system'.

[136] Lenin, *Selected Works*, op. cit., Vol. II, p. 354. In this connection it should be noted that Bernstein cites several times a statement of Marx's from the 1872 Preface to the *Manifesto*, that 'the working class cannot simply lay hold of the ready-made state machinery and wield it for its own purposes'. This means that the working class cannot restrict itself to taking power but must transform that power, '*smash*' the old structure and replace it by a new type of power. But Bernstein interprets it as a warning to the working class against too much revolutionary emphasis on the seizure of power.

It is impossible to show here how this conception – which, remarkably enough, is susceptible to two opposed interpretations: one sectarian and primitive, which considers *political equality* a mere 'trap'; and one 'revisionist', which sees the modern representative State as expressing the 'general interest' – has exhaustively nourished the two opposed traditions of the workers' movement. To show how much more realistic and complex Marx's analysis is, I shall restrict myself to one of his most successful and compressed formulations, discussing *The Class Struggles in France*:

The comprehensive contradiction of this constitution, however, consists in the following: the classes whose social slavery the constitution is to perpetuate, proletariat, peasantry, petty bourgeoisie, it puts in possession of political power through universal suffrage. And from the class whose old social power it sanctions, the bourgeoisie, it withdraws the political guarantees of this power. It forces the political rule of the bourgeoisie into democratic conditions, which at every moment help the hostile classes to victory and jeopardize the very foundations of bourgeois society. From the ones it demands that they should not go forward from political to social emancipation; from the others they they should not go back from social to political restoration.[137]

Unless I am mistaken, the first writer to 'rediscover' these lines and make them the central point of his own study of the relationship between liberal and socialist democracy was Otto Bauer, who, in a famous and in many respects important book published in 1936, *Zwischen zwei Weltkriegen?*,[138] gave an interpretation of them very similar to Bernstein's theses – an interpretation later taken over lock, stock and barrel by John Strachey in his book *Contemporary Capitalism*.[139]

According to this interpretation, Marx's test confirms the central thesis of at least one tendency in present-day Social Democracy: the idea that in the great 'Western Democracies' the 'basic tendencies in the political and economic fields', as Strachey puts it, 'move in diametrically opposed directions'. While 'the diffusion of universal suffrage and its use has become ever more effective, the growing strength of trades unionism' over the last half-century 'has diffused political power', placing it more and more in the hands of the working classes. In the very same period, by contrast, 'economic power has come to be concentrated in the hands of the largest oligopolies'.

It follows from this interpretation that in the 'great Western democ-

[137] Marx and Engels, *Selected Works* in two volumes, Moscow, 1962, Vol. I, p. 172.
[138] O. Bauer, *Zwischen zwei Weltkriegen?*, Bratislava, 1936, pp. 97 ff.
[139] J. Strachey, *Contemporary Capitalism*, London, 1956.

racies', the situation is basically characterized by a 'contrast' between politics and economy, between the constitution or *Rechtsstaat* or parliamentary government (the political form more or less common to all these countries) and their economy which remains capitalist. There is no question, in other words, of seeking to establish a new democracy or new type of democracy; the existing one is the only one possible. The problem is rather to transfer democracy from the political plane, where it is already alive, to the economic plane (without, on the other hand, 'subverting' the system), In other words, to use the most common formula, to give 'content' to the existing 'liberties' which are only 'formal' (as if they had no content already).

Turning to the passage from Marx, this interpretation seems to me to miss all its complexity. Marx certainly recognizes that through universal suffrage the modern constitution places the working classes in a certain sense 'in possession of political power'. But he also points out that it perpetuates their *'social slavery'*. He recognizes that it withdraws from the bourgeoisie the 'political guarantees' of its power, but also states that it sanctions its 'old social power'. In short, for Social Democracy the contradiction is only *between* constitution and capitalism; for Marx it is within society, traversing the constitution as well. On the one hand, through universal suffrage, the constitution brings *everybody* into political life, thus recognizing for the first time the existence of a common or public interest, a 'general will' or sovereignty of the people. On the other hand, it can only turn this common interest into a *formal* one, real interests remaining 'particularistic' and opposed to one another by the class divisions of society. ('The constitutional State', Marx wrote, 'is a State in which the "State interest" as a real interest of the people exists *only formally*. The State interest formally has reality as an interest of the people but it can only express this reality in formal terms.') Hence in the modern State 'general affairs and occupying oneself with them are a monopoly, while by contrast monopolies are the real general affairs.'

To conclude: the constitution of the bourgeois democratic republic is the *résumé*, the compendium of the contradictions between the classes in capitalist society. But since from one class 'it demands that they should not go forward from political to social emancipation', and 'from the others that they should not go back from social to political restoration', the republic is, for Marx, by no means the resolution or supersession of the basic antagonisms. On the contrary, it provides the best *terrain* for them to unfold and reach maturity.

Part Two

From Hegel to Marcuse

HEGEL AND THE REALIZATION OF PHILOSOPHY

Hegel's philosophy is based on three propositions. The first is that philosophy is always idealism:

The proposition that *the finite is ideal* constitutes *idealism*. The idealism of philosophy consists in nothing else than in recognizing that the finite has no veritable being. . . . This is as true of philosophy as of religion; for religion equally does not recognise finitude as a veritable being, as something ultimate and absolute or as something underived, uncreated, eternal.[1]

The second is that the problem of philosophy is *to realize* the principle of idealism:

Every philosophy is essentially an idealism or at least has idealism for its principle, and the question then is only how far this principle is actually carried out.[2]

The third is that the realization of the principle of idealism implies the *destruction of the finite and the annihilation of the world*, since, writes Hegel,

This carrying through of the principle depends primarily on whether the finite reality still retains an independent self-subsistence alongside the being-for-self.[3]

The first proposition does not have to be explained: the principle of idealism is the Idea, the infinite or the Christian Logos. The second will be clarified below. The most difficult to understand is the third, which, it might be added, has also been given the least attention in studies on Hegel. This can be stated as (a) why idealism must destroy the finite and annihilate the world in order to be realized, and (b) how this annihilation can take place.

[1] G. W. F. Hegel, *The Science of Logic*, trans. A. V. Miller, London, 1969, pp. 154–5. Modifications have been made in this translation to bring it into line with Colletti's usage.   [2] ibid., pp. 154–5.   [3] ibid., p. 161.

Point (a) is the easiest to solve. The principle of idealism implies the destruction of the finite because if the finite is allowed to survive, it becomes impossible to conceive of the infinite. Hegel writes:

The infinite, in that case, is *one of the two*; but as *only* one of the two is it itself finite, it is not the whole but only one side; it has its limit in what stands over against it; it is thus the *finite infinite*. There are present only *two finites*.[4]

And again (in the *Encyclopedia*):

Dualism, which renders the antithesis of the finite and the infinite insuperable, does not make the simple consideration that in this way the infinite is *only one of the two*; that in this way only something *particular* is yielded, of which the finite is the other particular. Such an infinite, which is only a particular, stands alongside the finite; in this it finds its limits or barrier; it is *not* what it should be, it is not the infinite but only *finite*. In such a relationship, where the finite is *on one side* and the infinite *on the other*, the former *here*, the latter *beyond*, the finite is credited with the same dignity of subsistence and independence that is attributed to the infinite. The being of the finite is made an absolute being; within this dualism it stands firm for itself. If, so to speak, it were touched by the infinite, it would be destroyed. But it cannot be touched by the infinite: an abyss, an unbridgeable gap is thus opened between the two; the infinite *is fixed* beyond, the finite here.[5]

We will offer a few explanations to help the reader to a full realization of the meaning of this text. The infinite as 'one of the two', that is, the false infinite, is the infinite of the 'intellect'. The infinite as entirety is the infinite of 'reason'. 'The main point is to distinguish the true concept of infinity from spurious infinity, the infinite of reason from the infinite of the intellect.'[6]

The 'intellect' (*Verstand*) is the principle of non-contradiction, the principle of the mutual exclusion or separation of opposites. 'Reason' is the principle of dialectical contradiction or coincidence of opposites. The first is the logical universal which has its particular or real object outside itself. The second is the unity of finite and infinite in the infinite, the unity of thought and being in thought, i.e. 'sameness' and 'otherness', tauto-heterology or dialectic.

The passage from the *Encyclopedia*, cited above, lists all the defects that Hegel attributes to the 'intellect'; (1) it lets the finite survive, it does not

---

[4] ibid., p. 144.
[5] Hegel, *Sämtliche Werke*, ed. Glockner, Stuttgart, 1929, Vol. 8, pp. 224-5.
[6] Hegel, *The Science of Logic*, op. cit., p. 137.

annihilate it but turns it into a 'firm being'; (2) it finitizes the infinite; (3) it poses the finite 'here' (*diesseits*), and the infinite 'beyond' (*jenseits*) – i.e. it makes the finite *real* or terrestrial existence, and the infinite something merely abstract or *ideal*.

The substance of the argument is that the 'intellect', the principle of non-contradiction, is common sense, the point of view of materialism (empiricism) and of science. Everything that philosophy or idealism asserts – that the finite 'is not' and the infinite 'is' – the 'intellect' presents in the reverse order. Materialism and science are, therefore, the *Unphilosophie*, that is, the antithesis or negation of philosophy.

Let us now consider briefly the problem of the old or precritical metaphysics (Descartes, Spinoza, Leibniz), which also adopts the method of non-contradiction. Hegel's thesis is that insofar as it is metaphysical, the principle of this philosophy is the infinite, the absolute; that this philosophy is therefore true philosophy or idealism. Its fault, however, lies in the method it uses. The content of this metaphysics is correct, the form is wrong.[7] The substance is 'philosophical', the method flatly 'scientific'. As a result, the use of the principle of non-contradiction prevents the old metaphysics from *realizing* idealism.

The argument to which Hegel frequently resorts in support of this is an examination of the metaphysical proofs of the existence of God. An excellent example is provided by the cosmological proofs. 'Their starting point,' says Hegel, 'is certainly a view of the world in some way as an aggregate of chance occurrences', namely, as an accumulation of things without value. But while in principle these proofs recognize that the world is merely ephemerality and valuelessness, and that God and God alone is the true reality, the demonstrative method that they adopt in fact subverts the direction of their argument. They want to derive the existence of God from that of the world, maintaining that the existence of the creature can demonstrate that of the creator. In so doing, they do not realize that in their syllogism, the world, which is 'nothing', becomes the *basis* of the proof, and that God, who is everything, becomes a mere consequence or something mediated. The creature, which is secondary, becomes primary; the creator, who is primary, becomes secondary. Thus,

---

[7] ibid., p. 816. On this most important page Hegel explains the difference between the critique advanced by Jacobi against the old metaphysics and that advanced by Kant. Jacobi's critique is directed against its 'intellectual' method; Kant's is a critique of its content, i.e. of the objects of the old metaphysics. Hegel declares himself on Jacobi's side.

says Hegel, Jacobi made the 'correct objection' that they 'seek the *conditions* (the world) for the *unconditioned*; the *infinite* (God) in this way is conceived as *caused* and *dependent*.'[8]

In other words,

> metaphysical proofs of the existence of God are unsuccessful accounts and descriptions of the elevation of the Spirit from the world to God, because they do not express, or rather they do not emphasize, the moment of *negation* contained in this elevation; since the world is *accidental* it is implicit that it is only something *ephemeral* and phenomenal, in and for itself a nullity. The meaning of the elevation of the Spirit is that, while being does indeed belong to the world, it is only appearance not true being, not absolute truth; that absolute truth lies only beyond that appearance in God – only God is true being. This elevation, being a *transition* and *mediation*, is also the *sublation* of the transition and mediation, because that in whose mediation God could appear – the world – is, instead, shown to be nullity. Only the *nullity of the being* of the world gives the possibility of elevation, so that whatever is the mediator disappears, whereby in this mediation itself, mediation is removed.[9]

The direction of the argument is, as we can see, that the 'intellect', the principle of non-contradiction, is so closely tied to materialism that even when it is applied to metaphysical or idealistic premises, it distorts the meaning of 'philosophy' and forces it to say the opposite of what it has in mind. The finite, which is nothing, is consolidated by the intellect, which renders it a 'stable being' or foundation. It reduces the infinite, which is the true reality, to something caused and dependent. The finite, which is the negative, becomes the positive, i.e. effective existence. The infinite, on the other hand, which is the true real, becomes something unreal or negative, a 'void' beyond, 'something mental or abstract'.

Intellect and reason, then, are two distinct logics:

> In ordinary inference the *being* of the finite appears as ground of the absolute; because the finite is, therefore the absolute is. But the truth is that the absolute is, because the finite . . . is *not*. In the former meaning the inference runs thus: the *being* of the finite is the *being* of the absolute; but in the latter thus: the *non-being* of the finite is the *being* of the absolute.[10]

Let us sum up what we have expounded. All 'true' philosophies are idealism, or at least they have idealism as their principle; materialism and

---

[8] Hegel, *Sämtliche Werke*, op. cit., Vol. 8, pp. 145–7. Jacobi's critique of the proofs of the existence of God is outlined in Appendix VII of his *Über die Lehre des Spinoza in Briefen an den Herrn Moses Mendelssohn*, 2nd edition, Breslau, 1789.

[9] ibid.   [10] Hegel, *The Science of Logic*, op. cit., p. 443.

science are *Unphilosophie*. Hence it all depends upon how far a philosophy can actualize this principle, that is, the *realization* of idealism. The condition upon which this realization depends is the destruction of the finite, the annihilation of the world. (Later we shall see how Hegel obtains this annihilation.) Once the finite is destroyed, the infinite, that is the Spirit or God, which 'intellectualist' metaphysics relegates to the 'beyond', passes from the beyond to the *here and now* and becomes existing and real. This is the realization of philosophy. It is the immanentization of transcendence, the 'secularization of Christianity',[11] the incarnation or actualization of the divine Logos. In other words, the difference between the old and the new metaphysics is the difference between ordinary theology and speculative theology, between theism and philosophy, between precritical metaphysics and absolute idealism.

Feuerbach saw this clearly. At the beginning of his *'Provisional Theses'* he wrote: 'Speculative theology may be distinguished from ordinary theology by the fact that the divine Being, which the latter removes to . . . the beyond, is transposed to the here and now, making it *present, determinate and actual.*'[12] Speculative philosophy, he adds in the *Principles*, 'has made the God which in theism is only an imaginary being, a remote, indeterminate, vague being, into an actual, determinate being'.[13]

THE PROBLEM OF THE HEGELIAN LEFT

The problem of the 'realization' of (Hegel's) philosophy was the main problem for the Hegelian left (excepting Feuerbach and Marx). The most important thing, however, is that the problem now became *political*. It became the problem of the liberal-radical revolution in Germany.

There is, so the argument ran, a contradiction in Hegel's philosophy between the 'principles' and the 'conclusions'. The principles are revolutionary, the conclusions conservative. The cause of this lies in the fact that the full maturity of Hegel's thought coincides with the period of the Restoration.

Hegel thus came to substantiate his own saying that every philosophy is only the thought content of its own age. On the other hand, his personal opinions were refined by the system, but not without their having influenced its conclusions. Thus, his philosophy of religion and right would certainly have

[11] L. Michelet, *Entwicklungsgeschichte der neuesten deutschen Philosophie*, Berlin, 1843, pp. 304 ff.

[12] L. Feuerbach, *Sämtliche Werke*, op. cit., Vol. II, pp. 222–3.   [13] ibid., p. 253.

emerged quite differently if he had abstracted more from the positive elements (*von den positiven Elementen*) that it derived from the education of the time, and had instead developed it from pure thought. All the inconsistencies, all the contradictions in Hegel come down to this. Everything in his philosophy of religion that seems too orthodox, and in his philosophy of the State too pseudo-historical, must be judged from this standpoint. The principles are always progressive and independent, the conclusions – it cannot be denied – are occasionally lagging and even illiberal.

This passage is taken from an early work, *Schelling und die Offenbarung*,[14] which Engels published in 1842 under the pseudonym of Oswald, as spokesman for the *Doktorclub* in Berlin. All the basic motifs of the interpretation of Hegel's philosophy then in vogue on the left may be found here: (a) the discovery of a (presumed) contradiction in Hegel's philosophy between the (revolutionary) *principles* and the (conservative) *conclusions*; (b) the thesis that all the 'inconsistencies', all the 'contradictions' present in Hegel, both in his philosophy of religion and in his philosophy of the State, do not spring from ideas intrinsic to his thought, but are merely the price he paid to his epoch, the period of the Restoration. They were the product of the personal compromise by which Hegel attempted to solve the conflict between the audacity of his principles and the backwardness of the German situation.

It is not possible to enter into a more detailed analysis here. The main point of this line of interpretation is that, according to the left, the celebrated Hegelian identity of the Real and the Rational should not be understood as the observation or consecration of an existing state of affairs, so much as a programme to be actualized. The Hegelian identity signifies that the rational *should* be realized. Everything which is and does not correspond to reason, seems to be but in fact, is not; it must be subverted to make way for a new reality. Formally, the problem is the same as in Hegel; it is a question of actualizing philosophy, of realizing the Idea. But in reality everything is transposed into the terms of political revolution. The programme of realizing the Christian Logos, of the immanentization of God, has become the programme of the liberal-radical revolution.

---

[14] MEGA (*Marx Engels Gesamtausgabe*), I, 2, pp. 183–4; *Werke*, op. cit., Supplementary Vol., Part 2, p. 176. We owe the rediscovery of these early writings of Engels to Gustav Mayer, the author of a monumental biography of Engels (*Friedrich Engels, Eine Biographie*, 2 volumes, The Hague, 1934; abridged English translation, *Friedrich Engels: A Biography*, London, 1936).

Some indications may be cited to illustrate the fortunes of this line of interpretation. After adopting it in his youth while he was still a left liberal, Engels resurrected this line of thought in 1888 in *Ludwig Feuerbach*, with the celebrated thesis of the contradiction in Hegel between the revolutionary dialectical method and the conservative idealist system. From Engels it passed to Plekhanov and Lenin, thus forming part of the orthodoxy of Russian 'dialectical materialism'.

Even before this, the interpretation of the *Doktorclub* and, in this case, of the young Engels had arrived in Russia in another way. It played a decisive part in the formation of the thought of the 'democratic revolutionaries' (Belinsky, Herzen, Chernishevsky), writers whose influence on Plekhanov and Lenin is well known.

This passage from the young Engels came to the knowledge of Belinsky (who warmly approved of it) through an almost literal transcription by his friend, the critic Botkin.[15] His text on *Schelling and Revelation* was also commented upon by Herzen in 1842 itself. Herzen wrote that Hegel lacked the 'heroism of consistency', the courage to accept the consequences of his own thought, the clear results of his own principles. He refused to do so because 'he loved and respected *das Bestehende*' (the existing state of things), because he 'realized that he would not bear the blow and did not wish to be the first to strike'. At the time it was enough for him to have achieved what he had; but his principles 'were *more faithful* to him than he was to himself, i.e. to him, as a thinker, detached from his accidental personality, the epoch, etc.' Hence these principles survived him in the school of his younger followers.[16]

Later I shall attempt to say something about the rather different interpretation of Hegel (in relation to that of the Hegelian left), given by Feuerbach and the young Marx.[17] Here I need only point out that both in the *Doctoral Dissertation* and the *Economic and Philosophical Manuscripts* (1844), Marx totally rejects the idea of explaining Hegelian philosophy and its presumed contradiction between 'principles' and 'conclusions', as the result of any compromise that Hegel might have made with the Prussian State.

[15] For further comparisons, see MEGA, I, 2, *Einleitung*, pp. xlvi–clix.

[16] A. Herzen, *Selected Philosophical Works*, Moscow, 1956, pp. 308–9.

[17] On the differences between Feuerbach and Marx on the one hand, and the young Hegelian left on the other, see the excellent study by M. G. Lange, 'L. Feuerbach und der junge Marx', in *I. Feuerbach: Kleine philosophische Schriften*, Leipzig, 1950.

Marx writes in his *Notes to the Doctoral Dissertation*:

In regard to Hegel, it is out of mere ignorance (*blosse Ignoranz*) that his disciples explain this or that determination of his system by accommodation and the like or, in a word, morally (*moralisch*). . . . It is conceivable that a philosopher commits this or that apparent *non-sequitur* out of this or that accommodation. He himself may be conscious of it. But he is not conscious that the possibility of this apparent accommodation is rooted in the inadequacy of his principle or in its inadequate formation. Hence, if a philosopher has accommodated himself, his disciples have to explain from *his inner essential consciousness* what *for him had the form of an exotic consciousness*. In this way what appears as progress of consciousness is progress of knowledge as well. It is not that the particular (*partikulare*) consciousness of the philosopher is suspect; rather, his essential form of consciousness is constructed, raised to a particular form and meaning, and at the same time superseded.[18]

However, the line of interpretation offered by Feuerbach and Marx, as is well known, has carried little weight in studies of Hegel. Even Lukács's monograph on *The Young Hegel*, which refers at several points to Feuerbach's writings of 1839–43 and to Marx's *Manuscripts* (though not to his *Critique of Hegel's Philosophy of Right*), nonetheless only accepts their interpretation in such a way as to adapt it to a quite differently directed discussion. It accepts it, so to speak, only to weaken its effectivity and the more actively . . . digest it.

Apart from the question of the 'dialectics of matter', which I shall discuss shortly, Lukács's monograph proceeds in the direction already traced out by the Hegelian left. This was the more inevitable for Lukács in as much as this interpretation, or at least its central argument (the contradiction between 'method' and 'system'), became, with Engels's

[18] L. D. Easton and K. H. Guddat, *Writings of the Young Marx on Philosophy and Society*, New York, 1969, pp. 60–1. Karl Rosenkranz has also opposed this idea of a compromise in his *Georg Wilhelm Friedrich Hegel's Leben*, Berlin, 1844, p. 332. He writes: 'Already at the end of the last century and the beginning of this one, Hegel had abandoned the seductive vagueness of the notions of people, liberty and equality in general, for the more precise concepts of State, estate divisions and government with universal obligations. At Jena he was even enthusiastic about the hereditary transmission of the monarchy as a basic determination of modern political life. Remembering this, we must dispel the notion that Hegel by deliberate deviation from his philosophic positions, created his concept of the State to accord with the interests of the Prussian government.' And further in the same text he sharply criticises the thesis that Hegel was 'senile, a man who unknowingly deviated from his own principles, since he did not have strength to deduce all their consequences' (p. 401).

Ludwig Feuerbach, as we have seen, the interpretative line of 'dialectical materialism'.

All the motifs indicated above, not excluding Hegel's substantial atheism and the 'diplomatic' duplicity of his thought (religious in the 'exoteric' form, atheist and revolutionary in the 'esoteric' form) – much in vogue in the *Doktorclub* and developed especially by Heine[19] are ably re-adopted and valorized in Lukács's monograph. From there they have spread to more or less the whole French *coterie* of neo-Hegelians. In short, the argument (already developed by B. Bauer, Ruge, etc.) of the *Zurück-gebliebenheit* of Germany, of the backwardness of contemporary German society as the 'key' to understanding Hegel's entire work, is given decisive importance in the work of Lukács.

Marcuse's *Reason and Revolution* operates entirely within this perspective. Hegel is the philosophical *pendant* to Robespierre.[20] ('Robespierre's deification of reason as the *Être suprême* is the counterpart to the glorification of reason in Hegel's system'.) Hegel's philosophy is the philosophy of the Revolution, because the identity of Real and Rational must be understood in the sense that Reason *must* be realized and that 'unreasonable reality has to be altered until it comes into conformity with reason'.[21] According to Hegel, the French Revolution enunciated reason's ultimate power over reality. 'The implications involved in this statement lead into the very centre of his philosophy. . . . What men think to be true, right and good ought to be realized in the actual organization of their societal and political life.'[22]

The 'compromise' argument is similarly given prominence. The 'reconciliation' of Reason and Reality proclaimed by Hegel, the famous *Versöhnung*, does not derive from the very principles of his philosophy, but is the result of a subjective accommodation.

However, the radical purport of the basic idealistic concepts is slowly relinquished and they are to an ever-increasing extent made to fit in with the

---

[19] Heine, *Werke* (ed. Elster), Vol. 5, pp. 148 ff.: '. . . I was following the *master* while he composed it [the music of atheism]; in obscure and circumlocutious terms, certainly, so that not everyone would decipher it; I often saw him looking anxiously about him for fear of being understood. . . . Once, when I was dissatisfied with the phrase "All that is real is rational", he smiled strangely and observed that it could also be read, "All that is rational must necessarily be".' The passage describing this (imaginary) meeting between Heine and Hegel is quoted by Lukács in *Der junge Hegel* (*Werke*, Vol. 8, Neuwied and Berlin, 1967, pp. 569–70).

[20] H. Marcuse, *Reason and Revolution: Hegel and the Rise of Social Theory*, New York, 1963, p. 5.   [21] ibid., p. 61.   [22] ibid., pp. 6–7.

prevailing societal form. . . . The particular form, however, that the reconciliation between philosophy and reality assumed in Hegel's system was determined by the actual situation of Germany in the period when he elaborated his system.[23]

Marcuse not only readopts the idea of the 'compromise', but even expands it – without it losing any of its psychologistic character, however. The conflict, the contradiction between Hegel's 'willingness to become reconciled with the social reality' of Germany and his critical rationalism or the impulse toward Revolution, that forms the basis of his philosophy, is not characteristic only of his thought, but of all German idealism. This 'will' towards reconciliation was instilled into German culture by the Lutheran tradition.[24]

This, in broadest outlines, is the interpretation of Hegel elaborated by Marcuse. But we should not have to preoccupy ourselves with it if he stopped there. In reality, what is new – and also in a certain sense important – in Marcuse, as compared with the whole left-wing interpretative tradition and 'dialectical materialism' itself, is the rediscovery of a central motif in Hegel's thought, which, as we have already indicated, has almost always remained in the background. This is the theme *of the destruction of the finite and the annihilation of the world*. The 'social function' of Marcuse's philosophy today has its roots here.

DIALECTICAL MATERIALISM AND HEGEL

We must now see how this destruction of the finite is achieved in Hegel and compare it with the significance it comes to assume in Marcuse. But before coming to this we should return to the interpretation of Hegel provided by 'dialectical materialism'.

Reduced to its essentials the interpretation is this: in Hegel the dialectic is a dialectic of *concepts*; after the materialistic 'inversion' affected by Marx and Engels, the Hegelian dialectic became, on the contrary, a dialectic of *matter* and of things. Marx inherited the 'dialectic' from Hegel, but rejected the 'system', i.e. idealism.

This interpretation of the 'inversion' is that elaborated by Engels in *Anti-Dühring* and *Ludwig Feuerbach*, which then became the 'orthodoxy' in Russian dialectical materialism. It is the result of the blending of two quite distinct interpretative formulae.

In the *Afterword* to the second edition of *Capital*, Marx had spoken of the 'mystification which dialectic suffers in Hegel's hands', recalling his

[23] ibid., p. 12.   [24] ibid., pp. 15 ff.

own early writings of 1843-4; and, he added, the Hegelian dialectic 'must be turned right side up again if you would discover the rational kernel within the mystical shell'.[25]

This formula from *Capital*, according to which we must distinguish between a rational kernel and a mystical shell *within Hegel's dialectic itself*, was married by 'dialectical materialism' with Engels's formula – born in the orbit of the Hegelian left – according to which the method represented the revolutionary aspect and the system the conservative side of Hegel's philosophy. The final result was that the rational nucleus became the Hegelian method itself, and the mystical shell merely the 'system'.

There is no need to prolong discussion of this question any further. The essential point which should be stressed is that both 'dialectical materialism' and its critics have always regarded the 'dialectics of matter' as the mark of 'dialectical materialism' itself. Marxism is held to be materialism by virtue above all of its dialectics of nature. The dialectic of 'things' and of 'matter' is held to be the pre-eminent distinctive feature, the most evident and macroscopic difference between Marxism and Hegel.

In reality the situation is different. Not only does Hegel's system contain a *Philosophy of Nature* that is identical in every way with Engels's *Dialectics of Nature*, but all Hegel's philosophy is based on the 'dialectics of matter' – the dialectics of things and of the finite. It is possible to show from the texts themselves that 'dialectical materialism' was from first to last merely a mechanical transcription of Hegel's philosophy (the assertion that everything consists of itself and its opposite, itself and the negative of itself at the same time; the definition of 'motion' as 'contradiction', etc.). The real point at issue – but one which has never been posed either by *Diamat* or by its critics – is different: what does a 'dialectics of matter' really mean and does it, as has always been assumed, really imply a materialistic conception?

Firstly, to give a rough idea of the hermeneutic situation that has been created, it is worth giving at least one example, from Hegel's *The Science of Logic*. The passage opens with the assertion that *all things are inherently contradictory*. Then follows the definition of the dialectical nature of

---

[25] This metaphor of the 'kernel' or nucleus' and the 'shell' or 'cover' is Hegel's own, as Mario Rossi has shown in his *Marx e la dialettica hegeliana*, 2 volumes, Rome, 1960, where he quotes from Hegel: '. . . the rational, which is synonymous with the idea, realising itself in external existence, presents itself in an infinite variety of forms, phenomena and aspects; and surrounds its nucleus with a varied husk *(seinen Kern mit der bunten Rinde)* . . .'

movement ('something moves, not because at one moment it is here and at another there, but because at one and the same moment it is here and not here, because in this "here" it at once is and is not').

Similarly, internal self-movement proper, *instinctive urge* in general . . . is nothing else but the fact that something is, in one and the same respect, *self-contained* and deficient, the *negative of itself*. Abstract self-identity is not as yet a livingness, but the positive, being in its own self a negativity, goes outside itself and undergoes alteration. Something is therefore alive only insofar as it contains contradiction within it, and moreover is this power to hold and endure the contradiction within it.[26]

Lenin's comment, accompanying his transcription of this passage in the *Philosophical Notebooks*, is revealing:

Movement and 'self-movement' . . . 'change', 'movement and vitality', 'the principle of all self-movement', 'impulse' (*Trieb*) to 'movement' and to 'activity' – the opposite to '*dead Being*' – who would believe that this is the core of 'Hegelianism', of abstract and abstruse . . . Hegelianism? This core had to be discovered, understood, *hinüberretten*, laid bare, refined, which is precisely what Marx and Engels did.[27]

Let us leave Marx aside. It is clear that Lenin, like Engels, sees in this passage from the *Logic* the 'kernel' to be saved from Hegel's philosophy, the point at which a genuine realism erupts in contradiction with the 'shell' of the system, the 'mysticism of the Idea'. The conviction governing him at this point is the one that he erected as the criterion in all his reading of Hegel: 'I am in general trying to read Hegel materialistically; Hegel is materialism which has been stood on its head (according to Engels) – that is to say, I cast aside for the most part God, the Absolute, the Pure Idea, etc.'[28]

In reality, Lenin's reading of these pages is based on a fundamental misunderstanding. He has 'forced' himself to read Hegel 'materialistic-

---

[26] Hegel, *The Science of Logic*, op. cit., p. 440. Cf. Engels, *Anti-Dühring*, Moscow, 1959, pp. 166–7; 'Motion itself is a contradiction: even simple mechanical change of position can only come about through a body being at one and the same moment of time both in one place and in another place, being in one and the same place and also not in it' – and a little further on, '. . . life consists precisely and primarily in this – that a being is at each moment itself and yet something else. Life is therefore also a contradiction which is present in things and processes themselves, and which constantly originates and resolves itself; and as soon as the contradiction ceases life, too, comes to an end, and death steps in.'

[27] Lenin, *Collected Works*, op. cit., Vol. 38, p. 141.   [28] ibid., p. 104.

ally' exactly at the point at which Hegel is in fact . . . annihilating matter. Far from representing the realistic moment in contradiction to the idealism of the system, the 'dialectics of matter' is the way in which Hegel destroys the finite and makes the world disappear.

This thesis may seem surprising but it is incontrovertible nonetheless. The chapter from *The Science of Logic* which opens with the assertion that 'all things are inherently contradictory', ends with a critique, as we have already noted, of the cosmological proofs of the existence of God. In these proofs God is made to depend on the world, because the 'intellectual' method used in these proofs was not capable of annulling the finite and making the world disappear. 'But the truth', says Hegel, 'is that the absolute is, because the finite is the inherently self-contradictory opposition, because it is *not*. . . . The *non-being* of the finite is the *being* of the absolute.'[29]

The possibility, therefore, of demonstrating God as the *unconditioned*, without repeating the mistake of the old metaphysics which made God something caused and dependent, presupposes precisely the 'dialectical' conception of the finite. The contradictoriness of things, in fact, goes together with the ephemerality and nullity. The 'good God' and the 'mysticism of the Idea' are thus lodged precisely in those pages where Lenin, and Engels before him, believed they had found Hegel's 'materialism'.

HEGEL AND THE DIALECTICS OF MATTER

We may now briefly deal with the dialectics of matter in Hegel, and exactly how this conception allowed him to destroy the finite. The question is dealt with at length in the *Logic*. Hegel's thesis is as follows. Philosophy has always considered the finite as ephemerality and non-being and, therefore, that philosophy 'worthy of the name' has always been idealism. But what prevented idealism from being 'realized' was the mistake of believing that the finite, precisely because it was ephemeral and valueless, should be kept separate and distinct from the infinite, itself kept 'pure and distant' from the former.

This 'intellectualist' separation of the two was, according to Hegel, the origin of all errors. Since the finite is 'incapable of union with the infinite, it remains absolute on its own side'. The possibility of 'passing over' into

---

[29] Hegel, *The Science of Logic*, op. cit., Vol. II, p. 443.

the other is denied it. Its ephemerality has no outlet. Also, since the *non-being* of the finite is understood here as a negation 'fixed in itself', which 'stands in abrupt contrast to its affirmative', the intellect does not become aware of taking the finite as 'imperishable and absolute'. Being unable to perish, the ephemerality of things becomes 'their unalterable quality, that is, their quality which does not pass over into its other, that is, into its affirmative'. The finite never stops finishing and 'is thus eternal'.[30] The *mors immortalis* of Lucretius!

The way in which Hegel corrects this imposture of the old metaphysics is simple. He adopts the negative conception of the sensory world (the finite or the perceptible as *non-being*) characteristic of the Platonic-Christian tradition. But at the same time he develops it. He does not restrict himself to the mere negation of the finite, but integrates this negation with an affirmative proposition, complementing the thesis that 'the finite is not a true being', with the thesis that the 'finite is ideal'. (I refer here to the basic propositions stated initially.)

This innovation means in practice that he no longer says only: the finite has no true reality, it does not have a genuine existence; he adds that the finite has as 'its' own essence and basis the 'other' of itself, that is, the infinite, the immaterial, thought. The consequence is decisive. If the finite does have as its essence the 'other' of itself, it is clear that to be truly, or 'essentially' itself, it must no longer be itself – that is, the self which it is 'in appearance': the finite – but the 'other'. The finite 'is not' when it *is* truly 'finite'. Vice versa, it 'is' when it is *not* finite but infinite. It 'is' when it 'is not', it is 'itself' when it is 'the other', it is born when it dies. The finite is dialectical.

The innovation is simple but decisive. Hegel could say that he does *not* consider the finite, that he abandons and transcends it. Indeed, he does so, but merely by formulating the procedure in another way. Instead of stating clearly that he does *not* consider the finite, he says that he considers the finite for what it *is not*, or better still, that the finite has its opposite for its 'essence'. The resulting advantage is evident; the act by which *he* abstracts or detracts from the finite, Hegel can now present as an *objective* movement achieved by the finite itself in order to move beyond itself, and so *pass* into the essence.

I will limit myself, for reasons of brevity, to giving an outline of this process, without citing the relevant documentation. The thesis that each particular or finite is itself and its opposite, 'is' and 'is not', gives rise to

[30] ibid., Vol. I, p. 130.

a two-fold movement, but of a different nature from that which 'dialectical materialism' has supposed. We are not dealing here with a horizontal movement from finite to finite but with a dual vertical passage: from 'here' to 'beyond' and from 'beyond' to 'here'.

The first movement. The finite has its opposite as its essence. This means that, in order to be itself, the finite must not be itself but the other, it must not be finite but infinite. That is, the *ideal* finite, the internal moment of the Idea, which is naturally no longer the eleatic idea, but 'sameness' and 'otherness', 'being' and 'non-being' together, the 'identity of identity and non-identity'. In order to grasp the finite in what it 'truly' is, we must not consider the finite but the infinite. To take the real particular, that is, the 'this', non-contradictory determinateness, it is necessary to take the logical totality, that is the 'this as much as that', the tautoheterology or dialectic. The true reality is not the world but the Idea, being is not being but thought, that is spirit, or the Christian Logos.

The second and simultaneous movement. As the 'essence' of the finite is in the infinite, so the infinite has its own 'existence' in the other. The essence of the 'here' is in the 'beyond', but the latter, no longer having a reality over against it that confines it to the supra-terrestrial world, passes from the 'beyond' to 'here'; that is, makes the finite its incarnation and terrestrial manifestation. The finite passes into the infinite, the infinite into the finite. The world is idealized, the Idea is realized.

Hegel calls this second movement *die positive Auslegung des Absoluten*, the positive exposition of the absolute. The finite, that is, the particular or the positive, does not express or represent itself, but becomes the means by which the absolute ex-poses itself, i.e. externalizes itself and assumes a terrestrial form. The second book of *The Science of Logic* dedicates an entire chapter to the explanation of this process.

The illusory being is not nothing, but is a reflection, a relation to the absolute; or, it is *illusory* being in so far as *in it the absolute is reflected*. This positive exposition thus arrests the finite before it vanishes and contemplates it as an expression and image of the absolute. But the transparency of the finite, which only lets the absolute be glimpsed through it, ends by completely vanishing; for there is nothing in the finite which could preserve for it a distinction against the absolute; it is a medium which is absorbed by that which is reflected through it.[31]

The world has disappeared. What seemed finite is, in reality, infinite. An *independent* material world no longer exists. On the other hand, insofar

[31] ibid., p. 532.

as the finite is arrested in its disappearance, it is restored as the 'other' of itself. It is not the finite, but the exposition of the absolute. It is not, does not signify this determinate object – bread and wine, for example – it signifies the Spirit. *Hier werden Wein und Brot mystische Objekte.*[32] Bread and wine become mystical objects. 'The spirit of Jesus, in which His disciples are One, is, by external sentiment, present as an object, it has become real.'[33] But this real is only *die objectiv gemachte Liebe, dies zur Sache gewordene Subjective.* 'In the banquet of love, the corporeal disappears and only the sensation of life is present.'[34]

In a certain sense, as Marx says, all things are 'left as they are, while at the same time acquiring the meaning of a determination of the Idea'.[35] There was a world there before and it still is there, only now the 'host' is no longer flour and water. The 'principle' of idealism has been actualized. 'True' reality has been substituted for the annihilated world. However, Revolution has not occurred, only Transubstantiation.

> Thus empirical reality is admitted just as it is and is also said to be the rational; but not rational because of its own reason, but because the empirical fact in its empirical existence has a significance which is other than it itself. The fact, which is the starting point, is not conceived to be such but rather to be the mystical result.[36]

It is not possible here to dwell further upon the subject. The 'dialectics of matter' is the Pyrrhonism, the destruction – by means of the famous tropes of scepticism – of the certainty that sensory reality exists. Hegel confronts the question with admirable clarity in his chapter on ancient scepticism in the *Lectures in the Philosophy of History* and in his early text *The Relation of Scepticism to Philosophy*, where he shows how the storehouse of this scepticism, so dear to him (because it is scepsis about the reality of external things), lies in Plato's *Parmenides*. Scepticism is the negative side of the knowledge of the absolute (*die negative Seite der Erkenntnis des Absoluten*) and immediately presupposes Reason as a positive (*und setzt unmittelbar die positive Seite voraus*).[37] In fact, 'precisely because the finite is the opposition which contradicts itself in itself, because it is *not*, thereby the absolute "is".' On the other hand, the whole mystical-religious slant hidden in this 'dialectical' concept of matter is explained by Hegel with a reference to Ficino.

[32] *Hegels theologische Jugendschriften*, Tübingen, 1907, p. 298.
[33] ibid., p. 299.   [34] ibid.
[35] Marx, *Critique of Hegel's 'Philosophy of Right'*, op. cit., p. 8.
[36] ibid., p. 9.   [37] Hegel, *Sämtliche Werke*, op. cit., Vol. I, pp. 230–1.

Here we have within our grasp the total and incurable theoretical inconsistency of 'dialectical materialism'. It mistakes the 'dialectics of matter' of absolute idealism for materialism. Instead, it considers the materialistic principle of non-contradiction or the 'intellect', which is the same thing, to be the principle of metaphysics. Engels takes metaphysics, that is, the romantic philosophy of nature, for science. For metaphysics he takes effective science, namely, modern experimental science. The result is a theoretical *débâcle*.

We may now briefly turn to two serious students of Hegel's thought: Feuerbach and Marx. Their criticism of Hegel is the exact antithesis of that made by the Hegelian left. For the left, there is a contradiction in Hegel between the Idea from which he starts, and the 'positive elements' which he presents as the contents of this Idea, that is, the real-empirical factual data that he derives from his own epoch. The critique of Feuerbach and Marx, on the contrary, is based on the complementary nature of the two processes. The *a priori* 'purity' of the Hegelian Idea implies its substantiation, its identification with a real particular. In other words, the fact that Hegel denies the real premises of the Idea means that any empirical reality must then be revealed as an incarnation of this Idea, that is, as a 'vessel' of the Absolute. The philosophy which begins without real presuppositions, begins by presupposing itself, that is, it presupposes the Idea or knowledge as 'already' given, as always having been in existence. But this presupposed knowledge belongs together with its empirical contents which are dogmatic, i.e. not controlled and mediated by thought. Hegel's philosophy is therefore simultaneously an 'acritical idealism' and 'a positivism equally devoid of criticism'. Or, as Feuerbach's anticipation of this formula of Marx's goes, 'the philosophy, which begins with thought *without reality*, concludes consistently *mit einer gedankenlosen Realität*'.[38] It is better, therefore, adds Feuerbach, 'to begin with non-philosophy and end with philosophy, than, on the contrary, like so many "great" German philosophers – *exempla sunt odiosa* – to open one's career with philosophy and conclude it with non-philosophy'.[39] That is, to begin as a philosopher and to end up as an apologist for the Prussian State. (The complex logico-gnoseological problems that this critique presupposes clearly cannot be dealt with here.)

Hence we conclude once again with the immanentization of God and the 'secularization of Christianity'. If there are commentators who cannot understand the concrete (historical) significance of this, the lengthy

[38] L. Feuerbach, *Sämtliche Werke*, op. cit., Vol. II, p. 208.   [39] ibid.

Anmerkung, that accompanies Section 552 of the *Encyclopedia*, is written for them.

The divine spirit must immanently penetrate the mundane: thus wisdom becomes concrete therein and its justification determined in itself. But this concrete inhabitation is the formations indicated by morality (*Sittlichkeit*): the morality of marriage against the sanctity of celibacy, the morality of wealth and income (*Vermögens- und Erwerbstätigkeit*) against the sanctity of poverty and its idleness, the morality of obedience towards the laws of the State against the sanctity of obedience without laws and obligations, slavery to conscience.[40]

Thus all the institutions of capitalist-protestant society or bourgeois 'civil society' such as marriage, the family, entrepreneurial activity, obedience to State laws, appear to be permeated and inhabited by the Logos; that is, they appear as immanent concretizations of the divine Spirit, not historical institutions but sacraments.

If, then, there are Marxists who still fail to grasp what this immanentism, this inhabitation of the sensory by the super-sensory means, let them rest assured; they, too, are provided for. The most rigorous definition given by Marx of the 'commodity' (the 'cell' of all contemporary society) in *A Contribution to the Critique* and in *Capital* is that it is 'sensory and super-sensory', *ein sinnlich-übersinnliches Ding* – 'a very queer thing, abounding in metaphysical subtleties and theological niceties'.[41]

REASON AND REVOLUTION IN MARCUSE

Finally, to Marcuse. Here the points to keep clear are as follows.

1. The interpretation of Hegelian Reason as mere subjective *raison*, the reason of the empirical individual, rather than the Christian Logos. *Ergo* – as on the left and especially in Bruno Bauer – a reading of Hegel along the lines of subjective idealism (Fichte). Reason is the 'Ich', the 'ego' and the 'mass', etc.; hence the interpretation of the Hegelian realization of the Christian Logos as a political programme through which to realize 'ideals', what reason prescribes for men. (The fundamental principle of Hegel's system, says Marcuse, is that, 'That which men believe to be true and good, should be realized in the effective organization of their social and individual life.' Compare instead Marx's letter to Ruge of September

---

[40] Hegel, *Encyclopedia*, in *Sämtliche Werke*, op. cit., Vol. 10, p. 439.

[41] K. Marx, *Capital*, Vol. I, p. 71. For a further development of this theme (the commodity as transcendent but real) see my *Il Marxismo e Hegel*, Bari, 1969, pp. 422 ff.

1843: 'we shall not confront the world in a doctrinaire fashion with a new principle – here is the truth, kneel here!')

2. The insertion of the Hegelian motif of the *destruction of the finite* into this liberal-radical idea of revolution (lacking in the entire interpretative tradition, except perhaps in Stirner and Bakunin); but while in Hegel this motif is linked to transubstantiation or the immanentization of God, lacking any theological significance, in Marcuse it tends to acquire the literal or ordinary meaning.

Hence the antithesis which is central to *Reason and Revolution* and also to *One-Dimensional Man*;[42] the opposition between 'positive thought' and 'negative thought'. The first corresponds to the 'intellect', i.e. to the principle of non-contradiction as a (materialist) principle of common sense and science. The second corresponds to dialectical and philosophical 'reason'. 'Positive' thought is the thought which recognizes the existence of the world, the authority and reality of 'facts', vice versa, 'negative' thought is the thought which denies 'facts'. The finite outside the infinite has no true reality. The truth of the finite is its ideality. (Hegel said that, 'The proposition that the finite is ideal constitutes idealism.') 'Facts', insofar as they are external to and different from thought, and, therefore, insofar as they constitute the opposite of reason, are not reality but non-truth. Truth is the realization of reason; it is the idea or philosophy translated into reality. Marcuse writes, 'According to Hegel the facts by themselves possess no authority. . . . Everything that is given must find a justification before reason, which consists of the reality of Man and nature's possibilities.'

The opposites of Hegel are Hume and Kant. Marcuse writes:

If Hume was to be accepted, the claim of reason to organize reality had to be rejected. For, as we have seen, this claim was based upon reason's faculty to attain truths, the validity of which was not derived from experience and which could, in fact, stand against experience. . . . This conclusion of the empiricist investigations did more than undermine metaphysics. It confined men within the limits of 'the given', within the existing order of things and events. . . . The result was not only scepticism but conformism. The empiricist restriction of human nature to the knowledge of 'the given' removed the desire both to transcend the given and to despair about it.

In Hegel, on the other hand,

the realization of reason is not a fact but a task. The form in which the objects immediately appear is not yet their true form. What is simply given is at first

[42] H. Marcuse, *One-Dimensional Man*, London, 1964, Chapters V and VI.

negative, other than its real potentialities. It becomes true only in the process of overcoming this negativity, so that the birth of the truth requires the death of the given state of being. Hegel's optimism is based upon a destructive conception of the given. All forms are seized by the dissolving movement of reason which cancels and alters them until they are adequate to their notion.

Hegel's philosophy is, therefore, a negative philosophy . . . It is originally motivated by the conviction that the given facts that appear to common sense as the positive index of truth are in reality the negation of truth, so that truth can only be established by their destruction.[43]

A formidable example of the heterogenesis of ends! The old spiritualist contempt for the finite and the terrestrial world re-emerges as a philosophy of revolution, or rather . . . of 'revolt'. It is not a fight against particular socio-historical institutions (such as 'profit', 'monopoly', or even 'socialist bureaucracy'); it is a fight against objects and things. We are crushed by the oppressive power of 'facts'. We suffocate in the slavery of recognizing that 'things' exist. 'They are there, grotesque, stubborn, gigantic, and . . . I am in the midst of Things, which cannot be given names. Alone, wordless, defenceless, they surround me, under me, behind me, above me. They demand nothing, they don't impose themselves, they are there.'[44] Before this spectacle of things, indignation grabs us by the throat and becomes Nausea. We may easily compare it with the roots of a tree! 'I was sitting, slightly bent, my head bowed, alone in front of that black, knotty mass, which was utterly crude and frightened me.' Here is the absurdity which cries vengeance to the sky: 'soft, monstrous masses, in disorder – naked, with a frightening, obscene nakedness'.[45] The absurdity is not that Roquentin should be pursuing his wretched little petty-bourgeois *débauche* in the public parks, while a Daladier or even a Laval is in power. The absurdity lies in the roots of the tree. 'Absurdity was not an idea in my head, or the sound of a voice, but that long-dead snake at my feet, that wooden snake. Snake or claw or root or vulture's talon, it doesn't matter. And without formulating anything clearly, I understood that I had found the key to Existence, the key to my Nauseas, to my own life.'[46]

The Manifesto of this destruction of things – which is what Marcuse too means by 'revolution' – he himself points out in Hegel's writings. Emancipation from the slavery of 'facts' coincides with the Night and

[43] Marcuse, *Reason and Revolution*, op. cit., pp. 26–7.
[44] J. P. Sartre, *Nausea*, London, 1965, p. 180.
[45] ibid., pp. 181–3.   [46] ibid., p. 185.

Nothingness, which Hegel discusses in an early text, *The Difference between Fichte's and Schelling's Systems of Philosophy*: 'Here in his first philosophical writings', Marcuse reveals, 'Hegel intentionally emphasizes the negative function of reason: its destruction of the fixed and secure world of common sense and understanding. The absolute is referred to as "Night" and "Nothing" in order to contrast it with the clearly defined objects of everyday life. Reason signifies the absolute annihilation of the common-sense world.'[47]

No-one will fail to realize that here we are dealing with familiar romantic themes. *The Difference* . . . is full of echoes of Schelling. But since Marcuse descends from Heidegger, perhaps we can see this celebration of Night and Nothingness (precisely where we were accustomed to expect the 'sun of the future') as an echo of *Was ist Metaphysik?* Heidegger is a master of the *Nichtung*. And if even *Nichtung* is not *Vernichtung* nor *Verneinung*,[48] this philosophical 'revolution' is hardly clear. It not only locates 'authentic' and no longer 'estranged' existence 'in the clear night of Nothing', but as if this were not enough, prey to some pedantic fury, it insists on specifying that 'Nothing itself annuls'.

THE IDEALISTIC REACTION AGAINST SCIENCE

To get straight to the point, the true direction of Marcuse's position lies in the so-called 'critique of science'. The opposition of 'positive thought' and 'negative thought', of 'intellect' and 'reason', of non-contradiction and dialectical contradiction, is above all else the opposition of science and philosophy. For Hegel, says Marcuse, 'the distinction between intellect and reason is the same as that between common sense and speculative thinking, between undialectical reflection and dialectical knowledge. The operations of the intellect yield the usual type of thinking that prevails in everyday life as well as in science.'[49]

This Hegelian and romantic critique of the 'intellect' re-emerged precisely at the turn of the century, with the so-called 'idealistic reaction against science'.[50] The two tendencies meet and coincide, as Croce saw

[47] Marcuse, *Reason and Revolution*, op. cit., p. 48.
[48] M. Heidegger, *Was ist Metaphysik?*, Frankfurt, a.M., 1949, p. 31.
[49] Marcuse, *Reason and Revolution*, op. cit., p. 44.
[50] This expression, 'the idealistic reaction against science', was originally used in a positive sense by Aliotta in his book of 1912; it has rightly been reproposed – but with the meaning of a regressive phenomenon – by F. Lombardi in *Il sense della storia*, Florence, 1965, pp. 165 ff.

well, in their critical-negative aspect. In *Logic as the Science of the Pure Concept*, he comments upon Bergson's critique of science:

All these criticisms directed against the sciences do not sound new to the ears of those acquainted with the criticisms of Jacobi, of Schelling, of Novalis and of other romantics, and particularly with Hegel's marvellous criticism of the abstract (i.e. empirical and mathematical) intellect. This runs through all his books from *The Phenomenology of Mind* to *The Science of Logic*, and is enriched with examples in the observations to the paragraphs of *The Philosophy of Nature*.[51]

It is not possible here to describe all the variations on this 'idealistic reaction' against science. *Entsteht die Wissenschaft vergeht das Denken*.[52] Science is born, thinking departs. Let it pass as far as Heidegger is concerned, since he no longer deceives anyone. But this same commodity is today sold . . . on the left. Horkheimer and Adorno:

Science itself has no consciousness of itself; it is a tool. But enlightenment is the philosophy which identifies truth with scientific system. The attempt to establish this identity which Kant undertook, still with philosophical intentions, led to concepts which made no sense scientifically. The concept of the self-understanding of science conflicts with the concept of science itself. . . . With the sanctioning – achieved as a result by Kant – of the scientific system as the form of truth, thought set the seal on its own nullity, because science is technical performance, no less remote from reflecting upon its own ends than other types of labour under the pressure of the system.[53]

The essential point to note is that this critique of science is immediately presented as a critique of society, too. The scientific intellect is the form of thought which prevails in practice and in everyday life. The *Allgemeingültigkeit* of science, i.e. the universality of its statements, is identical with the impersonality and anonymity of social life. These developments are all already present *in nuce* in Bergson. Our intellect, says *Creative Evolution*, is a function which is 'essentially practical, made to present to us things and states rather than changes and acts'. But things and states are only views, taken by our mind, of becoming. There are no things, there are only actions. Therefore, if 'the thing results from a solidification performed by our intellect, and there are never any things

[51] B. Croce, *Logic as the Science of the Pure Concept*, London, 1917, p. 556.
[52] M. Heidegger, *Über den Humanismus*, Frankfurt, 1949, p. 39.
[53] M. Horkheimer and Th. W. Adorno, *Dialektik der Aufklärung*, Amsterdam, 1947, p. 104.

other than those that the intellect has thus constituted',[54] this means that
the natural world, which science presents to us as reality, is in fact only
an artefact. Matter is a creation of the intellect, 'Things' are the crystals
in which form takes and coagulates our vocation to *objectify*, to 'solidify'
the world in order to act on it practically and transform it.

In addition to this original solidarity of science and materialism, there
is the solidarity of materialism and society, of science and communal life.
We objectify in order to act on the world, but this objectification is also
a means towards intersubjective communication. Authentic or personal
existence and social or impersonal existence result in two diverse subjects,
one 'fundamental' and the other 'superficial' and 'fictitious'; 'two different selves, one of which is, as it were, the external projection of the other,
its spatial and, so to speak, social representation'. The spatialization or
materialization of reality, says Bergson, is already an opening to social life.

> The greater part of the time we live outside ourselves, hardly perceiving
> anything of ourselves but our own ghost, a colourless shadow which pure
> duration projects into homogenous space. Hence our life unfolds in space rather
> than in time; we live for the external world rather than for ourselves[55] . . . This
> intuition of a homogeneous milieu . . . enables us to externalise our concepts in
> relation to one another, reveals to us the objectivity of things, and thus, in two
> ways, on one hand by getting everything ready for language, and on the other
> by showing us an external world, quite distinct from ourselves, in the percep-
> tion of which all minds have a common share, foreshadows and prepares the
> way for social life.[56]

All the essentials are here in embryo, as we can see; science as objectification or reification, and society as estranged as alienated existence.

It is impossible for me to discuss the elaboration and development these
themes underwent at the hands of the various currents of irrationalism
and German vitalism. Here I can only indicate the decisive 'turn' that was
signalled by Lukács's famous book in 1923. As the author himself recognized in a self-critical declaration in September, 1962,[57] and later in the
introduction to the English edition of *History and Class Consciousness*, it is
based on a move from the theory of 'alienation' ('fetishism' or 'reification') elaborated by Marx to that of Hegel. The analysis of capitalist
fetishism is expounded in this work in the terminology of the Hegelian

---

[54] H. Bergson, *Creative Evolution*, trans. A. Mitchell, London, 1911, pp. 261–2.

[55] H. Bergson, *Time and Free Will* (*Essai sur les données immédiates de la conséquence*),
trans. F. L. Pogson, London, 1910, p. 231. First French edition 1888.

[56] ibid., p. 236. [57] In I. D. Fetscher, *Der Marxismus*, Vol. I, München, 1962.

critique of the materialism of the scientific intellect and common sense. That is, the 'fetish' is not capital or commodities but natural objects external to thought. The division which capital introduces between the labourer and the objective conditions of labour is replaced by the distinction which the 'intellect' introduced between subject and object, with the consequence, as Lukács himself has since observed, that a 'socio-historical problem is thus transformed into an ontological problem'. Capitalist 'reification' in this way becomes the product of the materialist intellect and of science, whose analytical vision of reality is denounced as 'positivistic and bourgeois'. Meanwhile the proletariat is equated with philosophical Reason, i.e. with that 'reason' which unifies or 'totalizes' (as they say nowadays) what the intellect and common sense spend all their time distinguishing.

The most important consequence of this shift was that by confusing Marx with Hegel, *History and Class Consciousness* presented the obscurantist contents of the idealist critique of science in the 'revolutionary' form of a critique of bourgeois society. Emerging from the school of Rickert and Lask, and influenced to no small extent by the vitalist Simmel's *Philosophy of Money* (the German Bergson), Lukács ended up, in this work, by inscribing Marxism itself in the arc of the idealistic reaction against science inaugurated at the turn of the century, whose remote presuppositions lie, as we have seen, precisely in the Hegelian critique of the 'intellect'.

The 'fetish' is the natural object investigated by science. 'Reification' or, as Bergson said, *le chosisme*, is the product of the scientific intellect that chops and breaks up (the famous *morcelage*) the fluid and 'living' unity of the real into the 'fictitious' outlines of the objects that have to be used for practical-technical action. Alienation, in short, is science, technology. After absorbing these themes, Lukács broadcast them in his turn, enriched with fresh appeal. The old repugnance of philosophical spiritualism towards production, technology and science, in a word, the horror of machines, was now cloaked by the fascination of the critique of modern bourgeois society.

The kernal of Marcuse's philosophy is precisely here. Oppression is science. 'Reification' is to recognize that things exist outside ourselves. The dialectic of the 'here' and 'now' – i.e. the dialectic of the scepticism of antiquity – with which Hegel, at the beginning of the *Phenomenology*, destroys sensory certainty in the existence of external objects, appears to him as the emancipation of Man himself.

The first three sections of the *Phenomenology* are a critique of positivism and, even more, of 'reification'. . . . We borrow the term 'reification' from the Marxist theory, where it denotes the fact that all relations between men in the world of capitalism appear as relations between things. . . . Hegel hit upon the same fact within the dimension of philosophy. Common sense and traditional scientific thought take the world as a totality of things, more or less existing *per se*, and seek the truth in objects that are taken to be independent of the knowing subject. This is more than an epistemological attitude; it is as pervasive as the practice of men and leads them to accept the feeling that they are secure only in knowing and handling objective facts.[58]

The consequence of Marcuse's argument is an indiscriminate indictment of science and technology, or, to use Marcuse's expression, of 'industrial society'. If we examine it closely, the argument is the same as that which had already formed the basis for Husserl's *Krisis* (not to mention Horkheimer and Adorno's attacks on Bacon and Galileo). It has also been the theme which in recent decades has nourished all the publicity about the so-called 'crisis of civilization' (for example, Jaspers' *Vom Ursprung und Ziel der Geschichte*). The 'evil' is not a determinate organization of society, a certain system of *social relations*, but rather industry, technology and science. It is not capital but machinery as such. Marcuse, let no one be mistaken, is the product of that very tradition which today fears him so much.

CONCLUSION

In *One-Dimensional Man* there is a short section, where the author takes his distance from Marx, which can provide our concluding point. Marcuse writes:

The classical Marxian theory envisages the transition from capitalism to socialism as a political revolution: the proletariat destroys the *political* apparatus of capitalism but retains the *technological* apparatus, subjecting it to socialization. There is continuity in the revolution: technological rationality, freed from irrational restrictions and destruction, sustains and consummates itself in the new society.[59]

Marcuse does not agree with this analysis because he believes that the roots of today's evil lie precisely in the technological apparatus as such. But he is right to locate here the basis of Marx's entire thought.

Capitalist development is the development of modern industry. Under

[58] Marcuse, *Reason and Revolution*, op. cit., p. 112.   [59] ibid., p. 22.

capitalism this growth of modern industry is inseparable, according to Marx, from a series of seriously negative phenomena: exploitation, wage labour, the formation of the 'industrial reserve army', etc. But nevertheless, says Marx, under this cover capitalism prepares the conditions for the liberation of Man: an enormous increase in the productivity of labour (even though in the form of the 'intensification' of exploitation of labour power); the eradication of local and national boundaries and the unification of the world (even though in the form of a world 'market'); the socialization of Man, i.e. his unification with the species (although by means of the formation of the factory proletariat). The *Manifesto* states:

The bourgeoisie has through its exploitation of the world market given a cosmopolitan character to production and consumption in every country. To the great chagrin of Reactionists, it has drawn from under the feet of industry the national ground on which it stood. . . . In place of seclusion and self-sufficiency, we have intercourse in every direction, universal interdependence of nations.

The meaning of this passage is summarized by Marx in the following formulae: Contradiction between modern productive forces and the capitalist envelope in which they have developed. Between the social nature of industrial production and the still private mode of capitalist appropriation.

The use and abuse of these formulae have rendered them virtually meaningless. But beneath the veneer of time it is not difficult still to recognize in them two important points. The first is that Marx does not deduce the nature and quality of the forces concerned in the transformation and liberation of modern society from a mere 'ideal' of philosophic Reason (which is, anyway, always the 'reason' or 'ideal' of X or Y) but from a scientific analysis of modern society itself. This means, therefore, not from an *a priori* evasion of the object under examination (the so-called 'destruction' of the finite) but from the individualization of the rôle of the working class in the modern productive process. (Marx wrote to Ruge that: 'We do not anticipate the world dogmatically, but rather wish to find the new world through criticism of the old. Until now the philosophers had the solution to all riddles in their desks, and the stupid outside world simply had to open its mouth so that the roasted pigeons of absolute science might fly into it.') This means that the 'solution' is not deduced from any external *deus ex machina*, but that one appeals for it to *real* historical forces, internal to that society itself. The second is that precisely this function in the modern productive process makes the working class (from the mere manual labourer to the engineer) the historical agent through whom the new society can inherit the essentials of the old: the modern productive forces developed in its bosom, i.e. science, technology, industry, the critical spirit and the experimental style of life.

For Marx, and Marcuse is right this time, 'there is continuity in the revolution'. I would say that the difference between the revolution as a real historical act and the 'Promethean' attempt of the Great Refusal, is all here. The revolution is an act of real life; it is born from history and has the consciousness to give rise once again to real historical conditions. It is the liberation of forces accumulated by historical development. It is the recuperation, at a higher level, of all that humanity has seized in the course of its history. Seized from nature and seized from the irrational suggestions of myth.

Marcuse's Great Refusal, on the other hand, is defined precisely by its ahistoricity. It is a *total negation* of the existing. Having diagnosed that 'technology is the major vehicle of reification', he can only seek liberation either before history or after it. In either case, outside the bounds of common sense. 'Terror and civilization are inseparable.' 'The growth of culture has taken place under the sign of the hangman.' 'We cannot abandon terror and conserve civilization.'[60] These are aphorisms of Horkheimer and Adorno which help us to understand Marcuse's Great Refusal.

A barely cultivated literary taste would soon desire to turn elsewhere. A barely expert reader would recognize immediately their origin in Heidegger (*Der Mensch irrt. Die Irre, durch die der Mensch geht, ist nichts* . . .)[61] Yet we must make allowances for them. These are the last 'flowers of evil' of the old spiritualism and of its impotent desire to destroy things: the swansong of two old gentlemen, slightly nihilistic and *demodés*, in conflict with history.

Postscript on Marcuse

For Marcuse, alienation, fetishism is not the product of wage labour, of the world of commodities and capital. The 'evil' for him is not a determinate organization of society, a certain system of *social relations* but

[60] Horkheimer and Adorno, op. cit., p. 256.
[61] M. Heidegger, *Vom Wesen der Wahrheit*, Frankfurt, 1949, p. 22. On the same page, the notion of history as 'error'.

rather industry, technology and science. It is not capital but machinery as such.

It is a fact that *One-Dimensional Man* is entirely prisoner to this old assertion. The book is brilliant, it contains a series of minute and honest observations. But when the substance is examined it is easy to see that it is not an indictment of capital but of technology. Marcuse, who rebels against 'integrated thinking', does not realize that he is arguing like the most integrated of bourgeois sociologists. For him there is no difference between capitalism and socialism; what he fights is 'industrial society', 'industry' without class connotations, industry 'in itself'. Not machinery insofar as it is *capital*, not the capitalist employment of machinery, but machinery plain and simple.

In his analysis of the 'Industrial Revolution' in the chapter of *Capital* entitled 'Machinery and Heavy Industry', Marx frequently underlines the bourgeois economists' identification of machinery and capital.

Since, therefore, machinery *considered alone* shortens the hours of labour, but, when in the service of capital, lengthens them; since in itself it lightens labour, but when employed by capital heightens the intensity of labour; since in itself it is a victory of man over the forces of Nature, but in the hands of capital, makes man the slave of those forces; since in itself it increases the wealth of the producers, but in the hands of capital, makes them paupers – for all these reasons and others besides, says the bourgeois economist without more ado, the *treatment of machinery in itself* makes it as clear as noonday that all these contradictions are a mere *semblance* of the reality, and that, as a matter of fact, they have neither an *actual* nor a *theoretical* existence. Thus he saves himself from all further puzzling of the brain, and what is more, implicitly declares his opponent to be stupid enough to contend against, not *the capitalistic employment of machinery*, but *machinery itself*.[62]

Here Marx is aiming at the position of bourgeois apologetics. In this case, the identification of capital with machinery allows the determinate historical contradictions derived from the capitalist employment of machinery to be spirited away, i.e. to be presented as mere 'appearances'. On the other hand, it allows the positive advantage and qualification of machinery as such – i.e. the increase in the productivity of labour – to appear as a merit of capital itself. Marcuse's position, which is certainly not that of the economists, nevertheless repeats its operations – but in the opposite sense. Marcuse equates machinery and capital, not in order to attribute to the latter the advantages of the former, but rather to impute

[62] Marx, *Capital*, Vol. I, Chapter 15, p. 441 (my italics).

to machinery the enslavement and oppression of the labourer for which in fact capital is responsible. In the first case, the result is the apologetic approach of *Vulgärökonomie*. In the second case, it is that of the so-called 'romantic critique' of bourgeois society – i.e. a critique of the present, not in the name of the future but in the name of, and inspired by, 'nostalgia' for the past. For the economist, whoever wants modern productive forces, i.e. machinery and modern industry, must also want capitalist *relations of production*. (As Marx writes: 'No doubt he is far from denying that temporary inconvenience may result from the capitalist use of machinery. But where is the medal without its reverse? Any employment of machinery, except by capital, is to him an impossibility. Exploitation of the workman by the machine is therefore, with him, identical with exploitation of the machine by the workman.')[63] For Marcuse, on the contrary, whoever does not want exploitation, or rather (given that for Marcuse, in the final analysis, exploitation does not exist) whoever does not want . . . 'integration', must return to patriarchal conditions of life, or even perhaps to feudalism – a subject upon which our author expatiates like any high-thinking social prophet. Taken to its extreme, Marcuse's approach leads to that cult of 'primitivism' and 'barbarism' which the abstract spiritualism of the bourgeois intellectual so easily turns into. His perspective, like that of Horkheimer and Adorno, is one of *Luddism*, as Lukács recognized: 'If we say that manipulation has arisen as a consequence of technological development, then to fight manipulation we must transform ourselves into some kind of Luddites fighting technical development.' (See *Gespräche mit Georg Lukács*, Hamburg, 1969.)

This reference to the 'romantic critique' of bourgeois society may seem amazing. This is, in fact, an adversary about which we never think. In reality, there is not just Marxism on the one hand and bourgeois–capitalist ideology on the other; the game is more complex and has three players. No less than against bourgeois ideology, Marxism fights against 'the romantic conception that,' Marx says in his *Grundrisse*, 'will accompany the former as its legitimate antithesis until its dying day'.

Obviously, Marcuse is not Carlyle or Sismondi. But he is neither of these, apart from a series of obvious reasons, also because of the subtly apologetic implications of his entire argument. The concept of 'industrial society', the idea of 'industry' without class connotations, or industry 'in and for itself', that he shares with bourgeois sociology (see, for example, Dahrendorf), is to defer involuntarily to the great corporations. Industry

[63] ibid., pp. 441–2.

and technology are oppressors everywhere, in Russia no less than in America. 'Soviets plus electrification' (Lenin) is an empty illusion. If we wish to escape oppression it is pointless to attempt socialism. The remedy that Marcuse proposes is in keeping with the gravamen of his analysis. It is enough for us all to oppose the system with the 'Great Refusal' and set sail together, perhaps, for Tahiti.

I wish to make it perfectly clear that I am not criticizing Marcuse in the name of the ideology of the Soviet bureaucratic caste. Nevertheless, in the case of this author our judgement cannot be anything but severe. Marcuse is a critic of Marx of long standing, and the bases of his criticism (see, for example, *Soviet Marxism*, London, 1958) are derived essentially from the old Social-Democratic revisionism. His attribution to Marx of the theory of 'absolute immiseration' and the 'theory of collapse' are derived from Bernstein (see pp. 22–8). The theory of 'ultra-imperialism' which he uses again and again to illustrate how neo-capitalism is capable of anything, is derived from Kautsky (pp. 33ff.). His whole argument, from beginning to end, is an attempt to show that *Marx has been surpassed!* And the more general and vague the contents of his analysis, the more resolute Marcuse's conclusions. The Marxian theory of the proletarian revolution has been surpassed; 'the Marxist notion of the organic composition of capital', has been surpassed; and 'with it the theory of the creation of surplus value'.[64]

The first book by Marcuse that I read was *Reason and Revolution* in the second American edition (New York, 1965). The book contained a 'supplementary chapter' which was not reproduced in the recent Italian edition. If this chapter were translated today many ambiguities would disappear and Marcuse would be seen for what he is, a fierce critic of Marx and of socialism. Moreover, the concluding pages of *One-Dimensional Man* appear even more significant as to the point of view from which he conducts his criticism. Here Marcuse acclaims 'the interior space of the private sphere'; he invokes 'that isolation in which the individual, left to himself, can think and demand and find'; he acclaims the 'private sphere' as the only one which 'can give significance to freedom and independence of thought'. How can we fail to recognize in this the old liberal rhetoric?

[64] Marcuse, *One-Dimensional Man*, op. cit., p. 28.

Part Three

Rousseau as
Critic of 'Civil Society'

Let us make man – Hobbes

FOREWORD

The following notes arose from an attempt to pursue two aims at the same time: to give an account of a certain number of studies of Rousseau's political thought which appeared on the occasion of the 1962 celebrations; and to provide an interpretative sketch of the Genevan philosopher along the lines of the theme indicated in the title – the problem of modern 'civil society'.

As sometimes happens, the two aims, which ought to have merged, have remained separate. The result has been that, wavering between these contradictory demands, the pages I produced are therefore still halfway between the partial bibliographical survey which they might have been, but are only in part, and a short, straightforward essay.

I would also like to emphasize the provisional and incomplete character of this study in relation to some of the hypotheses it contains. The comparison drawn with Locke in some places, the comparison with Smith, which in some ways is more original, the references to Kant, and also the perhaps overstated thesis on the relationship between Rousseau and Marxist 'political' theory – these should all, it goes without saying, be taken as no more than *aperçus*, some at least of which I shall have to return to in time.

There is, I suppose, a certain 'political' slant which comes out at points in these pages, and which the reader might think too alien to Rousseau's thought. I appeal to the authority of the French editors of the very elegant and scholarly edition of Rousseau's political writings now appearing in the 'Pléiade' series. They remind us that 'many French-speaking African or Asian politicians began reading Rousseau at the time when their countries gained independence'; that 'some eminent statesmen in Vietnam, Guinea, Senegal, etc., have declared that they were directed into politics by reading the works of Rousseau', and finally that 'Fidel Castro . . . told a French journalist that Jean-Jacques had been his teacher and that he had fought Batista with the *Social Contract* in his pocket'. And though the French authors may not agree, I do not think that Castro disowned this last statement when he added, 'that since then, he has preferred reading Marx's *Capital*'.

MORALITY AND POLITICS

In the proceedings of the seminar held at Dijon on 3–6 May 1962, to celebrate the 250th anniversary of Rousseau's birth and the bicentenary of the *Social Contract*, there is an essay by S. Cotta on 'La position du problème de la politique chez Rousseau'[1] which is worthy of note. His thesis is that Rousseau's thought gives primacy to politics. Rousseau sees politics as the global response to the problems of man. 'It is my opinion that in Jean-Jacques, politics is presented as the solution (the only possible solution) to the problems of human existence.'[2] This primacy of politics stems from a particular view of evil, whose origins Rousseau attributes wholly to society. Evil is 'inequality', social injustice. The ethical task of the triumph of good over evil is therefore necessarily identified with the political task of the transformation of society.

The sense of the argument goes beyond the mere affirmation of the unity of morals and politics. The thesis is really that politics 'founds' morals. A morality in itself, anterior to and independent of politics, and restricted just to the 'inner life' of man, is ultimately inconceivable for Rousseau. For, says Cotta, 'the supreme criterion of moral life is exclusively the civil community, the city – this is the "grand tout" which in Jean-Jacques' words appears as the global horizon of human existence, based as it is on reason and the general will'.[3]

After Christianity with its claim for the supremacy of the spiritual, Rousseau's primacy of politics signals a profound transformation of the whole conception of life. Not only does it invalidate the Christian concept of the fall, the idea of original sin, but it subverts the very basis of secular Christianity and the school of natural law. The distinction of Pufendorf and still more of Thomasius, the distinction to which Kant was to return between morality and law (the former belonging to the 'inner' world, the latter only to 'external' relations), falls. With it also falls the classic Christian-liberal distinction between the 'virtuous man' and the 'good

---

[1] *Études sur le Contrat social de J.-J. Rousseau* (proceedings of the seminar held at Dijon 3–6 May 1962), Paris, 1964, pp. 177–90. Henceforth *Dijon*.
[2] *Dijon*, p. 179. [3] ibid., p. 182.

'citizen' – this being the distinction which has traditionally prevented the identification of morality with politics.

Cotta's essay recalls to mind the famous interpretation first put forward in 1932 by Cassirer in *Das Problem J-J. Rousseau*[4] (strictly speaking Cotta himself does not refer to this work but to the later pages of *The Philosophy of the Enlightenment*). Cassirer's thesis is that the deepest meaning of Rousseau's thought lies in his transposition of the problem of evil from the camp of 'theodicy' into that of 'politics'. The problem of justifying God in the face of the evil in the world, which was so important in the metaphysical religious thought of the seventeenth and eighteenth centuries (Leibniz, Shaftesbury, Pope, etc.) is radically transformed with Rousseau, according to Cassirer, in that the responsibility for the origins of evil is no longer attributed to an obscure wish of God's, or to some presumed original sin by man, but is placed squarely on society.

Rousseau's solution of this dilemma lies in his placing responsibility at a point where no one before him had looked for it. He created, as it were, a new subject of responsibility, of 'imputability'. This subject is not individual man, but human society.[5]

The main consequence of this view of evil as the product of a determinate organization of society is that the problem of the elimination of evil from the world comes to coincide with the problem of revolution.

In its present form society has inflicted the deepest wounds on humanity, but society alone could and should heal these wounds. The burden of responsibility rests upon it from now on. That is Rousseau's solution of the problem of theodicy.[6]

The old problem of evil is thus pushed out of the sphere of metaphysics and transferred to the centre of ethics and politics, and turns into the problem of the critique of society, releasing a stimulus of unprecedented power.

All contemporary social struggles are still moved and driven by this original stimulus. They are rooted in that consciousness of the *responsibility* of society which Rousseau was the first to possess and which he implanted in all posterity.[7]

A further consequence emphasized by Cassirer is the extent to which Rousseau finds himself in opposition to Christianity. In spite of his genuine and profound religious pathos, the determination with which he

[4] Translated into English as *The Question of Jean-Jacques Rousseau*, New York, 1954.
[5] ibid., p. 75.　　　　　[6] ibid., p. 76.　　　　　[7] ibid.

rejects the idea of man's original sin distinguishes Rousseau once and for all from all the traditional forms of faith. In the seventeenth and eighteenth centuries the dogma of original sin was the kernel and linch-pin of both Catholic and Protestant doctrine. All the great religious movements of the period hinge on this dogma and are encompassed in it. But this conviction that the roots of evil are in human nature finds in Rousseau an inexorable and dangerous enemy.

The Church fully understood this situation; it at once stressed the decisive issue with clarity and firmness. The *mandement* in which Christophe de Beaumont, Archbishop of Paris, condemned *Émile* laid the chief emphasis on Rousseau's denial of original sin.[8]

In conclusion, Rousseau signals a profound and radical transformation of man's whole perspective on his existence. 'Salvation' is no longer entrusted to religion but to politics. Redemption is no longer attainable by external aids ('no God can give us it'), but only by man. 'When the present coercive form of society is destroyed and is replaced by the free form of political and ethical community,' Cassirer says, then we shall have reached 'the hour of salvation'.[9]

This is also one of the main motives for the break with the Encyclopedists. Where Voltaire, d'Alembert, Diderot and all the *philosophes* see 'mere defects of society, mere mistakes in organization which must be gradually eliminated'.[10] Rousseau sees a 'sin' which can be redeemed only by an act which transforms society from its very foundations.

Cotta, although he agrees with Cassirer's interpretation of Rousseau, does not agree with Rousseau himself. In opposition to the Genevan philosopher he poses anew the case for realistic Christian pessimism. The idea of the fall is the idea of man's imperfection, his fallibility. The dialectic which Christianity presumes between creatural imperfection and man's aspiration to the absolute prevents any deification of society.[11] Rousseau, on the other hand, resolving man's destiny into the political community, has opened the way to 'democratic totalitarianism'. This is the well-known thesis of J. L. Talmon's book,[12] which Cotta in fact quotes, and it is also the thesis of the nineteenth-century liberal critique of Rousseau. In the light of this, Cotta concludes with the significant observation that 'there has been much discussion of Kant's debt to

[8] ibid., p. 74.   [9] ibid., p. 70.
[10] ibid., p. 71.   [11] *Dijon*, pp. 185 ff.
[12] *The Origins of Totalitarian Democracy*, London, 1955.

Rousseau, but this should not make us forget the perhaps still more important debt owed him by Hegel and especially Marx'.[13]

Morality – and this is Derathé's thesis too – is therefore resolved for Rousseau into politics. Derathé puts strong emphasis on this point in his introduction to the *Social Contract* and to the *Political Fragments* (in the third volume of the *Oeuvres Complètes*[14] in course of publication by the 'Bibliothèque de la Pléiade' and edited by B. Gagnebin and M. Raymond, which makes it possible to regard C. E. Vaughan's still admirable edition of the *Political Writings of J. J. Rousseau*[15] as at least in part superseded). Derathé also starts from the problem of evil, observing that Rousseau denies not man's wickedness, but only the view that 'wickedness is innate in the species as the "sophist" Hobbes teaches, or that it is necessary to accept the doctrine of original sin popularized by the "rhetorician Augustine".'[16] He goes on to recall the preface to *Narcisse* (1752) and the *Lettre à Ch. de Beaumont* (1763) in which Rousseau traces the genesis of his own ideas. These texts make it clear that for Rousseau the origin of evil does not lie in individuals but in nations, and still more in their systems of government ('a distinction I have always been careful to make, and which none of those who have attacked me has ever been able to grasp'). They also make it clear, according to Derathé, how Rousseau makes the passage from morality to politics. 'If we wish to follow evil back to its source, it is not enough to study social life in general. . . . In accusing society Rousseau in effect has his eye on a certain social order – what in the *Confession* he calls "nos sottes institutions civiles".'

The conclusion Derathé draws from these premises is a further confirmation of the central position of the political problem in Rousseau's work, and at the same time a critique of the traditional understanding of the relationship between the moral problematic of *Émile* (the work of Rousseau's which was dearest to Kant) and the political principles of the *Contract*. According to Derathé, it is wrong to maintain as is often done that the principles formulated in *Émile* are precursors to the principles of legislation laid out in the *Contract*, as if the latter were only an 'appendix' to the former. For insofar as in Rousseau morality does not govern politics, but politics itself is the solution to the moral problem, while *Émile* is devoted to the education of the individual in the 'old' society, the

---

[13] *Dijon*, p. 190.   [14] *Écrits politiques*, Paris, 1964.

[15] Cambridge, 1915, reprinted Oxford, 1962.

[16] Rousseau, *Écrits politiques*, op. cit., p. xci.

true education offered to the 'new citizen' of the *Contract* lies in participation in public life itself.[17]

Politics, then, is *supreme*. And the thesis is important, not only because it suggests that one should look in the political writings for a unitary criterion in the reading of all Rousseau's works – thus for one thing making it possible to break, as has rightly been pointed out,[18] with 'the hackneyed picture of Rousseau as "precursor" and interpreter of the romantic sensibility' (an idea, by the way, still active in many texts on Rousseau's 'egotism')[19] but also because it makes it possible to appreciate the difference in orientation between the 1962 Rousseau celebrations and those held in 1912. The former, closer to our own times, tended for the most part to take up the political or 'external' projection of the moral problem in Rousseau; the earlier ones tended rather to absorb the political problem into the moral one, and the moral, in its turn, into the subjective 'interiority' of the individual as such.

Having emerged in its most significant forms in 1912 in the *Revue de Métaphysique et de Morale*, in the work of writers like Boutroux, Delbos, Jaurès, Stammler, etc. (whose interpretation was then adopted by R. Mondolfo in *Rousseau e la coscienza moderna*), this orientation, which tended to lead the thought of the Genevan philosopher back into the sphere of Kant's moral problematic, is also at the basis of some more recent works,[20] works whose well-foundedness is certainly open to doubt, but not their link with a very worthy tradition of interpretation, even though it may appear historically outmoded.

But other, different, routes, which nonetheless still tend to lead Rousseau's 'politics' back to the 'interiority' of the moral subject seem to reach more dubious conclusions. This is true, for example, of Otto Vossler's book, *Rousseaus Freiheitslehre*,[21] in which although he does stress that Rousseau had broken with natural-law theory as early as the *Discours sur l'inégalité*,[22] he does so only to rediscover in Rousseau's work (in terms which seem at times to echo actualistic formulations) an internalization of

[17] ibid., p. xcviii.

[18] P. Casini, *Rousseau*, Rome and Milan, 1966, p. 75.

[19] cf., for example, P. D. Jimack, 'Rousseau and the Primacy of Self', in *Studies on Voltaire and the Eighteenth Century*, Geneva, 1965, Vol. XXXII, pp. 73–90.

[20] See, for example, A. de Regibus, *Il problema morale in J.-J. Rousseau e la validità dell' interpretazione kantiana*, Turin, 1957, or, more briefly, Aimé Forest, 'Les principes du droit politique, selon Rousseau', in *Il problema del potere politico*, Records of the XVIIIth Congress of the *Centro di Studi filosofici di Gallarate*, Brescia, 1964.

[21] Göttingen, 1963.   [22] ibid., p. 67.

society in man (*ein Hereinverlegen der Gesellschaft in die Brust des Menschen*),[23] or in other words the transformation of the 'social question into a moral question'. He then concludes by presenting the *Social Contract* as a 'mere fragment'[24] of *Émile* – *Émile*, which had already been elevated in Martin Rang's book, *Rousseaus Lehre vom Menschen*[25] as the key to the 'rationalistic theological anthropology' of Rousseau.

THE STATE OF NATURE

The problem is posed above all in relation to the interpretation of the second *Discourse*. More recent studies seem to have definitively cleared the field of two old commonplaces. The first was that Rousseau claims the 'state of nature' as a real condition which actually existed, whereas this supposed 'state' basically represents for him, as Starobinski notes,[26] a 'reference concept', a hypothesis, a degree zero, by which to measure the 'divergence' of each individual phase of human civilization with respect to the original conditions. The second, much more serious position, is that in his works Rousseau is inviting society to choose the savage existence rather than society ('he wants to walk on four legs', Voltaire wrote sarcastically). This error, as Derathé has observed (but there is an essay on it by A. O. Lovejoy, 'The supposed Primitivism of Rousseau's Discourse on Inequality',[27] which is generally accepted as decisive, though I have been unable to obtain it), has survived from the eighteenth century to our own day, despite the warning in the *Discourse* itself, where Rousseau exclaims:

What, then, is to be done? Must societies be totally abolished? Must *meum* and *tuum* be annihilated, and must we return again to the forests to live among bears? This is a deduction in the manner of my adversaries, which I would as soon anticipate as let them have the shame of drawing.

Though the ground has been cleared of these mistakes first propagated by the *philosophes* (and not even disinterestedly) we still have to analyse what Rousseau meant by the 'state of nature'. The way to do this is to compare and contrast it with the natural-law tradition. In the natural-law view, the state of nature is already a 'moral' state. The individual in it has

---

[23] ibid., p. 93.   [24] ibid., pp. 208-9.
[25] Gottlingen, 1959.
[26] Rousseau, *Écrits Politiques*, op. cit., p. lviii.
[27] Now in *Essays in the History of Ideas*, Baltimore, 1948.

'innate' and 'inalienable' rights, which he derives not from society and therefore from his historical relations with the species, but from a direct transcendental investiture. Gierke[28] says 'the individual is destined for eternity and his essence is therefore absolutely sacred and inviolable'. He is 'man', a moral subject, a 'person' before and independently of history and society. His 'humanity' is his spirituality – his soul. His 'social nature' is in his relationship to God.

Nothing is added to this 'moral' condition, which is already perfect in the 'state of nature', by the establishment of society (through the contract), except for the protection of positive law guaranteeing and hence securing the exercise of the 'original rights' which man has 'from all time' possessed, but which are exposed in the state of nature to violence and mutual oppression.

The whole liberal-natural-law conception descends from these principles. Society is not an end, i.e. the indispensable condition for man to be made 'man', but a mere means. It is a means which men decide to form in order to defend, with all the strength they have between them, the person and the goods of each individual member. The 'contract' is not intended to unite and integrate man and man, i.e. to give life to a 'real' association, an effective community of interests; rather its only task is to create an external 'formal' order, i.e. a politico-juridical order which, through the law, consolidates and reinforces the absolute prerogatives of the 'natural man' in his isolation and separation from others. 'Political power, then, I take to be a right of making laws, with penalties of death, . . . for the regulating and preserving of property' – so says Locke in the *Second Treatise* (chapter I, art. 3). True freedom is, therefore, freedom 'from' society. The only task of the State is to use the 'law' – 'the limitation of every other man's freedom, such that it may coexist with my own according to a universal law' (Kant) – to regulate the coexistence of private parties, that is of the antagonistic and mutually exclusive spheres of individual action which express the dissociation and 'competition' of real interests.

In Rousseau the idea of the 'state of nature' is quite different. In fact such a state to him is not a 'moral' condition but a state of innocence, a purely animal condition, beyond the distinction between good and evil. Strictly speaking, in it man cannot be either good or evil because he is not yet really 'man' or a moral subject, but only a natural being. In other

[28] Otto von Gierke, *The Development of Political Theory: On the life and work of Johannes Althusius*, London and New York, 1939.

words because, as Jacques Dehaussy perceptively observed at Dijon,[29] 'value judgements about the individual's behaviour towards his own kind are possible only when there are relationships between them; whereas Rousseau's man of nature is man in isolation, lacking continuous contact with his own kind'.

It is immediately obvious where the difference lies. Whereas for Locke the state of nature is in fact already a perfect 'moral' state, where man has 'always' (by reason of the metahistorical contact with transcendence whereby he is constituted as a 'soul') realized his 'humanity', 'before and independently of every social relationship'; for Rousseau, on the other hand, man's nature is definitely not realized in the 'state of nature' but can be actualized only 'in and through society'. 'When man passes from the state of nature to the "civil state",' says Burgelin, 'not only has he gained access to morality, but he sees developing within himself the faculties he possessed only in the seed.'[30]

In other words, the natural man is only potentially 'man'. His truly human faculties – reason, language, moral responsibility, – which are superfluous and, so to speak, unawakened in the isolation of the state of nature, can only be realized and activated in society, which is both the precondition and the context for their operation. 'Human nature,' as Derathé said in his intervention at Dijon, 'is only able to show its full potential in social life, which, in the famous lines from the *Contract*, "instead of a stupid and unimaginative animal, made him an intelligent being and a man". Life in society, the relations of man with his own kind, are the condition for the development of our highest faculties, such as reason and consciousness.'[31] Whereas for Locke the 'state of nature' contains 'more' than life in society, in which 'civil liberty is narrower than natural liberty as measured by the law of nature alone',[32] to Rousseau on the contrary, as P. Burgelin has rightly emphasized 'man's "present" nature is infinitely greater than "natural man".'[33]

The main consequences are these. Firstly, to Rousseau freedom is no longer liberal freedom or individual freedom 'from' society, but freedom realized in and through the latter. This means that man is liberated by

---

[29] 'La dialectique de la souveraine liberté dans le Contrat social', in *Dijon*, op. cit., p. 124.
[30] 'Le social et le politique chez Rousseau', *Dijon*, p. 171.
[31] 'L'homme selon Rousseau', *Dijon*, p. 207.
[32] R. Polin, *La politique morale de J. Locke*, Paris, 1960, p. 193.
[33] P. Burgelin, *La philosophie de l'existence de J.-J. Rousseau*, Paris, 1952, pp. 218–19.

liberating society, that his freedom is not an area which 'excludes' others, but is achieved with the 'positive' implication of freedom for all: and from this, as we shall see, there comes a new relationship between freedom and equality. ('According to Rousseau,' Burdeau observes,[34] 'freedom is not the residue of some primitive anarchy nor the faculty of opposing some rights against the initiatives of power: it is not a sheltered garden, an *enclave* of individual autonomy in the web of social regulation.') Secondly, while to Locke and Kant and to the whole liberal-natural-law tradition in general, the contract 'is not an innovation in the natural-legal order but tends only to consolidate it, to realize it in a more perfect and rational form', to Rousseau on the other hand, 'the contract means the renunciation of the state and freedom of nature, and the creation of a new moral and social order.'[35]

I shall return to these questions later. I wish now to turn to an examination of the kind of philosophy of history which stands at the centre of the *Discourse on Inequality*. A vast interval, says Rousseau, separates man's loss of his primitive animal condition and the transition to modern 'civil society'. The phases in this interval have been usefully summarized by Starobinski.[36]

(a) Man, who in the 'state of nature' lived in isolation and had a few elementary, easily appeased needs, discovers the utility and effectiveness of labour. Without yet having given up their primitive dispersal, men begin to associate, to collaborate occasionally and to create a degree of provisional order.

(b) A first revolution comes about, according to Rousseau as the result of technical progress. Men begin to build themselves shelters. Families begin to stay grouped together. Humanity enters the patriarchal period. If there is a golden age worth regretting, Rousseau thinks it is this.

(c) Just as man lost the idle condition of the 'state of nature', giving himself up to labour and to thought (to the use of reason, which together with language develops from the consolidation of the first social relations), so now he comes to a new fall which wrenches him from the happiness of the 'patriarchal' state. By an 'unhappy chance' men discover the advantages of the 'division of labour', which enables them to pass from a subsistence economy to an economy of productive development. The appearance of metallurgy and agriculture amounts, says Rousseau, to

[34] 'Le citoyen selon Rousseau', *Dijon*, p. 224.
[35] G. Solari, *Studi storici di filosofia del diritto*, Turin, 1948.
[36] Rousseau, *Écrits Politiques*, op. cit., pp. lxii–lxiii.

a great revolution. 'It was iron and corn which first civilized men, and ruined humanity.' Now producing more than they really need, men vie for the surplus. They want not only to use things but to possess them. They want not only present goods, but the abstract tokens of possible and future goods.

(d) We have therefore reached the unstable situation, already described by Hobbes, in which the war of all against all necessitates the creation of a civil order. With their security threatened, men come together to complete their socialization. But the move goes wrong. The *Discourse* shows us the conclusion of a 'contract' which is an iniquitous contract. Instead of founding the just society, it perfects and consecrates 'the bad socialization' (Burgelin).

There are three essential points arising from Rousseau's description of the course of history, which I have just described, and we should now concentrate on them. They are: Rousseau's view of history; his view of the rôle of the rise of private property; and finally his view of the nature of modern 'civil society'.

On the first point, Starobinski's position should at once be noted. For Rousseau, he says, history is 'essentially degradation. Salvation cannot then come in or through history, but by opposition to destructive development. By exalting Geneva as an example, and offering himself as one, Jean-Jacques invites us to believe that there is an exception to the general corruption in small cities faithful to their principles, and in the brave spirits who stand apart. . . . Rousseau is therefore in his day the most important witness to the discovery of history and temporality, *not* through any theory of progress but through his horrified consciousness of the simultaneous risk and promise of temporal existence.'[37]

Starobinski's interpretation undoubtedly has more than one argument on its side, but it rings perhaps with too contemporary a *Stimmung*. What truth there is in the statement that Rousseau sees no prospect for salvation in history can be explained other than 'existentially' – it can be done with historical arguments, as I shall try to show. Moreover, in my opinion, the rather widespread explanation of Rousseau's attitude to history as an echo, in rationalist terms, of the Christian conception of the fall and redemption is also unsatisfactory.

J. H. Broome has maintained this in *Rousseau, a Study of his Thought*[38] – a book which, with its strong liberal stamp, shows little understanding of Rousseau – but in a feeble and conventional manner. There is, however,

[37] ibid., pp. lxviii–ix. [38] London, 1963, pp. 48–9.

a noteworthy essay on the subject by Lionel Gossman, 'Time and History in Rousseau'.[39] Gossman resolutely rejects the interpretations of Rousseau in terms of romantic sensibility, and affirms that his tragic ambiguity towards history, like all his other contradictions, is '*no* accidental spiritual dilemma, the offshoot of an "interesting" psyche, but the expression in the work of an unusually sensitive and original thinker of a crucial moment in the history of society and of the human spirit'.[40] Rousseau is neither a primitivist nor a mystic trying to flee from history and immerse himself in a kind of timeless *Weltall*;[41] on the contrary, he has an 'acute awareness of history as the mode of being of all things'. 'Rousseau, the explorer of the individual in all his richness, found that the individual could fulfil himself only in relations with others, only as part of a wider (social) whole beyond himself.'[42] Rousseau's 'modern sensibility' arises from conflict with the society of his own times ('Rousseau's unhappiness has, in the first instance, a specific cause in the alienation and dehumanization that he observes in the social world and experiences in his own life'[43]). It is an effect of the antagonistic and divided character of this society. Rousseau's historical pessimism must be explained, says Gossman, by his negative attitude towards economic progress and 'capitalist development'. This pessimism, although it is a contradictory element in the historical orientation of Rousseau's thought, still does not prevent Rousseau from looking for a solution to man's problems in history itself. (On Rousseau's attitude towards capitalist development, a number of studies, to which I shall shortly return, are worth noting: B. de Jouvenal, *Rousseau the Pessimistic Evolutionist*;[44] Iring Fetscher, *Rousseaus politische Philosophie: zur Geschichte des demokratischen Freiheitsbegriffs*;[45] Jean Fabre, *Réalité et utopie dans la pensée politique de Rousseau*;[46] Launay and Bronislaw Baczko, *Rousseau et l'aliénation sociale*.[47])

As for the second theme I have extracted from the *Discourse*, the idea of private property, it should be sufficient to recall the famous statement in the *Discourse* itself:

The first man who, having enclosed a piece of ground, bethought himself of saying, '*This is mine*' and found people simple enough to believe him, was the

---

[39] *Studies on Voltaire and the Eighteenth Century*, Geneva, 1964, Vol. XXX, pp. 311–49.

[40] ibid., p. 312.   [41] ibid., p. 348.

[42] ibid., p. 329.   [43] ibid., p. 343.

[44] *Yale French Studies*, 1961–2, Vol. XXVIII, pp. 83–96.   [45] Neuwied, 1960.

[46] *Annales J.-J. Rousseau*, 1959–62, Vol. XXV, pp. 181–216.   [47] ibid., pp. 223–31.

real founder of civil society. From how many crimes, wars and murders, from how many horrors and misfortunes might not any one have saved mankind, by pulling up the stakes, filling up the ditch, and crying to his fellows, 'Beware of listening to this impostor; you are undone if you once forget that the fruits of the earth belong to us all, and the earth itself to nobody.'

It now remains for us to look at the third point: Rousseau's analysis of 'civil society'. But here a broader investigation is called for.

ROUSSEAU AND SMITH

I have already observed that the *Discourse on Inequality* contains a critique of the division of labour and the transition from a subsistence economy to an economy of productive development. This kind of question, which (I think) is only just beginning to be appreciated in the literature on Rousseau, undoubtedly represents a focal point for research on the Genevan philosopher. What is unique in this respect in Rousseau's position can be brought out quite clearly by comparing him with Smith. The 'Early Draft' of *The Wealth of Nations*, which was discovered and published for the first time in 1937, is presumed to date from 1763. In two points at least it seems to give evidence of knowledge on Smith's part of the *Discourse on Inequality*. Smith presents Rousseau's argument that inequality or difference in talents (which is very small, or almost non-existent, in the 'state of nature') must basically be considered as a product of history and an effect of the development of the social division of labour, and he presents it in almost the same terms. 'In reality the difference of natural talents in different men is perhaps,' he says, 'much less than we are aware of, and the very different genius which appears to distinguish men of different professions when grown up to maturity, is not, perhaps, so much the cause as the effect of the division of labour.'[48] If they had all done the same work and performed the same functions, such a deep differentiation of character and attitudes would not have occurred (Smith uses the example of the porter and the philosopher). In evidence of this: 'A much greater uniformity of character is to be observed among savages than among Civilized nations.'[49]

From this initial point of contact, however, the two thinkers go in opposite directions. For Smith the division of labour is the basic means

---

[48] Adam Smith, 'An Early Draft of Part of *The Wealth of Nations* (c. 1763)', in William Robert Scott, *Adam Smith as Student and Professor*, Glasgow, 1937, pp. 315–56, hereinafter referred to as *Draft*. This quotation is from p. 341.   [49] ibid., p. 342.

for increasing the productivity of human labour. Since the development of this productivity is the essential condition for the improvement or economic progress of a country (or strictly speaking 'one' of the two conditions, together with the one represented by the ratio between the people in a nation who are occupied in useful or 'productive' labour and those who are not), Smith makes the development of the division of labour coincide with the development of human civilization. 'What is the work of one man in a rude state of society', he says in *The Wealth of Nations*, '[is] generally that of several in an improved one. In every improved society, the farmer is generally nothing but a farmer; the manufacturer, nothing but a manufacturer.'[50]

Iron and corn are for him as for Rousseau the protagonists of historical development. But there is a difference; whereas in Rousseau civilization goes together with the ruin of the human race ('it was iron and corn, which first civilized men and ruined humanity'), for Smith the opposite is true. Not that he does not see the shadows surrounding the light, for Smith is no blind apologist for the rise of bourgeois society. In the *Draft* he already recognizes the division into classes and 'oppressive inequality'.

In a Civilized Society the poor provide both for themselves and for the enormous luxury of their Superiors. The rent, which goes to support the vanity of the slothful Landlord, is all earned by the industry of the peasant. . . . Among savages, on the contrary, every individual enjoys the whole produce of his own industry. There are among them, no Landlords, no usurers, no tax-gatherers.

For Smith the wage labourer or productive worker who

bears, as it were, upon his shoulders the whole fabric of human society, seems himself to be pressed down below ground by the weight, and to be buried out of sight in the lowest foundations of the edifice. . . . In a Society of an hundred thousand families, there will perhaps be one hundred who don't labour at all, and who yet, either by violence, or by the orderly oppression of law, employ a greater part of the labour of the society than any other ten thousand in it. The division of what remains, too, after this enormous defalcation, is by no means made in proportion to the labour of each individual. On the contrary those who labour most get least.[51]

But although he sees the deepening of social inequality, Smith is absorbed above all by the idea of economic development. The division of

[50] Adam Smith, *The Wealth of Nations*, ed. Cannan, London, 1961, p. 2.
[51] *Draft*, pp. 326–8.

labour determines such a great increase in wealth that, despite exploitation and inequality, the benefit becomes 'general' i.e. it extends to all classes. He says that 'a common day labourer in Britain or in Holland' has not only more wealth and goods than 'the most respected and active savage', but even in the case of the 'lowest and most despised member of Civilized society', thanks to prodigious economic development, 'his luxury is much superior to that of many an Indian [i.e. North American Indian] prince, the absolute master of the lives and liberties of a thousand naked savages'.[52]

It is a fact that Rousseau did not even remotely perceive this problem of development. 'Rousseau,' writes Iring Fetscher, 'who still adhered to a completely undynamic view of economics, was convinced that one man's wealth arose *directly* from the impoverishment of another.'[53] The *Projet de Constitution pour la Corse*, Fetscher adds, clearly shows how 'reactionary' was his 'economic plan'; and in fact Rousseau's programme here foresees a regression from a developed market economy to the economic self-sufficiency of small tenant farming.[54]

Although Rousseau's France is in no way comparable to Smith's England, which was already on the threshold or even at the take-off point of the 'industrial revolution', and although the backwardness of French society must be taken into account in an appreciation of Rousseau's thought, it is well known that the first analysis of modern capitalism had in fact been developed in France (although as Marx pointed out it still wore a 'veil of feudalism') and that Rousseau had responded precisely to this analysis - i.e. physiocracy - with a complete *fin de non-recevoir*. Henri Denis has shown, in particular, the distance between Quesnay's contribution to the *Encyclopédie* and Rousseau's articles on 'Political Economy'.[55]

Yet despite this insuperable limitation, it is true that from another point of view Rousseau's argument does contain an analysis of 'civil' or bourgeois society. The comparison with Smith can be of service again here. Smith attributes the division of labour to one of man's 'innate' attitudes. The division of labour is, he says, 'the necessary, tho' very slow and

[52] ibid., pp. 328 and 323.
[53] Iring Fetscher, 'Rousseau's Concepts of Freedom in the Light of his Philosophy of History', in *Nomos*, Vol. IV - 'Liberty', ed. Carl J. Friedrich, New York, 1962, pp. 40–1.
[54] ibid., p 46.
[55] 'Deux collaborateurs de L'Encyclopédie: Quesnay et Rousseau', in *La Pensée*, 1951, n.s. XXXVIII, pp. 44–54.

gradual consequence, of a certain principle or propensity in human nature'. This 'propensity, common to all men, and to be found in no other race of animals' is 'a propensity to truck, barter and exchange one thing for another'.[56]

For Smith, these exchange or trading relationships provide the only context in which a society truly conforming to the 'nature' of man, that is bourgeois 'civil' society, can really develop. ('Every man', writes Smith in Book I, Chapter 4, of *The Wealth of Nations*, 'thus lives by exchanging, or becomes in some measure a merchant, and the society itself grows to be what is properly a commercial society.') They are, as Smith saw clearly, relationships based on selfish 'interest'. Man, who has 'almost constant occasion for the help of his brethren', would expect it in vain 'from their benevolence only'. 'He will be much more likely to prevail if he can interest their self-love in his favour, and show them that it is for their own advantage to do for him what he requires of them.' Smith adds: 'It is not from the benevolence of the butcher, the brewer and the baker that we expect our dinner, but from their regard to their own interest. We address ourselves, not to their humanity, but to their self love, and never talk to them of our own necessities, but of their advantages.'[57]

The model of society that emerges from these pages is extremely important. Relationships between men are relationships of interest, of mutual 'competition'. What unites men is not their 'humanity', a 'co-operative' or associational link but, on the contrary, the fact that each makes the other into the 'means' or instrument for the satisfaction of his own interests. '*Society*, as it appears to the economist,' says Marx in the *Economic and Philosophical Manuscripts of 1844*, 'is *civil society* [*die bürgerliche Gesellschaft*], in which every individual is a totality of needs and only exists for the other person, as the other exists for him, insofar as each becomes a mean for the other.'[58] Further on, commenting on just the passage of Smith which we have been looking at, Marx adds: '*Division of labour* and *exchange* are the two *phenomena* in connection with which the political economist boasts of the social character of his science and in the same breath gives expression to the contradiction in his science – the establishment of society through unsocial, particular interests.'[59]

This contradiction, in which social relations – as commercial or trading relations and therefore relations in which one man's gain is another man's loss and vice versa – are discovered to be 'unsocial' relationships, is

[56] *Draft*, pp. 338–9.   [57] ibid., p. 340.
[58] Moscow, 1959, p. 119.   [59] ibid., p. 124.

resolved by Smith by the use of 'philosophy', that is by recourse to the metaphysics of natural-law utilitarianism. Although each individual pursues only his own interest, the 'invisible hand' of competition and the market finally composes the conglomeration of conflicting private interests, in the 'harmony' of the common and general interest. The only power which can bring men together and make them relate to each other is that of their 'own good', their individual advantage, their private interests. But, Marx notes with irony,

each looks to himself only, and no one troubles himself about the rest, and just because they do so, do they all, in accordance with the pre-established harmony of things, or under the auspices of an all-shrewd providence, work together to their mutual advantage, for the common weal and in the interests of all.[60]

A short aside, before going back to Rousseau. The plan of society developed in *Wealth of Nations* is the same as that found in Kant. Competition is the basis of 'civil society'. This form of society into which 'nature' forces the human species is the 'only' order which guarantees human progress and civilization. Such are the fourth and fifth theses of the *Idea of a universal history from a cosmopolitan point of view* (1784):

By this antagonism, I mean the *unsocial sociability* (*ungesellige Geselligkeit*) of men; that is, their tendency to enter into society, conjoined, however, with an accompanying resistance which continually threatens to dissolve this society. The disposition for this lies manifestly in human nature. Man has an inclination to *socialize* himself . . . He has, moreover, a great tendency to *individualize* himself by isolation from others, because he likewise finds in himself the unsocial disposition of wishing to direct everything merely according to his own mind; and hence he expects resistance everywhere just as he knows with regard to himself that he is inclined on his part to resist others. Now it is this resistance or mutual antagonism that awakens all the powers of man, that drives him to overcome all his propensity to indolence, and that impels him through the desire of honour or power or wealth, to strive after rank among his fellow men – whom he can neither bear to interfere with himself, nor yet let alone. Then the first real steps are taken from the rudeness of barbarianism to the culture of civilization. . . . Without those qualities of an unsocial kind, out of which this antagonism arises – which viewed by themselves are certainly not amiable but which everyone must necessarily find in the movements of his own selfish propensities – men might have led an Arcadian shepherd life in complete harmony, contentment and mutual love, but in that case all their talents would have for ever remained hidden in their germ. As gentle as the sheep they tended, such

[60] Marx, *Capital*, Vol. 1, op. cit., p. 176.

men would hardly have given for their existence a higher worth than belonged to their domesticated cattle. Thanks be then to Nature for this unsociableness, for this envious jealousy and vanity, for this unsatiable desire of possession, or even of power! Without them all the excellent capacities implanted in mankind by nature would slumber eternally undeveloped. Man wishes concord; but Nature knows better what is good for his species, and she will have discord.[61]

The argument could not be clearer. Firstly, 'civil society' is the society of progress: 'only in society, and precisely in that society in which there is both the greatest liberty conjoined with a general antagonism of its members, and on the other hand the strictest definition and security of the limits of such liberty, so that it may coexist with the liberty of others' is there progress, that is the 'further development of [man's] natural capacities'.[62] Secondly, the law of this progress is the law of competition: 'in such a complete growth as the Civil Union', Kant says, the competitive impulse of men gives the best results, for 'it is with them as with trees in a forest; for just because everyone strives to deprive the other of air and sun, they compel each other to seek them both above, and there they grow beautiful and straight, whereas those that in freedom and apart from one another shoot out their branches at will, grow stunted and crooked and awry'.[63] Thirdly, this law of the forest is also the law which moves civilization forward: 'All the culture and art that adorn humanity, and the fairest social order, are fruits of that unsociableness which is necessitated of itself to discipline itself and which thus constrains man, by compulsive art, to develop completely the germs of his nature.'[64]

I regret having to lean so heavily on quotations, but there is a part of the preface to *Narcisse* (1752) where Rousseau replies to Kant thirty years in advance. This passage contains the essence of Rousseau's critique of modern bourgeois society.

Our writers all consider the *chef d'oeuvre* of the politics of our century to be sciences, arts, luxury, commerce and other ties, which *tightening the bonds of society* among men *by personal interest*, place them all in mutual dependence, and give them reciprocal needs ... obliging each to concur in the good of others to achieve his own. ... These ideas are undoubtedly pleasant, and presented in a favourable light. *But, examining them carefully* and impartially, many drawbacks are to be found which modify the advantages at first apparent. For it is an astonishing thing to have made it *impossible for men to live together without being constantly on their guard, usurping each other's places, deceiving, betraying and*

---

[61] Kant, *Principles of Politics*, Edinburgh, 1891, pp. 10–11.
[62] ibid., p. 12.   [63] ibid., p. 13.   [64] ibid.

destroying each other! From now on we must guard against being seen for what we are; for, *where two men have common interests, a hundred thousand may be opposed to them, and the only way to succeed is to deceive or ruin them all.* Such is the unhappy source of violence, betrayals, and all the horrors compelled by a state of things in which every man who pretends to work for the fortune or reputation of others, is trying only to lift his above theirs, at their expense.

This is evidently the exact opposite of the arguments advanced by Smith and Kant. In Kant, we find praise of competition, of mutual unsociability and the resulting desire for 'honour, power and wealth'; in Smith, praise of 'commercial society', where everyone can satisfy his own needs, not by relying on the 'humanity' of others, but by interesting 'their self love in his favour', and showing that 'it is for their own advantage to do for him what he requires of them.' In Rousseau, on the other hand, we find a critique of the very point on which this society rests, the division and opposition of private interests; a critique of competition, in which one man's success is another man's ruin; a critique of the general deceit which must preside over these relations in which everyone, in order to live, needs to bring others down for his own advantage. To complete the examination of texts: Marx's 1844 Manuscript on *Human Requirements . . . and the Division of Labour* opens with an unconscious return to Rousseau's critique:

. . . every person speculates on creating a *new* need in another, so as to drive him to a fresh sacrifice, to place him in a new dependence and to seduce him into a new mode of *gratification* and therefore economic ruin. Each tries to establish over the other an *alien* power, so as thereby to find satisfaction of his own selfish need. The increase in the quantity of objects is accompanied by an extension of the realm of the alien powers to which man is subjected, and every new product represents a new *potency* of mutual swindling and mutual plundering.

I would like to attempt a provisional systematization of the series of relations briefly analysed here. In Iring Fetscher's essay (which seems to me, I should add, to contain more new ideas than most recent studies of Rousseau), the author draws attention to these two points: 1. that the physiocratic thesis of the relationship between 'private interests' and 'general or common interest' is analogous, as we already know, to the theory of 'harmony' which Smith was to develop; 2. that precisely in this thesis we should see Rousseau's main reason for refusing to accept the physiocrats' arguments. Fetscher concludes on this point with the words that 'Rousseau judged bourgeois society by moral categories, the physiocrats by economic categories.'[65]

There is some truth in this information, but only if it is correctly understood. Fetscher is basically saying: Rousseau rejected the physiocratic doctrine of *laisser-faire* because, given the 'reactionary' character of his economic views, which deny 'development', he never believed that free enterprise could produce a 'general' enrichment, but rather held that the 'individual' always grew rich at the expense of his fellows; whereas the physiocrats were for the greatest use of capital because, as the first to assert that there was 'economic development', they saw its ability to produce 'general' well-being.

The backward and backward-looking character of Rousseau's economic views is beyond question. In a fragment relating to the *Social Contract* he even went so far as to state that 'in everything depending on human industry, it is essential to be careful to proscribe every machine and every invention which might shorten labour, reduce the number of workers and produce the same result with less trouble'. But if Rousseau's views in this field should certainly be rejected, it is also true that capitalist 'economic development', though representing a 'general' advance of society, has failed to produce the enrichment of all at cost to 'none', but has taken place at the expense of the 'wage labourer' the 'productive worker' who 'bears, as it were, upon his shoulders the whole fabric of human society', and, says Smith, is 'pressed down below ground by the weight, and . . . buried out of sight in the lowest foundations of the edifice'.

In the Physiocrats and in Smith, the phenomenon of impending 'economic development' obscures (without completely obliterating) class differences and hence social inequality. On the other hand, Rousseau's insensitivity to the phenomenon of 'development' sharpens his dramatic perception of the new 'social inequality' which is emerging and prevents him from seeing the progressive significance of the rise of industrial capitalism and the concomitant rise of bourgeois 'civil society'. Lastly, Marx, who inherited the analysis of 'economic development' worked out by Smith, and that of 'social inequality' developed above all in France, unified and combined the two arguments. Capitalist development is pregressive; it therefore advances the 'whole' of society. On the other hand, if the modern wage labourer is indisputably better off and more advanced than the savage described by Smith, it is also true that his social condition is continually 'getting worse'. This is not because of the

[65] Fetscher, op. cit., p. 54.

truth of the theory of the 'absolute immiseration' or secular impoverishment of the masses (which would contradict this recognition of 'development') it is, as Marx explains in typically Rousseauesque style, because inequality and poverty are not measured by 'absolute' yardsticks, or in terms of metahistorical, abstract needs, but 'in relation' and therefore proportionally to the conditions and prospects of others.

An appreciable rise in wages presupposes a rapid growth of productive capital. Rapid growth of productive capital calls forth just as rapid a growth of wealth, of luxury, of social needs and social pleasures. Therefore, although the *pleasures of the labourer have increased, the social gratification which they afford has fallen in comparison with the increased pleasures of the capitalist*, which are inaccessible to the worker, in comparison with the stage of development of society in general. Our wants and pleasures have their origins in society; we therefore measure them in relation to society; *we do not measure them in relation to the objects which serve for their gratification. Since they are of a social nature, they are of a relative nature.*[66]

ROUSSEAU AS CRITIC OF 'CIVIL SOCIETY'

The critique centres on themes already stated in the preface to *Narcisse*. The society arising out of the dissolution of patriarchal conditions of life, under the impact of the division of labour and the development of private property, 'gave rise' says the *Discourse*, 'to a horrible state of war.' All the natural qualities which had previously lain unused and unawakened now came into play. And, 'these being the only qualities capable of commanding respect, it soon became necessary to possess or affect them'. Hence there arose the necessity of appearing to be what one is not. The corrupt and deceitful man of modern 'civil society' was born.

To be and to seem became two totally different things; and from this distinction sprang insolent pomp and cheating trickery, with all the numerous vices that go in their train.

The cause of this corruption lies in the fact that relationships between men are 'exchange' relationships, that is – as Rousseau explains with a formulation similar to Smith's – relationships in which each individual must make the others his 'tools', and in which, he

must now, therefore, have been perpetually employed in getting others to interest themselves in his lot, and in making them, apparently at least, if not

[66] Marx, *Wage Labour and Capital*, in *Selected Works* in one Volume, op. cit., pp. 84–5.

really, find their advantage in promoting his own. Thus he must have been sly and artful in his behaviour to some, and imperious and cruel to others; being under a kind of necessity to ill-use all the persons of whom he stood in need, when he could not frighten them into compliance, and did not judge it his interest to be useful to them.[67]

These exchange relationships

inspired all men with a vile propensity to injure one another, and with a secret jealousy, which is the more dangerous, as it puts on the mask of benevolence, to carry its point with greater security. In a word, there arose rivalry and competition on the one hand, and conflicting interests on the other, together with a secret desire on both of profiting at the expense of others. All these evils were the first effects of property, and the inseparable attendants of growing inequality.

According to the *Discourse*, from this permanent state of competition and social conflict, 'when men are forced to caress and destroy one another at the same time; when they are born enemies by duty, and

---

[67] At this point the reader's attention should be drawn to an error shared by Rousseau and Smith: the identification of the 'division of labour' and 'exchange'. 'Society' and 'social division of labour' are the same thing. Living in society, in fact, means living within a division of labour, where, unlike Robinson, who must do all his work himself, everyone labours for others as they labour for him. This division of labour or 'co-operation' is inevitable in any society. And it naturally presupposes a 'mutual dependence' of all the members of the society, as if they were, for example, in an orchestra. The 'particular' historical form of the social division of labour which is called 'exchange' and presupposes 'commodity' production is quite a different matter. In this case the men who attend to the different labours are independent 'private' producers, each of whom decides on his own account how much of what to produce. Here the social bond, the mutual integration of their labours is not immediate but is realized only indirectly, through 'exchange' and the 'market'. The social division of labour has the nature of 'competition' rather than co-operation. Mutual dependence turns into the dependence of all on the 'market', whose workings escape the control of society. Smith always confuses the two, because for him the only possible society is the society of commodity production, 'commercial society', the society of exchange (bourgeois society is for Smith 'natural' society). Rousseau often if not always confuses them. The result is at times that rather than criticizing the social relationships 'of exchange', he unwittingly criticizes social relationships as such, the mutual connection and interdependence of men. The critique of a 'determinate' organization of society then becomes the critique of *society* in general. And Rousseau inevitably finds himself driven, against his intentions, to counterpose life in solitude and life in society. This explains why the thesis that Rousseau upholds 'unsocial' life, although it does his thought some injustice, still has a certain foundation. It is my impression that some uncertainty about the relationship between 'division of labour' and 'exchange' is also to be found in Marx.

knaves by interest', there arises the last of the stages of historical development summarized above. With their very security threatened, men draw together to complete their socialization. Rousseau shows us the conclusion of a 'social contract' between them. But the opportunity is bungled. Rather than abolishing the state of competition and inequality, the contract confirms and reinforces it with the power of 'law'.

In Rousseau's account, the expedient of the contract is thought up by a rich man to the detriment of the poor. The former addresses the latter as follows:

'Let us join', he said, 'to guard the weak from oppression, to restrain the ambitious, and secure to every man the possession of what belongs to him. . . . Let us, in a word, instead of turning our forces against ourselves, collect them in a supreme power which may govern us by wise laws, protect and defend all the members of the association, repulse their common enemies, and maintain eternal harmony among us.'

The result, says Rousseau, was

the origin of society and law, which bound new fetters on the poor, and gave new powers to the rich; which irretrievably destroyed national liberty, eternally fixed the law of property and inequality, converted clever usurpation into unalterable right, and, for the advantage of a few ambitious individuals, subjected all mankind to perpetual labour, slavery and wretchedness.

The 'strength of all', the 'public power', is thereby placed at the service of private property. It became the instrument legalizing each man in the possession of his own – the rich of their wealth, and the poor of their poverty. The law, the common rule, thus becomes 'the law of property and inequality'. 'According to Rousseau', Jacques Dehaussy commented at Dijon,[68] 'this is the objective of all existing civil societies. In effect they stabilize and give a legal status to inequalities originally based on force, ensuring that they are allowed an almost indefinite legal development.' Dehaussy concludes:

For the rest, in transposing the dialectic of relations of forces from the individual sphere to the collective sphere of social classes, the Marxists, especially Lenin, are saying nothing else when they see in the institutions of modern 'bourgeois' States (constitutions, laws, collective labour contracts, etc.), which appear uninvolved in class struggle, the means for attenuating such struggles – attenuations from which only the propertied classes gain.

[68] *Dijon*, p. 126.

Apart from these considerations, which support what I said at the beginning, namely that while in the 1912 Rousseau celebrations the dominant theme was Rousseau and Kant, in 1962 this was often replaced by Rousseau and Marx, the section of the *Discourse* I have just examined raises a serious problem of interpretation.

The *Discourse on Inequality* is generally taken to be a document of the period in which Locke and his *Treatise on Civil Government* had their greatest influence on Rousseau. On the other hand, the *Social Contract* is taken to be evidence of a considerable shift by Rousseau towards the thought of Hobbes, whom he had previously criticized in the harshest terms. This view, strengthened by all Rousseau's declarations of esteem and appreciation for Locke in the second *Discourse*, has been advanced anew in one of the most important works produced since the Second World War: R. Derathé's *J.-J. Rousseau et la science politique de son temps*.[69] Now, though great caution is called for here, it seems to me that – irrespective of how aware Rousseau may have been of it – the 'evil contract' described in the *Discourse* has many features in common with the 'compact' which Locke makes the origin of 'civil government'.

The men of the 'state of nature' are for Locke the holders of innate 'original' rights, 'moral' subjects who are already perfect and complete. But as Polin[70] says, Hobbes and Locke work from the same basic premise: that man is really wicked and evil. Natural freedom, then, degenerates into caprice and oppression. No one is secure in his own possessions. Therefore men decide to give up a part of the limitless freedom which they enjoyed in the 'state of nature' and to establish a common power, which will guarantee each of them in the undisturbed exercise of his rights, above all the 'right of property'.

The basic features that emerge from this construction should at least be noted.

(a) The social state arising out of the contract is the state of nature itself, only confirmed and made compulsory by law. Positive laws consecrate and strengthen natural rights, that is the rights of man 'independent' of society. They protect but cannot violate them. Freedom is the right to be separate from others, freedom 'from' society. When the State invades the sphere of private rights, it loses its legitimacy and the contract is broken (the right of resistance).

(b) The contract does not really create a 'society' but only a 'State'. More precisely, the society which is created by the contract is only a

---

[69] Paris, 1950.　　　　　　　　　　　　　[70] Polin, op. cit., p. 205.

'formal', juridical society, with no 'real' association at its base, no effective community of interests, but only unsociability and the competition of private interests. The unifying or common moment is no more than this: that everyone agrees (the contract!) that, within the limits of the law, everyone should pursue his own particular interests. The agreement, therefore, the moment of 'general' or common will, is only 'negative': the positive content is not general, but is constituted by individual or pre-social interests. 'The community as such,' says Polin, 'can only exist, so to speak, in a provisional way, in the act by which it acquires a government: as a community it is unable to survive over time. Ultimately it is even incapable of any will or act other than the will and act of acquiring a government.'[71]

(c) At the basis of this whole construction aimed at guaranteeing individual freedom by law, lies 'property', the property which for Locke is always linked with liberty.

For Locke freedom is identical with the property of oneself: being free means disposing of oneself without anyone having the right to violate or limit this right. It is therefore clear that man, as master and proprietor of his own person, . . . carries within himself the basis of his own property just as he carries the power to establish it in fact.[72] . . . The right of property is the first right, the right without which there would be no proprietors of other rights.[73] . . . The reader of Locke has the impression that not only is property presented as the means to liberty and the point of its application, . . . but that property is dearer to Locke's heart than liberty. Liberty, as he understands it, is the liberty of property which incorporates the whole human person. In this sense it could be said that liberty is defended to guarantee property and not vice versa. Liberty of property has the advantage over the property of liberty.[74]

(d) Freedom of property, which has now been found to be the basic 'right of man', for the protection of which Locke's compact establishes a society, is compatible only with 'formal' equality. Equality can only be the equality of all 'before the law', that is the right of all to be 'free' and hence to dispose freely of their property – be they landowners, merchants, bankers or mere workers who own only their labour power (*Second Treatise*, chapter 5, article 50). 'Real' equality, on the other hand, is incompatible with freedom. Yet for its free development the latter requires 'inequality of property' and therefore competition: 'an important observation', Polin comments, 'because it appears to condemn the concomitance

[71] ibid., p. 208.
[73] ibid., p. 260.

[72] ibid., p. 259.
[74] ibid., p. 281.

of the ideals of liberty and equality – for liberty to appear, it does of course require civil equality among individuals, but also at the same time actual inequality of possessions'.[75]

Now it is enough to take a look at the *Discourse on Inequality* to see that the main supports of this construction are already being criticized by Rousseau. In the *Discourse*, the law is considered to be the guarantee of private property; the 'common rule' of 'civil law' as mere means to reinforce inequality and make it irrevocable. Moreover, Rousseau understands the 'formal', i.e. negative, character of the society established by the contract (negative because free of general positive content).

Society consisted at first merely of a few general conventions, which every member bound himself to observe; and for the performance of covenants the whole body want security to each individual.

Rousseau further observes:

what particular interests have in common is so little that it never counterbalances what they have in opposition.

Certainly, in so far as Rousseau's text combines in the same critique two such different historical objects as 'civil society' proper on the one hand, and the institutions of the *ancien régime* on the other, it was inevitable that the line of the *Discourse* should occasionally be ambiguous and contradictory. Still, it seems to me that my anti-Lockean hypothesis is shown to be not far from the truth, on the one hand by the increasingly widespread awareness of the preparatory nature of the *Discourse* in relation to the *Contract* (as against the traditional line of interpretation which often contrasted the 'liberal' Rousseau of the earlier work to the 'totalitarian' Rousseau of the second); and on the other by the recognition which seems to have prevailed definitively in recent years, of the seriousness of the reasons – their 'objective' rather than merely 'temperamental' character – for Rousseau's break with the liberalism (derived from Locke) of even the most radical of the *philosophes*, particularly his break with Diderot.

On the last point, there is a very interesting and comprehensive essay by Jean Fabre,[76] which not only analyses the different philosophical premises of the two thinkers (such for example as the opposition between

---

[75] ibid., p. 274.
[76] 'Deux frères ennemis: Diderot et Jean-Jacques' in *Diderot Studies*, Vol. III, Otis Fellows and Gita May, Geneva, 1961, pp. 155–213.

their concepts of 'nature' arising from the antithesis between Diderot's mechanistic materialism and Rousseau's spiritualism),[77] but also stresses their different attitudes towards society, demonstrating in particular that with the passing of the years Diderot had increasingly felt 'growing in him to the point of obsession, that care for bourgeois worth and position from which he had never been free'.[78]

In *Diderot Studies*, Vol. III, we should also note G. R. Havens' essay, 'Diderot, Rousseau and the *Discours sur l'inégalité*'[79] (see also Havens' article on the 'Hardiesse de Rousseau' in *Europe*, November–December 1961 – a special issue on the Genevan philosopher). In this essay a careful comparison is made of the orientations of the two philosophers at the time of the writing of the second *Discourse*, bringing to light in particular the different view of the 'natural man' revealed by Diderot's article on 'Droit naturel'[80] (a view which, of course, remains entirely within the natural-law framework, and is influenced especially by Pufendorf). Among many other points I cannot describe here, the author also notes Diderot's 'usually more conservative'[81] attitude towards property.

On Rousseau's relations with the *philosophes*, the best work is still the old book by R. Hubert,[82] but we should also note: J. Robert Loy's essay, 'Nature, Reason and Enlightenment: Voltaire, Rousseau and Diderot' (which promises more in its title than it is able to fulfil);[83] R. A. Leigh (who is editing the new edition of the *Correspondance complète*), on 'Rousseau's letter to Voltaire on Optimism' (18 August 1756);[84] and finally, but only because it appeared in such a respectable place (it has no intrinsic worth), Virgil W. Topazio's essay, 'Rousseau, Man of Contradictions[85] (where for one thing it is surprising to find R. Mondolfo's work, *Rousseau e la coscienza moderna*, described as 'recent').

The truth is that the main reason for the break between Rousseau and the *philosophes* is to be found in their differences of principle, and above all, in their different attitude towards 'civil society'. In an age in which all the most advanced thinkers were interpreters of the rights and reasons of rising bourgeois society, its prosperity and industry (and in France struggled to give this new society adequate political forms), the

---

[77] ibid., pp. 170–5.
[78] ibid., p. 195.
[79] ibid., pp. 219–61.
[80] ibid., p. 251.
[81] ibid., p. 239.
[82] *Rousseau et l'Encyclopédie*, Paris, 1928.
[83] *Studies on Voltaire and the Eighteenth Century*, Geneva, 1963, Vol. XXVI, pp. 1085–107.
[84] ibid., Geneva, 1964, Vol. XXX, pp. 247–310.
[85] ibid., Geneva, 1961, Vol. XVIII, pp. 77–94.

critique of 'civil society' in the *Discourse* irretrievably isolated Rousseau from his contemporaries, and made his thought appear absurd and paradoxical to them. Hume, Bordes, *père* Castel, Dupan, Frederick II, Gauthier, Helvétius, Leboeuf, Turgot and d'Alembert were all agreed that his work was a 'mixture of eccentric parade and insincere sensationalism' (cf. Samuel S. B. Taylor, 'Rousseau's Contemporary Reputation in France'[86]). A standard vocabulary for Rousseau spread among his contemporaries, and its most benevolent terms were: *Diogène, charlatan, apôtre de l'ignorance, esprit de contradiction, homme paradoxe, cinique, sophiste, misanthrope*, etc.[87] Even those who recognized his genius were persuaded that his theses were the result of exhibitionism, no more than artificial paradoxes made in bad faith. These paradoxes, Turgot wrote to Hume, 'seem to me as to you to be a game, a kind of *tour de force* of eloquence . . . I think there is some charlatanry here on his part, rising out of misguided self-love'. Lack of interest, incomprehension and silence also greeted the *Social Contract*, which only began to be read after the Revolution. (Taylor writes, 'the myth that the *Social Contract* was influential in undermining the *ancien régime* and in precipitating the Revolution has led a charmed life. It came into being with the French Revolution itself . . .')[88]

It is significant that this impression of paradox is also found in Kant's assessment. The first thing one feels on reading Rousseau, according to him, is that one is in the presence of a rare intellectual penetration, a force of nobility and genius and a soul full of sensibility. But 'the impression which immediately follows is one of stupefaction caused by the extraordinary and paradoxical views of the author. They are so far opposed to what is generally thought that it is easy to suspect him of trying only to display his extraordinary talent and the magic of his eloquence, of wanting to appear the original who far outstrips his rivals in brilliance with the startling and seductive novelty of his ideas.'[89]

But it should also be said that if Rousseau was not understood, this was essentially a function of the extraordinary uniqueness of his historical position. A critic of 'civil society' in a period in which a critique could only even begin to be developed by thinkers like James Steuart who, as aristocrats at variance with the eighteenth century, were as Marx said on 'firmer historical ground', Rousseau not only distinguished himself from

---

[86] ibid., Geneva, 1963, Vol. XXVII, pp. 1545–74.

[87] ibid., p. 1552.   [88] ibid., p. 1563.

[89] V. Delbos, *La Philosophie pratique de Kant*, Paris, 1926, p. 118.

them but, despite the backwardness of his economic thought, was the most resolute adversary of the nobility in his time. On the other hand, although he was potentially linked by this aversion to the *ancien régime* with the radical *intelligentsia*, he dissociated himself from them, and was fiercely fought by them, over something which today must still seem a paradox, and in a way a historical aberration: the anticipation – in the eighteenth century – of the critique of the rising bourgeois society and its 'social inequality'. Hence Rousseau's extraordinary historical destiny: it was no accident that he was execrated both by the 'reactionary' critics of bourgeois society, such as Bonald, Joseph de Maistre, Seillière and Maurice Barrès, and by the representatives of French nineteenth-century liberalism, from Benjamin Constant to Hyppolite Taine, through Royer-Collard, Lamartine and Barbey d'Aurevilly.

MAN'S LOSS OF NATURE, AND HIS TRUE SOCIALIZATION

The theme comes out clearly in *Émile* and the *Social Contract*. But it is more easily understood by comparison with the 'evil contract' described in the *Discourse on Inequality*. Starobinski[90] has a brief passage on this contract which goes straight to the point:

Stipulated in inequality, the effect of the contract is to consolidate the privileges of the wealthy, and to give inequality the value of an institution: under the guise of peace and right, economic usurpation becomes political power; the rich safeguard their property with a right which did not previously exist, and from then on they are the masters. This abusive contract is a caricature of the true social pact.

The situation described by Rousseau is so far from fantasy that it reappears precisely in *The Wealth of Nations*: but with the difference that, as he is arguing from the point of view of capital, Smith of course supports 'civil government'.

Wherever there is great property, there is great inequality. For one very rich man, there must be at least five hundred poor, and the affluence of the few supposes the indigence of the many. The affluence of the rich excites the indignation of the poor, who are often both driven by want, and prompted by envy, to invade his possessions. It is only under the shelter of the civil magistrate that the owner of that valuable property, which is acquired by the labour of many years, or perhaps of many successive generations, can sleep a single

[90] Quoted in Rousseau, *Écrits Politiques*, op. cit., pp. lxiv–xv.

night in security. . . . The acquisition of valuable and extensive property, therefore, necessarily requires the establishment of civil government.[91]

Rousseau's opinion of this situation, in which 'civil institutions' arise only to confirm the 'state of nature' and the unsocial character of private interests, is that it makes man a 'mixed' creature, belonging at the same time to 'nature' and to 'society', or rather, that it denatures man both too much and too little. Too much, because it wrenches him from his primitive isolation and simplicity; too little, because, having taken from him his first nature, it is unable to provide him with another which could make him a social being in the full sense of the word. In *Émile* Rousseau writes:

He who wishes to keep the first place in the civil order for the feelings of nature, does not know what he wants. Forever in contradiction with himself, forever veering between his inclination and his duty, he can never be either man or citizen. He can be no good to himself, or to others. He will be a man of our times: a Frenchman, an Englishman, a Bourgeois. He will be nothing.

The problematic of the 'man of our time' therefore lies in the fact that, as Löwith has perceived,[92] 'the modern bourgeois is neither a citizen in the sense of the ancient *polis*, nor a whole man'. He is two things in a single person, belonging on the one hand to himself, and on the other to the 'civil order'. He is a man of individual and unsocial interests – a *bourgeois* – and at the same time a member of the political community, a *citoyen*.

In this diagnosis, all the deepest motifs of Rousseau's thought recur and intersect: (a) the idea that the man of the 'state of nature' is not a 'man', i.e. that the 'state of nature' is not already a 'civil state' in its own right, merely lacking the safeguard of positive laws, but is only the 'animal' state; (b) the idea that in the motives that bring men to unite in 'civil society' (as Rousseau says in an attack on Diderot in the *Geneva Manuscript*, the first version of the *Social Contract*), 'there is nothing relating to the matter of reunion; far from proposing for themselves the objective of a common happiness from which each may draw his own' (note the critique of the purely formal or 'negative' nature of Locke's idea of society), 'the happiness of one is the unhappiness of another' to the extent that 'instead of all moving towards the general good, they draw closer together only in moving away from it' (cf. Kant's *ungesellige Geselligkeit!*); (c) the idea that therefore 'it is untrue that in the state of

[91] *Wealth of Nations*, Vol. II, p. 202.
[92] *From Hegel to Nietzsche*, London, 1965, pp. 235 ff.

independence, reason brings us to agree to the common good' (one again thinks of Smith, the Physiocrats and Mandeville); (d) the idea that 'this supposed social treaty, dictated by nature (and favoured by the natural-law school), is nothing but a mirage' – because 'if the notions of the great Being and natural law were innate in the minds of all, there be no point at all in expressly teaching either'.

But finally, the decisive theme which emerges is that, precisely because society is not decreed *a priori* by any 'natural' transcendental law, but is on the other hand the only way in which man can really become 'man', it must start as an 'artificial' or 'moral body' consciously instituted by men, and therefore as a radically new order, in relation to the state of nature (and Kant's law of the forest), in which man is organically integrated with his whole being and his will. In *Émile*, Rousseau says:

The man of nature is everything to himself; he is the numerical entity, the absolute whole . . . Civil man is only a fraction of a whole, his value lying in his relation to the whole, which is the social Body. Good social institutions are those which best strip man of his nature, taking away his absolute existence to give him a relative one, and transferring his *self* into a common unity; so that each individual no longer believes himself to be one, but a part of a unit, and is no longer aware except in the whole.

As Burdeau has correctly observed,[93] in the century of Diderot, Helvétius and Holbach, such language could not but appear 'extravagant'. And yet, however little the situation today may have changed in this respect, if one thinks about it a little, the opposite assumption to Rousseau's seems much more extravagant: that a 'society' can be built while private interests remain 'dissociated'. To create a society is to create a common interest, an association or real socialization of interests. If the common interest is restricted to the agreement or contract by which all agree that each shall follow his own private interests, society does not exist (it is only 'formal'), and the socialization of man has not taken place: he has remained in the 'state of nature' with the sole addition of the safeguard of the State.

This is the basic originality of Rousseau's 'contract'. As Burdeau writes,[94]

the *Social Contract* is not the circumspect undertaking, the procedural bargaining, which it was in his predecessors and especially in Locke. It is not

[93] *Dijon*, p. 221.   [94] ibid., p. 223.

a matter, by the pact, of giving up some pre-existing rights in order to consolidate others. From the moment in which he enters society, man alienates all previous rights without restriction.

The pact, in other words, is not there to 'safeguard' the 'natural man', but to wrench him from that state; to integrate him into society and alienate him entirely to it; in short, to socialize him, to make a new being of him, a 'social being' – 'instead of a stupid and unimaginative animal, an intelligent being and a man'. According to the *Contract*,

he who dares to undertake the making of a people's institution ought to feel himself capable, so to speak, of changing human nature, of transforming each individual, who is by himself a complete and solitary whole, into part of a greater whole from which he in a manner receives all his life and being; of altering man's constitution for the purpose of strengthening it; and of substituting a partial and moral existence for the physical and independent existence nature has conferred on us all.

It is a fact that Rousseau sees this 'socialization' essentially in moral and political terms, not yet in economic ones; he sees it as giving rise to the *volonté générale* and the *loi commun*, but not to the socialization of property too. As Jacques Dehaussy has observed,[95] this would seem to be a 'weakness in logic'. But if one understands the real historical conditions in which Rousseau lived and thought, one also understands that this 'weakness in logic' stems not so much from the limitations of his own subjective logic as from an objective historical limitation inevitable in his times, i.e. from the impossibility, in the conditions of eighteenth-century France, of thinking concretely of a solution of that kind.

In fact, if one thinks seriously of the 'problem of Jean-Jacques', it is difficult to escape the impression that everything which we see today as a 'limitation' of his thought is an inevitable consequence of what on the other hand constitutes his greatest 'merit': the extraordinary foresight with which, while historical conditions were not yet ripe, he sketched the first and basic chapters of a 'critique of modern bourgeois society'. Rousseau's 'organicism', his cult of the ancient republican 'virtues', the exemplary value he accords the *polis*, and his 'patriotism' too, are of course solutions drawn from the 'past', and as such, incapable of giving an answer to the problems of modern 'civil society'. But in the eyes of historical consideration they are in a sense compensated for, and their meaning salvaged, by the fact on the one hand that Rousseau seized on

[95] ibid., p. 140.

them in a period when the objective conditions for realistically seeking a solution 'in advance' did not yet exist, and on the other hand, that behind the inadequacy of these old solutions there still flourish new rubrics for an analysis of modern society.

The prime example of this is the much-debated chapter on 'civil religion' in the *Contract*. At first sight, if taken literally, it seems to be (as in part, of course, it is) a desperate attempt to reproduce in modern conditions the ancient unity of religion and politics. A more careful examination, however, shows it to be the birthplace of the analysis of the relations between Christianity and modern 'civil society' (the relationship which – after Marx – Weber, Troeltsch and Löwith synthesized in the concept of 'Christian-bourgeois' society); or, which is the same thing, the birthplace of the modern duality of *citoyen* and *bourgeois*.

CHRISTIANITY AND POLITICS

Rousseau's analysis develops out of one of the most important historical problems of the Enlightenment: the question of the part played by the rapid diffusion of Christianity in the fall of the Roman Empire. The advent of Christianity, says Voltaire in his *Essai sur les moeurs* (chapter 11), led to there being more monks than soldiers in the Empire. Divided by the most absurd 'theological disputes', these monks yet united to fight the old religion – 'a false, ridiculous religion, no doubt, but one beneath which Rome had marched from victory to victory for six centuries'. Therefore,

Scipio's descendants having become controversialists, bishoprics being more solicited than triumphal crowns had been, personal consideration having left the Hortensius and Ciceros for the Cyrils, the Gregorys and the Ambroses, everything was lost; and if there is anything to be astonished by, it is the fact that the Roman Empire survived even a short time longer.

The motifs in this analysis – which are completely lacking from Montesquieu's *Considérations sur les causes de la Grandeur des Romains et de leur décadence* – had already been partly anticipated by Pierre Bayle in his *Pensées sur la comète* (para. 141). The Christian religion, he says, which urges us to suffer insults, to be humble, to love our neighbour, seek peace and return good for evil, is quite incapable of producing good soldiers, just as all the principles of the Gospel are ill-suited to governing the public good.

These arguments were criticized and rejected by Montesquieu in *De l'Esprit des Lois*, Book XXIV, chapter 6 ('Mr Bayle, after having abused all religions, endeavours to sully Christianity: he boldly asserts that true Christians cannot form a government of any duration'). Only with Voltaire did they acquire their full polemical strength and sharpness. The civil dissension and argumentative spirit introduced into the ancient world by *l'Infâme* were *the* cause of the ruin of the Empire; but they could not have done so much harm had not Christianity brought with it, on the one hand, the destructive principle of the separation of man from terrestrial things and therefore also from the prosperity of the *res publica* ('Christianity', Voltaire says, 'opened Heaven, but it lost the Empire'); and on the other hand, the tendency for the Church to turn itself into a State within a State.

In the 'English Voltaire school' (to use Eduard Fueter's historiographical categories) this interpretation culminated in Gibbon's *Decline and Fall of the Roman Empire* (1776), in which the problem is no longer treated in passing or in an epigrammatic manner, but at length and as a central theme of research. But in both Voltaire and Gibbon, the critique of Christianity is conducted in the name and from the point of view of 'civil society', in whose progress they identified the economic and moral progress of modern Europe and its 'improvement'. In Rousseau, however, although he has some motives broadly similar to those of Bayle and Voltaire, a different and more complex analysis is covertly coming into being.

The common critical ideas are those connected with the theme that Christianity is not of this world, as Rousseau repeatedly states in the *Geneva Manuscript*.

Christianity is a wholly spiritual religion which removes men from worldly things. The fatherland of the Christian is not of this world. He does his duty, it is true: but he does it with a deep indifference to the success of what he undertakes. Little does it matter to him whether things go well or ill down here: if the State is strong, he modestly enjoys the public welfare; if the State is in decline, he blesses the hand of God which burdens his people.

And again:

Christianity preaches only servitude and dependence. The spirit of Christianity is too favourable to tyranny for it not to benefit from it. True Christians are made to be slaves. They know it and are undisturbed; this short life has too little value for them.

The aspects of Christianity most strongly attacked by Voltaire (who derived his view of the world from the English empiricists and deists) are the fantastic superstructures with which fanaticism, theological sectarianism, superstition and credulity have encrusted it, thus placing it in contradiction – in 'this' form – with the causes of the progress of society. In Rousseau's argument, however, the ideal term is not modern 'civil society', but *le noeud et l'unité du Corps moral* which a true society must have in order to call itself such: he finds this not in modern conditions but in the 'patriotism' of the ancients (Sparta, Rome).

This different slant to the argument is already very clear in the *Geneva Manuscript* and the *Social Contract*, but it emerges especially sharply in two letters to Usteri on 30 April and 18 July 1763:

The patriotic spirit is an exclusive spirit which makes us look on everyone but our fellow citizens as strangers, and almost as enemies. Such was the spirit of Sparta and Rome. The spirit of Christianity on the contrary makes us look on all men as our brothers, as the children of God. Christian charity will not allow of odious differences between the compatriot and the foreigner, it is neither good to make republicans nor warriors, but only Christians and men; its ardent zeal embraces indifferently the whole human race. Thus it is true that Christianity is in its very sanctity contrary to the particular social spirit.

The ideas are still to some extent those of Bayle and Voltaire; the emphasis here falls on the consequences for the aims of the government of worldly things of Christianity's orientation towards transcendence. Yet, setting aside the tone of religious seriousness which seems despite everything to be present even in these polemical pages, an idea is laboriously sorting itself out in Rousseau's text which seems to me to be quite new and which would have been unthinkable for Voltaire and the *philosophes* as a whole: it is the antithesis between cosmopolitanism and local society, or to follow his text more closely, between 'general' society and 'particular' society. Christianity is not only contrary to 'the particular social spirit' because it is otherworldly, but because its otherworldliness is in itself another 'society'.

Wider society, human society in general, is based on humanity, on universal well-doing. I say and I have always said that Christianity is favourable to the latter. But particular societies, political and civil societies, have a quite different principle: they are purely human establishments, and consequently true Christianity separates us from them, as from all worldly things.

This 'abstract' general society, which potentially includes the whole human race and – as the first of the *Lettres de la montagne* says – makes Christianity the 'universal social institution', is what Rousseau now understands (by contrast with Voltaire) to be the complement and the very basis of modern 'civil society', i.e. of that intrinsic dissociation by which men live 'both in the liberty of the state of nature and subject to the needs of the social state'. The 'ideal' society for Christianity, according to the *Geneva Manuscript*, is the very same 'natural and general society' discussed by natural-law theory ('the ideas of natural right and the common fraternity of all men have spread rather late and progressed so slowly in the world that only Christianity has sufficiently generalized them'). And this 'abstract' general society, placed above particular or 'real' society, is only the expression of the internal contradiction which separates modern man into *bourgeois* and *citoyen*, making him on the one hand, the member of an imaginary or unreal 'community', and on the other, the egoistic and unsociable individual of the terrestrial world. ('Hence', says Rousseau, 'we see what we should think of the supposed cosmopolitans who justify their love for their country by their love for the human race, and boast of loving all the world, so that they may have the right of loving no one.')

There is no point here in trying to drag from Rousseau's text more definite meanings than it can reasonably give us. The problem is only embryonic here; the investigation still in its initial stages. But it is still a fact that the 'general society', the 'human society *in general*', which he sees Christianity as establishing, shifts with Rousseau from a debate about the causes of the ruin of the anciety world, and enters the horizon of a new problematic. Löwith, who has understood that 'Rousseau's writings contain the first and clearest description of the human problematic of bourgeois society', has also seen this difference of context. He affirms that Rousseau's argument about 'civil religion' starts from the statement that 'Christianity separated religion from politics, and proclaimed a heavenly kingdom superior to all earthly realms'; he understands the link between this religious problematic and the division of modern man into *bourgeois* and *citoyen*. Understanding this, he makes it possible for us to understand that the place in which this aspect of Rousseau's thought can be found in its highest and most mature form is in Marx's *The Jewish Question* (for obvious reasons, we cannot deal here with the contributions of Hegel and Feuerbach, important though they are).

The 'abstract' general society of Christianity is the very same political or 'celestial' sphere (celestial in its separation from real 'economic' society) of which Marx speaks in this text of 1843, analysing the liberal-democratic Constitutions produced by the French Revolution:

The difference between the religious man and the citizen is the difference between the shopkeeper and the citizen, between the day labourer and the citizen, between the landowner and the citizen, between the *living individual* and the *citizen*. The contradiction between the religious and political man is the same as that between *bourgeois* and *citoyen*, between the member of civil society, and his *political lion skin*.[96]

Marx continues:

. . . man leads a double life, a heavenly and an earthly life, not only in thought or consciousness but in *actuality*. In the *political community* he regards himself as a *communal being*; but in *civil* society he is active as a *private individual*, treats other men as means, reduces himself to a means and becomes the plaything of alien powers. . . . The members of the political state are religious by virtue of the dualism between individual life and species-life, between the life of civil society and political life. They are religious inasmuch as man regards as his true life the political remote from his actual individuality, inasmuch as religion is here the spirit of civil society expressing the separation and withdrawal of man from man. Political democracy is Christian in that it regards man – not merely one but every man – as *sovereign* and supreme. But this means man in his uncivilized and unsocial aspect, in his fortuitous existence, and just as he is, corrupted by the entire organization of our society, lost and alienated from himself, oppressed by inhuman relations and elements – in a word, man who is not yet an actual species-being[97] [that is a truly social being].

This is obviously not the place to go into the analysis of an argument which is, as one might suspect, rather complex. The connection between Christianity and bourgeois society is, however, a central (if unexplored) theme in all Marx's work, from the *Manuscripts* to *Capital*, from *The Jewish Question* to *Theories of Surplus Value*. Here it is only important to note the persistence in Marx of the original Rousseauan problematic – a persistence which, I would almost say, is the stronger for the ignorance he always reveals of his enormous debt to the great Genevan. Man 'in his uncivilized aspect', man 'corrupted by the entire organization of our society', is the very man of the 'state of nature' who survives, according to Rousseau, within modern 'civil society', for the latter has been unable to 'denature' him to the point of giving him a new nature. The dissociation

[96] *Writings of the Young Marx*, ed. Easton and Guddat, op. cit., p. 226.
[97] ibid., pp. 225 and 231.

of this man, his duplication into *bourgeois* and *citoyen*, the double earthly and heavenly life he leads, are the result of the merely abstract, formal or 'negative' character of the society that emerges out of the 'evil contract'. All equal and all members of the political 'community' as parties to the original agreement or contract, men in this way establish, however, only an abstract or a heavenly community, because their agreement does not represent an effective socialization of their interests and wills but only tends to guarantee them the mutual 'dissociation' and separation of the 'state of nature'.

In other words, society is born to confirm the 'rights of man' 'before' society, that is the rights directly invested in him by the transcendental, in that all are 'sons of God' before they are sons of the 'real' society to which they belong: so that the contract establishes not a real society but only a 'State' to protect the competition and struggles of private interests.

The model of the 'Declaration of the Rights of Man', as Jellinek has shown,[98] is the Christian idea that all men, as creatures of God, are born equal. Through this 'Declaration', the *Civitas Dei* on earth has become the social contract, and the Christian creature has been converted into the 'natural man' whose civil liberty 'from' society must be guaranteed by the State. Marx writes:

Thus none of the so-called rights of men goes beyond the egotistic man, the man who, in bourgeois society, is separated from the community and withdrawn into himself, his private interest and his private choice, and separated from the community as a member of civil society. Far from viewing man in his species-being, his species-life itself – society – rather appears to be an external framework for the individual, limiting his original independence. The only bond between men is natural necessity, need and private interest, the maintenance of their property and egotistic persons.[99]

POPULAR SOVEREIGNTY
AND THE CRITIQUE OF REPRESENTATION

It now remains to say something about two central concepts of political theory developed in the *Contract*: the concept of sovereignty and the critique of parliamentary representation. The decisive position – further confirmed by some of the more recent studies I have been able to examine – still seems to me to be that of Otto von Gierke in his classic work, *The*

[98] *Die Erklärung der Menschen-und-Bürgerrechte*, Munich, 1927.
[99] *Writings of the Young Marx*, op. cit., pp. 236–7.

Development of Political theory (*On the life and work of Johannes Althusius*).[100] The old natural-law theory presupposed a double contract: the
one by which men agree to unite to regulate their safety and preservation
by common consent, which is the *pactum societatis*; and the *pactum subjectionis*, by which, after their agreement, they transfer power to the
hands of the sovereign. This 'dualistic' position, adopted by Pufendorf
and continuing to Locke, was rejected by Hobbes and Rousseau from
opposing points of view. Hobbes eliminated the *pactum societatis*, sub-
suming it wholly into that of domination, so that 'when the State is
instituted the whole personality of the people is merged in the person of
the sovereign ruler, be it the natural person of one man or the artificial
person of an assembly', with the result that the people now become a
person, that is a subject, only through and 'in' the person of the sovereign,
while 'without him it is a mere multitude, and hence it cannot be regarded as the "subject" of any right against the ruler'.[101] Rousseau, on
the contrary, resolves the dualism by doing away with the *pactum subjectionis*, that is by attributing sovereignty wholly and exclusively to the
people and transforming the 'institution of government' – which was
originally a pact between the people and the sovereign – into a mere
'commission', not even a bilateral relationship, by which the sovereign
(in this case the people themselves), requires that certain officials or
'commissars' subordinate to it exercise various functions.

A multitude of historical references and connections can clearly be
developed on the basis of the formulation of the problem by Gierke. It
enables us to locate the central point which, despite their opposing
positions, links Hobbes and Rousseau: the fact that with them a unified
and complete concept of 'sovereignty' became possible for the first time.
This concept was absent in Locke, as Harold Laski in particular has
stressed;[102] indeed it was absent in the whole traditional natural-law
position, in which the centres of power and decision are always formally
at least double, the sovereign 'and' the people, and in reality infinite,
given that the fictitious generality of the people is in turn composed of
innumerable individuals, all holding innate and inalienable natural rights.
(On the medieval genesis of the modern liberal conception of the limits of
power, see C. H. McIlwain's classic work).[103]

---

[100] v. Gierke, op. cit.   [101] ibid., p. 96.
[102] *Political Thought in England from Locke to Bentham*, London, 1955, p. 32.
[103] *Constitutionalism Ancient and Modern*, revised edition, New York, 1947.

In this respect it can be said that, just as no study of Rousseau can avoid taking a position on the problem of his relation to Hobbes, so conversely, Rousseauesque elements seem somehow to reverberate, with an enlivening effect, on the study of the evolution of Hobbes's political thought. Warrender[104] notes, for example, that 'particularly in his earlier writings Hobbes appears almost to have foreshadowed Rousseau's theory of the General Will'. Davy has also developed a similar position in his long essay in the proceedings of the Dijon seminar ('Le Corps politique selon le "Contrat social" de J.-J. Rousseau et ses antecedents chez Hobbes'). Davy, who lays great stress on the modifications made in Hobbes's original theory by the addition of chapter 16 of *Leviathan*, states that 'the key idea of the early Hobbes was realistic and democratic in the sense of direct democracy, as the *De Cive*, after the *Elements*, expressly specifies'.[105] He also notes – though the observation is not new, it is even to be found in the pages devoted to Hobbes by Friedrich Meinecke in *Machiavellism* – that Hobbes makes a distinction between 'right of nature' and 'law of nature'; a distinction which with some uncertainties in terminology is to be found later in Rousseau too, making no small contribution to the crisis he induced in natural-law thought (on Hobbes it is also important to read the relevant chapter of C. E. Vaughan's old book, *The History of Political Philosophy before and after Rousseau*[106]).

In the same way, the link between *The Social Contract* and Hobbes is also stressed by Polin,[107] who notes that Rousseau's thesis that popular sovereignty is so 'absolute' as to be able to infringe the law it has itself made, derives from the *De Cive*. It should, however, be added that Polin himself is to be congratulated on having opportunely set limits in this direction, by showing that Hobbes's concept, developed between 1642 and 1651, of the sovereign as a 'person' 'representing' the rights and strength of individuals,[108] is *en route* for the theory of *translatio* or *concessio*, which came to maturity in the liberal theory (therefore in Locke rather than Rousseau) of political 'representation'.

To go back to Gierke, the value of his interpretation is that, despite all his intense resistance to Rousseau's thought, he resolutely picked out the two key concepts of *The Social Contract*: the distinction between sovereign

---

[104] *The Political Philosophy of Hobbes*, Oxford, 1957, pp. 129–30.
[105] *Dijon*, p. 72.
[106] Manchester, 1925, reprinted New York, 1960.
[107] R. Polin, *Politique et philosophie chez Thomas Hobbes*, Paris, 1953, p. 248.
[108] ibid., pp. 231 ff.

and government and the theory of popular sovereignty. The first point, following directly from Rousseau's repudiation of the *pactum subjectionis* ('there is only one contract in the State', says Rousseau, 'and that is association: it excludes all others. No public contract can be imagined which would not violate the first.'), amounted to a real revolution in the field of political theory, as Gierke clearly recognizes, In fact, it implies that the government no longer appears as the 'receptacle' of a sovereignty transferred to it by the people (as is the case in Locke), but as a mere executive organ, or precisely, a 'commission'. As *The Social Contract* says,

. . . the basis of government [is] often wrongly confused with the sovereign, whose minister it is. . . . It is simply and solely a commission, an employment, in which the rulers, mere officials of the sovereign, exercise in their own name the power of which it makes them depositories. This power it can limit, modify or recover at pleasure.

And here, Gierke comments, the 'true basic concept' of Rousseau's doctrine, is developing, the concept

from which there followed all the propositions first announced by him and unheard before. For the destruction of the contract of rulership cleared the way for the destruction of every right of the ruler; and from the permanent and absolute omnipotence of the assemblage of the people, suspending the executive power and the whole jurisdiction of government as soon as it is assembled, he developed his programme of permanent revolution.[109]

The second point – that Rousseau affirms the sovereignty of the people to be 'inalienable', 'untransferable' and 'indivisible' – results in the radical critique in the name of 'direct democracy' of the representative State or parliamentary Government. The *Contract* states:

Sovereignty, for the same reason as makes it inalienable, cannot be represented; it lies essentially in the general will, and will does not admit of representation: it is either the same, or other; there is no intermediate possibility. The deputies of the people, therefore, are not and cannot be its representatives: they are merely its stewards, and can carry through no definitive acts. Every law the people has not ratified in person is null and void – is in fact, not a law. The people of England regards itself as free; but it is grossly mistaken; it is free only during the election of members of parliament. As soon as they are elected, slavery overtakes it, and it is nothing. The use it makes of the short moments of liberty it enjoys shows indeed that it deserves to lose them.

[109] v. Gierke, op. cit., p. 98.

It is not particularly difficult now to understand the meaning of these theses of Rousseau's. The theory of popular sovereignty as inalienable and indivisible, carries with it the abolition of the *pactum subjectiònis* as the transmission of sovereignty from the people to the government; the elimination of this contract of domination implies in its turn the downgrading of government from the 'supreme power' it was traditionally understood to be to a mere 'commissarial' organ of the people. The meaning of the theory, in short, is that of a direct resumption, on the part of society, of the power or sovereignty which, in natural-law contractualism, was alienated to the separate and independent sphere of 'politics'. This resumption – signifying in fact the suppression of the division between civil 'society' and civil 'government', or 'civil' society and 'political' society, between society and State and therefore between *bourgeois* and *citoyen* – is expressed on the one hand in the unification (against the 'division of powers') of government and parliament, of executive and legislature; and on the other, in their 'common reduction' to mere 'commissions' or 'working' functions, which society not only requires some of its members to do (in the same way as with all other work functions), but which are carried out on behalf of and under the direct control of the mandators (the theory of the *mandat impératif*) who retain full power to effect their immediate 'recall'.

The necessary conclusion is that the meaning of the 'new pact' founding society, the ultimate development to which all the theory of *The Social Contract* tends, literally constitutes the need for the abolition or 'withering away of the State'. Society is a true 'society' when it is the expression of the 'general will', of a real socialization, a real common interest; but the overcoming of the dissociation of private interests simultaneously implies the annulment of the 'civil government' or State, whose birth is connected, as we have seen, to the need to confirm and guarantee social inequality. The meaning of the theory is this. As for the fact that Rousseau nevertheless continued to speak of the *État*, it can only be explained (and A. D. Chajutinis's article, *Zur politischen Terminologie J.-J. Rousseaus*,[110] is useless in this respect) by the fact that he was using State in the sense of the *civitas* of antiquity, or, as J.-J. Chevallier[111] observed at Dijon, that 'strictly, in the author's terms, the State is the congregation of *subjects*, or rather the people' and it is the people precisely insofar as it observes the norms it has set down for itself.

[110] *Neue Beiträge zur Literatur der Aufklärung*, Berlin, 1964, pp. 215 ff.
[111] *Dijon*, p. 294.

Let us take the argument to its furthest conclusion. My thesis is that revolutionary 'political' theory, as it has developed since Rousseau, is already foreshadowed and contained in *The Social Contract*; or to be more explicit, that so far as 'political' theory in the strict sense is concerned, Marx and Lenin have added nothing to Rousseau, except for the analysis (which is of course rather important) of the 'economic bases' for the withering away of the State.

The immediate verification of this is to be found in the *Critique of Hegel's 'Philosophy of Right'*. Although it was presumably written by Marx in 1843, and therefore several years before the real birth of 'historical materialism', this work already contains the essential outlines of all his later political theory: (a) the announcement of the 'dissolution (*Auflösung*) of the State'[112] at the same time as the 'dissolution of civil society' (the fall of one implying the fall of the other and vice versa); (b) the critique of Parliament as the 'people in miniature' – a concept reminiscent, critically, of Junius Brutus's *epitome regni* or, still better, of Nicolas of Cusa's maxim that the assembled representatives *substitute* for the whole people *in uno compendio repraesentativo*;[113] (c) the recognition of the contradiction inherent in parliamentary representation ('the contradiction', Marx says, 'appears to be double: 1. Formal. The delegates of civil society are a society whose members are connected by the form of instruction or commission with those who commission them. They are formally commissioned, but once they are actual they are no longer commissioned. They are supposed to be delegates, and they are not. 2. Material [This is] in regard to the interests. Here, we find the opposite of the formal contradiction. The delegates are commissioned to be representatives of public affairs, but they really represent particular affairs.'); (d) the substitution of representation as a 'working function' for representation in the 'political' sense (Marx says that 'here, the legislature is a representation in the same sense in which every function is representative. For example, the shoemaker is my representative in so far as he fulfils a social need . . . representative not by virtue of something other than himself which he represents, but by virtue of what he is and does.')[114]

A further verification for my thesis of the essential dependence of Marxist 'political' theory on Rousseau is to be found in Marx's work on *The Civil War in France*, where he analyses the experience of the Paris

---

[112] Marx, *The Critique of Hegel's 'Philosophy of Right'*, op. cit., p. 121.

[113] cf. v. Gierke, op. cit., pp. 243–4.

[114] Marx, *Critique of Hegel's 'Critique of Right'*, op. cit., pp. 123 and 119–20.

Commune, and its non-State character. He emphasizes that 'the Commune was to be a working, not a parliamentary, body, executive and legislative at the same time', and that this required that 'each delegate' was 'at any time revocable and bound by the *mandat impératif* [formal instructions] of his constituents'; concluding that in these new conditions, 'instead of deciding once in three or six years' – remember Rousseau on the English parliament! – 'which member of the ruling class was to misrepresent (*ver- und zertreten*) the people in Parliament, universal suffrage was to serve the people, constituted in Communes, as individual suffrage serves every other employer in the search for the workmen and managers in his business.'[115] Concepts, these, which, as we know, were not only repeated word for word by Lenin in *State and Revolution* (cf. particularly the chapter on the 'Abolition of parliamentarism'), but which, while (except, I repeat, for the analysis of the 'economic foundations' of the withering away of the State) they exhaustively summarize the significance and implications of Marxist 'political' theory, nonetheless still clearly remain within the horizons of Rousseau's thought. (There are some interesting reflections on this in Guy Besse's essay, 'De Rousseau au Communisme',[116] in which, after examining Rousseau's 'antiparliamentarism', he writes: 'Here the *Social Contract* is undoubtedly close to Lenin's theses, to the principles of proletarian democracy. Thus the *Social Contract*, which a moment ago seemed too 'abstract' to us, finally, after the eighteenth and nineteenth centuries, is reunited with contemporary experience.')

On the other hand, I think there is a further argument to support my theory in the fact that authors like Hans Kelsen, who are a long way from Marxism, still share some of its basic principles of political theory whenever they return (however consistent this is with the rest of their thought) to Rousseau's teaching. There is evidence of this in statements in the chapter of the *General Theory of Law and the State*[117] on 'The Fiction of Representation'. After noting that under a parliamentary regime, 'the function of government is transferred from the citizens organized in a popular assembly to special organs', Kelsen writes that 'this is a considerable weakening of the principle of political self-determination' and that 'it is characteristic of so-called indirect or representative democracy', arriving at the conclusion that 'there can be no doubt that . . . none of the existing democracies called "representative" are really representative'.

[115] Marx, *Selected Works* in One Volume, op. cit., pp. 291–2.
[116] In *Europe*, Nov.–Dec. 1961, pp. 167–80.   [117] London, 1945, pp. 289 ff.

In fact, while 'it is not enough, to establish real representation, that the representative be elected or nominated by the represented' but 'it is necessary that the representative be legally obliged to execute the will of the represented and that the fulfilment of this obligation be legally guaranteed', the elective members of a modern parliament, Kelsen says, 'are not legally responsible to the electorate', nor does their legislative mandate have 'the character of a *mandat impératif*'.

The formula that the member of parliament is not the representative of his electors but of the whole people, or, as some writers say, of the whole State, and that therefore he is not bound by any instructions of his electors and cannot be recalled by them, is a political fiction. Legal independence of the elected from the electors is incompatible with legal representation.

Therefore,

if political writers insist on characterizing the parliament of modern democracy, in spite of its legal independence from the electorate, as a 'representative' organ, if some writers even declare that the *mandat impératif* is contrary to the principle of representative government, they do not present a scientific theory but advocate a political ideology. The function of this ideology is to conceal the real situation, to maintain the illusion that the legislator is the people, in spite of the fact that, in reality, the function of the people – or, more correctly formulated, of the electorate – is limited to the creation of the legislative organ.

Kelsen concludes with a typically Rousseauesque argument:

Legal independence of a parliament from the people means that the principle of democracy is, to a certain extent, replaced by that of the division of labour. In order to conceal this shifting from one principle to another, the fiction is used that parliament 'represents' the people.

ROUSSEAU AND MARX

One point that is embarrassing and hard to explain in this whole affair is that in spite of the fact of his debt to Rousseau, Marx never gave any indication of being remotely aware of it. Della Volpe in an article in the number of *Europe* already referred to ('Du "Discours sur l'inégalité" a "l'État et la Revolution" '), René de Lacharrière[118] in his contribution at Dijon,[119] B. Gagnebin in his introduction to the above-mentioned

---

[118] René de Lacharrière has also written a book, *Études sur la théorie démocratique* (*Spinoza, Rousseau, Hegel, Marx*), Paris, 1963, but this is weak in analysis, and modest in every respect. [119] 'Rousseau et le Socialisme', *Dijon*, pp. 515-35.

edition of the *Écrits Politiques* and Della Volpe again in his contribution to the Dijon seminar,[120] have more or less extensively demonstrated this incomprehension. It is the more surprising in the light of the fact that in such a work as *The Jewish Question* – literally inconceivable without Rousseau – Marx not only refers only once to the Genevan philosopher, but he misinterprets on that one occasion a fundamental passage from the *Contract* (which I have already quoted) on the 'de-naturalization' that society must carry out on man to transform him from a mere 'natural' man into a truly 'social' being.

One possible explanation of this could perhaps be found in the interpretation of Rousseau current in Germany at the time when Marx's thought was formed. Hegel, for example, gave the *Contract* an essentially natural-law interpretation. Rousseau, to him, is the theorist of 'atomistic' liberal individualism. In the Notes to paragraph 258 of the *Philosophy of Right* (see also paragraph 98 of the *Encyclopedia*), he says that

unfortunately, however, as Fichte did later, he takes the will only in a determinate form as the *individual* will, and he regards the universal will not as the absolutely rational element in the will, but only as a *'general' will* which proceeds out of this individual will *as out of a conscious* will. The result is that he reduces the union of individuals in the State to a *contract* and therefore to something based on their arbitrary wills, their opinion, and their capriciously given express consent; and abstract reasoning proceeds to draw the logical inferences which destroy the absolutely divine principle of the state, together with its majesty and absolute authority.

(Similar opinions are also expressed in Appendix I to paragraph 163 of the *Encyclopedia*).

It seems that this reading of Rousseau by Hegel may have decisively conditioned Marx's opinion (as occurs in several other cases, not excluding his view of Kant's *Critique of Pure Reason*). The '1857 Introduction' to *A Contribution to the Critique of Political Economy*, for example, begins by noting that the *Robinsonaden* of the economists, starting from the 'solitary and isolated hunter or fisherman' like Smith and Ricardo, 'despite the assertions of social historians, . . . by no means signify simply a reaction against over-refinement and reversion to a misconceived natural life. No more is Rousseau's *contrat social*, which by means of a contract establishes a relationship and connection between subjects that are by nature independent, based on this kind of naturalism.' If anything, Marx continues,

[120] 'Critique marxiste de Rousseau', ibid., pp. 503–14.

this is an illusion and nothing but the aesthetic illusion of the small and big Robinsonades. It is, on the contrary, the anticipation of 'bourgeois society', which began to evolve in the sixteenth century and in the eighteenth century made great strides to maturity. The individual in this society of free competition seems to be rid of natural ties, etc., which made him an appurtenance of a particular, limited aggregation of human beings in previous historical epochs. The prophets of the eighteenth century, on whose shoulders Adam Smith and Ricardo were still wholly standing, envisaged this eighteenth-century individual – a product of the dissolution of feudal society on the one hand and of the new productive forces evolved since the sixteenth century on the other – as an ideal whose existence belonged to the *past*. They saw this individual not as an historical result, but as the starting point of history.[121]

This rather remarkable passage recalls the real historical roots (the development of commodity production and the resulting configuration of all social relations as 'contractual' or 'exchange' relations) of the 'independent' individual of eighteenth-century natural-law theory; and it clearly shows how fully Rousseau has been assimilated to that tradition. But whatever the reasons conditioning Marx's view, it is a fact that it acted as a retarding factor until Marxists reached the point of being able to re-examine Rousseau's thought. It is necessary to stress this in order to understand correctly the originality and novelty – and not only in the field of Italian Marxist studies – of Della Volpe's book *Rousseau e Marx*,[122] a work which has contributed considerably to the reopening of the question of the relations between the two thinkers, so long locked up in the archives.

Without embarking on a comprehensive examination of this book, which I have discussed elsewhere, I should like simply to discuss an appendix added to the later editions (in particular, to the fourth, of 1964) which deals with the interpretation of the *Discourse on Inequality*. Della Volpe's thesis, to summarize it schematically, starts from the distinction Rousseau introduced into his writings between 'two' kinds of inequality.

I conceive [says Rousseau] that there are two kinds of inequality among the human species; one, which I call *natural* or physical, because it is established by nature, and consists in a difference of age, health, bodily strength, and the qualities of the mind or of the soul; and another, which may be called *moral or political* inequality (or also '*institutional* inequality'), because it depends on

---

[121] Marx, 'Introduction' to *A Contribution to the Critique of Political Economy*, op. cit., p. 188.
[122] First edition, Rome, 1957.

a kind of convention, and is established, or at least authorized, by the consent of men. This latter consists of the different privileges which some men enjoy to the prejudice of others; such as that of being more rich, more honoured, more powerful or even in a position to exact obedience.

The conclusion of Rousseau's *Discourse* centres around the argument that a relationship or 'proportion' must exist between these two kinds of inequality; and that inequality is 'unjust' wherever the moral or 'political' disparity (and hence the disparity of 'rank') is not proportional to 'natural' inequality, that is difference in talents, merit and ability. At the end of the *Discourse* Rousseau writes,

it follows from this survey that . . . moral inequality, authorized by positive right alone, clashes with natural *right*, whenever it is not proportionate to physical inequality – a distinction which sufficiently determines what we ought to think of that species of inequality which prevails in all civilized countries; since it is plainly contrary to the law of nature, however defined, that children should command old men, fools wise men, and that the privileged few should gorge themselves with superfluities, while the starving multitude are in want of the bare necessities of life.

From this reading of the *Discourse on Inequality*, which once it is put forward seems quite natural (though it is certainly not traditional), Della Volpe draws two conclusions, which are both of great interest. The first is that Rousseau's 'egalitarianism' is 'not' a levelling egalitarianism *à la Baboeuf* (with which it has often been confused), but, on the contrary, an egalitarianism which takes into account 'differences' between individuals and therefore gives rise to an equality which is not in conflict with freedom but rather a 'mediation of persons' (a statement he supports with Rousseau's argument that 'the rank of citizens ought therefore to be regulated . . . according to the actual services done to the state'). The second conclusion is that this non-levelling egalitarianism of Rousseau's foreshadows and brings to mind the problematic of the *Critique of the Gotha Programme*, in which Marx states the necessity that in the 'second' stage of socialist society – 'communist' society strictly speaking – the criterion of distribution on the basis of 'equal' or 'bourgeois' rights still in force in the 'first' or 'socialist' phase, be overcome: this for the reason that the application of an 'equal' norm to 'unequal' persons is an evident injustice.

'*Equal right*', according to which, in the first phase of socialism everyone is compensated according to the quantity of labour he performs, 'is still in principle *bourgois right*', Marx says. Here, in effect, the right of producers is *proportional* to the labour they supply; the equality consists in the fact that measurement is made with an *equal standard*, labour. But one man is superior to another physically or mentally and so supplies more labour in the same time, or can labour for a longer time. . . . This *equal* right is an unequal right for unequal labour. It recognizes no class differences, because everyone is only a worker like everyone else; but it tacitly recognizes unequal individual endowment and thus productive capacity as natural privileges. *It is, therefore, a right of inequality, in its content, like every right.* Right by its very nature can consist only in the application of an equal standard; but unequal individuals (and they would not be different individuals if they were not unequal) are measurable only by an equal standard insofar as they are brought under an equal point of view, are taken from one *definite* side only, for instance, in the present case, are regarded *only as workers*, and nothing more is seen in them, everything else being ignored. Further, one worker is married, another not; one has more children than another, and so on and so forth. Thus, with an equal performance of labour, and hence an equal share in the social consumption fund, one will in fact receive more than another, one will be richer than another, and so on. To avoid all these defects, right instead of being equal would have to be unequal.

Marx concludes:

In a higher phase of communist society . . ., after labour has become not only a means of life but life's prime want; after the productive forces have also increased with the all-round development of the individual, and all the springs of co-operative wealth flow more abundantly – only then can the narrow horizon of bourgeois right be crossed in its entirety and society inscribe on its banners: from each according to his ability, to each according to his needs![123]

Let us return to Della Volpe's two conclusions. His interpretation of Rousseau's *Discourse* seems to me to be correct (in a sense which I shall explain shortly): it has also been welcomed and adopted by Starobinski in his introduction to the *Écrits Politiques* volume. But I feel I have to correct my previous agreement[124] when Della Volpe establishes a link between the end of Rousseau's *Discourse* and the text by Marx reproduced above.

I think it incontrovertible that the problematic of the *Discourse* is centred on the 'proportion' of the two kinds of inequality, just as I think it is also correct both that Rousseau's egalitarianism is not a levelling one, and that egalitarianism of such a kind is not in general a good thing. My

---

[123] Marx, *Critique of the Gotha Programme*, in *Selected Works*, op. cit., pp. 324–5.
[124] cf. 'Rousseau politico' in *Cultura e Scuola*, December 1962–February 1963.

doubts centre rather on the homogeneity of the two solutions in Rousseau and Marx, which is the point most stressed in Della Volpe's argument.

To put it briefly, it is my contention that whereas Rousseau stresses the need for social recognition of the individual's 'merits', Marx on the other hand appeals to social recognition of his 'needs'. Both foresee an equality based on the recognition of the 'differences' that exist between individual and individual. But with this distinction: that Rousseau holds it to be necessary to take individual differences into account so that society can recognize different 'merits' and consequently arrange social 'ranks' to conform with the 'services' given by individuals, and therefore with their different capacities and products; while Marx hopes that, in the future, society will be able to take differences between individuals into account, precisely in order to face up to the 'needs' of the less gifted and prevent the emergence of any kind of hierarchy.

Rousseau's argument is that society should take 'natural differences' into account, by recognizing and in some sense confirming them. Marx argues that society should do this not to confirm these differences but rather so as to be able to suppress disadvantages by recognizing them, and therefore prevent 'unequal individual attributes and hence capacity to produce' operating – 'tacitly' – 'as natural privileges'. This I think means pushing the argument even beyond class differences, to confront the still more radical question of 'natural differences' (Rousseau never reaches the point of posing this question). And, obviously, not to abolish them (as would be the case if equal production were required of all or if the social 'task' of the individual did not take his individual abilities into account), but to prevent the varying individual attributes from crystallizing into privileges (which is what Rousseau, on the contrary, could not see, in that his polemic was conditioned by the survival in France of the hierarchies and 'orders' of the *ancien régime* and he therefore became the interpreter of the thoughts and talents of the new man of the Third Estate).

As for the fact that the difference between the two types of social recognition – the recognition of *merits* and the recognition of *needs* – is not an artificial difference or a small one, I think this is proved by a little-known passage of *The German Ideology*[125] which anticipates and clarifies the argument of the *Critique of the Gotha Programme*. Marx writes that

one of the most vital principles of communism, a principle which distinguishes it from all reactionary socialism, is its empiric view, based on a knowledge of

[125] Marx and Engels, *The German Ideology*, London, 1965, p. 593.

man's nature, that differences of *brain* and of intellectual capacity do not imply any differences whatsoever in the nature of the *stomach* and of physical *needs*; therefore the false tenet, based upon existing circumstances, 'to each according to his abilities', must be changed, insofar as it relates to enjoyment in its narrower sense, into the tenet, *'to each according to his need'*; in other words, a *different* form of activity, of labour, does not justify *inequality*, confers no *privileges* in respect of possession and enjoyment.

This means, in relation to Rousseau, that one cannot avoid acknowledging the still inevitably libertarian and individualistic (and hence insufficiently egalitarian) character of the *Discourse on Inequality* as compared with the later, more mature *Social Contract* – despite the genius of the critique of 'civil society' outlined in it. And in general, one has to acknowledge that it is impossible, even for the greatest and most prophetic mind, to transcend the historical limitations and causes of his own time.

Mandeville, Rousseau and Smith

I

In considering Smith's relationship to Rousseau it is especially interesting to read his letter of 1755 to the *Edinburgh Review*,[1] in which he enters into a full discussion of the *Discourse on the Origin of Inequality*. The way in which the discussion of Rousseau's work is introduced into the letter is most significant. Smith recalls England's supremacy over France in modern times, not only in the field of 'natural philosophy' (Bacon, Boyle, Newton, etc.), but also in that of 'morality' and 'metaphysics'. 'The Meditations of Des Cartes excepted,' he writes, 'I know nothing in French that aims at being original upon these subjects; for the philosophy of Mr Régis, as well as that of Father Malbranche, are but refinements on the Meditations of Des Cartes'. In England, however, 'Mr Hobbes, Mr Lock, and Dr Mandevil, Lord Shaftesbury, Dr Butler, Dr Clark, and Mr Hutcheson', each by his own system, which is 'different and inconsistent' with the rest, 'have endeavoured at least to be, in some measures, original'.[2] But this situation of English supremacy in the field of moral philosophy has, according to Smith, been changing in recent years. 'This branch of the English philosophy, which seems now to be entirely neglected by the English themselves, has of late been transported into France. I observe some traces of it, not only in the Encyclopedia, but in the Theory of agreeable sentiments by Mr De Pouilly, a work that is in many respects original; and above all, in the late Discourse upon the origin and foundation of inequality amongst mankind by Mr Rousseau of Geneva.'[3]

After some remarks on the relation between Rousseau's text and Mandeville's *Fable of the Bees*, which I shall come to in a moment, Smith gives the readers of the *Edinburgh Review* an idea of the content of the work by reproducing a few pages of extracts, specifically, pages 117, 126

---

[1] *Edinburgh Review*, July 1755 to January 1756, 2nd edition 1818: 'A Letter to the Authors', pp. 121–35.

[2] ibid., pp. 129–30.   [3] ibid.

and 134 of the first edition of the *Discourse*. The exceptional interest of these extracts from our point of view is that they contain some of the most important passages in which Rousseau summarizes and lays bare the structure of the competitive relationships of modern 'civil society'; passages so vivid and significant that they are worth bringing to the attention of the reader in the order (and translation) in which Smith transcribed them:

He [the individual in 'civil society'] is obliged therefore to endeavour to interest them [others] in this situation, and to make them find, either in reality or in appearance, their advantage in labouring for his. It is this which renders him false and artificial with some, imperious and unfeeling with others, and lays him under a necessity of deceiving all those for whom he has occasion, when he cannot terrify them, and does not find it in his interest to serve them in reality. To conclude, an insatiable ambition, an ardour to raise his relative fortune, not so much from any real necessity, as to set himself above others, inspires all men with a direful propensity to hurt one another; with a secret jealousy, so much the more dangerous, as, to strike its blow more surely, it often assumes the mask of good will; in short, with concurrence and rivalship on one side; on the other, with opposition of interest, and always with the concealed desire of making profits at the expense of some other person. All these evils are the first effects of property, and the inseparable attendants of beginning inequality.

In the previous essay on Rousseau I have already noted – together with other points of contact – the analogy there is (in structure, of course: for they diverge radically in meaning and evaluation) between certain formulations in the *Discourse* and others which appear in the *Early Draft* and *The Wealth of Nations* (the best example is the one in which Smith remarks that man, who has 'almost constant occasion for the help of his brethren', would in vain expect such help 'from their benevolence only'; rather, 'he will be much more likely to prevail if he can interest their self-love in his favour, and show them that it is for their own advantage to do for him what he requires of them'). At the time, however, I was unaware of the contents of the letter to the *Edinburgh Review*, from which it becomes plain that Smith had direct knowledge of Rousseau's *Discourse*. The relation I posited between the two authors was therefore in some sense only supposed or, so to speak, advanced as a mere hypothesis; whereas it is now fully confirmed.

To go back to Smith's letter, it is noteworthy that it establishes a connection between Mandeville's *Fable of the Bees* and Rousseau's *Discourse*.

Whoever reads this work with attention, will observe, that the second volume of the Fable of the Bees has given occasion to the system of Mr Rousseau, in whom however the principles of the English author are softened, improved and embellished, and stript of all that tendency to corruption and licentiousness which has disgraced them in their original author. Dr Mandeville represents the primitive state of mankind as the most wretched and miserable that can be imagined; Mr Rousseau, on the contrary, paints it as the happiest and most suitable to his nature. Both of them however suppose there is in man no powerful instinct which necessarily determines him to seek society for its own sake; but according to the one, the misery of his original state compelled him to have recourse to this otherwise disagreeable remedy: according to the other, some unfortunate accidents having given birth to the unnatural passions of ambition and the vain desire of superiority, to which he had been a stranger, produced the same fatal effect. Both of them suppose the same slow progress and gradual development of all the talents, habits and arts which fit men to live together in society, and they both describe this progress pretty much in the same manner. According to both, these laws of justice, which maintain the present inequality amongst mankind, were originally the inventions of the cunning and powerful, in order to maintain or acquire an unnatural and unjust superiority over the rest of their fellow creatures.[4]

This juxtaposition of Rousseau and Mandeville may cause some legitimate surprise. But restricted to the points within which Smith circumscribed it – i.e. 1. the attribution to the natural man of a feeling of 'pity' (for which Rousseau himself refers to Mandeville in the *Discourse*) and 2. the denial of 'original sociability', the refusal to see man as already by 'nature' and therefore *a priori* a 'social' being and 'moral' person – restricted to these points, as I have said, the juxtaposition Smith makes seems well founded. But for the rest, i.e. for the substance of their views, it is clear that Rousseau is diametrically opposed to Mandeville (Smith himself notes that 'Rousseau criticizes upon Dr Mandeville').[5] This opposition emerges very clearly in the preface to *Narcissus*, to which I have referred above: here Rousseau's critique of 'civil society' appears to be designed in direct and conscious antithesis to Mandeville's which he cites explicitly.

The basic theme of these pages is the contrast Rousseau establishes between the ties or *social relationships* based on mutual *solidarity* and therefore on 'good will', and the social relationships based rather on *competition* and trade, that is on exchange and personal interest. 'Neither

[4] ibid.   [5] ibid., p. 131.

of these bonds can be tightened,' he says, 'without the other being loosened.' A little further on he adds:

I think there is a way of judging quite accurately the morals of men in the many transactions they have with each other: the more they trade and the more highly they regard their industry, the more are they skilfully and successfully cheating each other, and the more they deserve to be suspected.

The tone of the argument may call to mind what I have already said about the backward and archaic nature of Rousseau's economic thought. Still, the most important point is that – through his reference to Mandeville (much more than to the Physiocrats) – Rousseau is led to discover some of the most significant *contradictions* of modern 'civil society': contradictions which, needless to add, are never denounced by Mandeville but exalted as the motive forces of 'modern' development.

From this point of view, the juxtaposition of the two writers which Smith makes has a wider and deeper meaning. Both Mandeville and Rousseau see the laws of justice as an instrument for maintaining inequality among men. Both think that in modern society 'virtue' is only a mask hiding 'self-love', 'vanity', and the egoistic interests of men. Both see that the mechanism of economic prosperity presupposes inequality – i.e. wealth and dissipation at one pole of society, depravity and poverty at the other. Rousseau writes:

A strange and tragic constitution under which accumulated wealth always affords the means for accumulating still more, and it is impossible for him who has nothing to acquire anything; where the good man has no means for rising out of poverty; where the greatest cheats are the most honoured, and where it is essential to renounce virtue to be an 'honnête homme'!

The viewpoint is evidently in a certain sense the same as that of Mandeville. What in modern society appears in the guise of 'virtue' is in effect 'egoism'. The 'bourgeois', exalted by Voltaire as the 'honnête homme', is and cannot fail to be a 'cheat': not because a moralistic critique so wills it, but because he is compelled to be so by the *competitive relationships* within which he operates ('In Europe', Rousseau explains, 'everything – governments, laws, customs, interest – obliges individuals to deceive each other unendingly; they are obliged to be bad to be good, for there is no greater folly than making swindlers happy at one's own expense.')

Yet the coincidence in the two arguments comes about on the basis of a diametrical opposition between them. For Mandeville, the struggle of private interests, the seething of conflicting egos, is what gives vitality and *élan* to modern society: 'private vices' are 'publick benefits'; competition is the lever of progress; individual egoisms form the basis of national prosperity.[6] For Rousseau, on the other hand, the picture Mandeville draws of modern society, though accurate, contains all the arguments for its denunciation. The savagery of the man of 'civil society' makes Mandeville *rejoice*.[7] 'His ethics', Kaye says, 'are a combination of philosophic anarchism in theory and utilitarianism in practice.'[8] Man is an *animal* in permanent conflict with his kind. For Rousseau, however, Mandeville to some extent repeats Hobbes's error: he mistakes man in the state to which he has been reduced in this society, for man in general; he does not see that 'all these vices are not so much of man, as of man when he is ill-governed'.

I observe that the world is at present ruled by a host of little maxims which reduce fools with a false appearance of philosophy. . . . Such as this: 'men everywhere have the same passions, are led by the same self-love and interest; so they are everywhere the same'.

This is true today, in this society dominated by private property, where relations between men are based on trade and competition. However, it is not true where – in the absence of property – individuals co-operate towards a common end and personal interests are in solidarity with one another.

Among the Savages [cf. Marx and Engels's 'primitive communism'], personal interest has as loud a voice as with us, but it does not say the same things: love of society and regard to their common defence are their only ties: the word *property*, cause of so many crimes among our 'honest' people, has scarcely any meaning for them. No arguments of interests divide them; nothing leads them to deceive each other; public esteem is the only good to which all aspire, and which they all deserve.

II

This link between Rousseau and Mandeville acquires its full importance in the light of Mandeville's place in the history of economic thought and the relations in which he stands to the founders of political economy. In this way it in fact becomes possible to understand what I have up to now

[6] D. Mandeville, *The Fable of the Bees: or Private Vices, Publick Benefits*, with a Commentary critical, historical and explanatory by F. B. Kaye, Oxford, 1924, Vol. I, p. xlvii.　　　　　　　　　[7] ibid., p. liii.　　　　　　　　　[8] ibid., p. lvi.

been trying to show, i.e. that Rousseau's critique of 'civil society' is not (or not only) a moralistic critique, but is above all a historically circumscribed critique. It is a critique which, despite serious limitations and misunderstandings, has in some sense come to terms with the first theoretical 'models' of nascent economic reflection. But it also becomes much easier to understand, especially bearing in mind Smith's relations with Mandeville, that through its criticism of the latter Rousseau's thought retains some of its effectivity even in the face of the author of *The Wealth of Nations*, thus acquiring, so to speak, a projection into the future.

The basic theme which comes out here is the complex process which was coming to maturity, particularly in England in the last decades of the seventeenth century and the early decades of the eighteenth, with the zenith of the mercantilist doctrine and, simultaneously, the beginnings of its decline. This was the time at which Mandeville too was thinking and writing. Contemporary students have paid greater attention to the so-called 'predecessors of Adam Smith'[9] and to identifying the themes then in process of elaboration (to be gathered up, unified and organized in the grand schema of *The Wealth of Nations*); in particular, this has led them to stress the definitive turn which was effected in that period in the relations between *ethics* and *economics*, between the 'general interest' and the 'private interest'.

In this case too it can of course be said: *nihil novi sub sole*. In his *Studies in the Theory of International Trade*,[10] Jacob Viner has shown the wealth and variety of 'antimercantilist' motifs in the works of the so-called 'mercantilist school': a school often traditionally considered, a little too conveniently, as a compact, homogeneous body of thought. 'If Adam Smith,' he writes, 'had carefully surveyed the earlier English economic literature . . ., he would have been able to find very nearly all the materials which he actually used in his attack on the protectionist aspects of the mercantilist doctrine.'[11] In the same way, 'the concept of the "economic man", instead of being, as is often alleged, an invention of the nineteenth-century classical school, was an important element in the mercantilist doctrine'.[12]

---

[9] The classic work of this kind is E. A. J. Johnson, *Predecessors of Adam Smith* (*The Growth of British Economic Thought*), New York, 1937, and 1965. For a critique of Steuart, there is an interesting essay by R. L. Meek, 'The Rehabilitation of Sir James Steuart', in *Economics and Ideology and Other Essays* (*Studies in the Development of Economic Thought*), London, 1967.

[10] Jacob Viner, *Studies in the Theory of International Trade*, London, 1937.

[11] ibid., p. 92.   [12] ibid., p. 93.

Yet as Viner himself recognizes, at the same time, one should not exaggerate 'the extent to which free-trade views already prevailed in the English literature before Adam Smith', and it is still true that there is a profound divergence in the methods of understanding economic activity between the classical school and mercantilism.

Between the attitudes of the two schools toward the 'economic man', if the extreme positions of both may be taken for purposes of contrast, there was this important difference, however, that the classical economists argued that men in pursuing their selfish interests were at the same time, by a providential harmony of interests, either rendering the best service of which they are capable to the common good or at least rendering better service than if their activities were closely regulated by government, whereas the mercantilists deplored the selfishness of the merchant and insisted that to prevent it from ruining the nation it was necessary to subject it to rigorous control.[13]

This is well known as the problem of the different way of conceiving the relationship between ethics and economics, between the interest of the communal body and the interest of the individual, which distinguishes the Middle Ages from the modern era proper. In medieval theory there is no place for economic activity without a moral goal. Economics is still a branch of ethics. The activity and interests of the individual are subordinated and made to conform to the end of the 'common good'. The social order is seen as a well-articulated 'organism' whose parts contribute, in different ways, to the common goal. All human activities are treated as part of a single system, the nature of which is determined by the spiritual destiny of humanity. The idea of property following from this is well illustrated, as Tawney showed, by the question of the 'common lands'. In the Middle Ages, 'the theoretical basis of the policy of protecting the peasant by preventing enclosure had been a conception of landownership which regarded its rights and duties as inextricably interwoven. Property was not merely a source of income, but a public function, and its use was limited by social obligations and necessities of State.'[14] In connection with this view of property, the attitude towards *pauperism* seems inspired by

---

[13] ibid., p. 94, where in discussing Malynes, Viner also observes that 'in extreme cases this attitude tended to lead to wholesale denunciation of the merchants, and the belief that merchants were governed only by self-interest underlay the fundamental mercantilist doctrine of the need for State regulation of commerce.' On Gerard de Malynes, see also E. A. J. Johnson, op. cit., pp. 41–54.

[14] R. H. Tawney, *Religion and the Rise of Capitalism*, London, 1936 (first published 1926), p. 258.

measures for aid and assistance. The dominant criterion is that of *charity*. 'Peasant and lord, in their different degrees, are members of one Christian commonwealth, within which the law of charity must bridle the corroding appetite for economic gain. In such a mystical corporation knit together by mutual obligations, no man may press his advantage to the full, for no man may seek to live outside "the body of the Church".'

After the 'glorious revolution', however, 'the theory which took its place,' Tawney writes, 'and which was to become in the eighteenth century almost a religion, was that expressed by Locke, when he described property as a right anterior to the existence of the State, and argued that "the supreme power cannot take from any man any part of his property without his own consent".'[15] Here, it need scarcely be remarked, society does not appear to be

a community of classes with varying functions, united to each other by mutual obligations arising from their relation to a common end. It is a joint-stock company rather than an organism, and the liabilities of the shareholders are strictly limited. They enter into it in order to insure the rights already vested in them by the immediate laws of nature. The State, a matter of convenience, not of supernatural sanctions, exists for the protection of those rights, and fulfils its object in so far as, by maintaining contractual freedom, it secures full scope for their unfettered exercise.[16]

Although he cannot be made out to be an economist *strictu sensu*, Mandeville is one of the chief interpreters of the new situation emerging in the phase of the decline of mercantilism, when the motor of 'capitalist accumulation' was already at full throttle. In a particularly fine passage, recalling a key part of Dialogue III of the second part of the *Fable of the Bees*,[17] Macfie has recently observed that not only is it clear that Mandeville has a concept of 'economic development', but that Smith's idea of *economic growth* 'must have drawn inspiration from this source'.[18] Similarly, after recording the contribution of such important writers on economic matters as Davenant and North, Viner observes that 'more important, in preparing the way for Adam Smith, was Mandeville's more elaborate reasoning in support of individualism and *laissez faire*, resting on his famous argument that "private vices" such as "avarice" and luxury were "public benefits" '; adding in a footnote, that 'Mandeville

[15] ibid., p. 255.   [16] ibid., p. 189.
[17] B. Mandeville, op. cit., Vol. II, p. 141.
[18] A. L. Macfie, *The Individual in Society* (*Papers on Adam Smith*), London, 1967, p. 116.

deliberately stated his conclusions in such a manner as to make them offensive to moralists, but Smith accepted them in substance while finding a more palatable form for their expression'.[19]

This is not the occasion to dwell on other aspects of Mandeville's thought. The rôle he played in the development of the theory of the division of labour, and the especial influence he exercised in this respect, too, on Smith's thought, were noted by Marx in his time. In the chapter on 'The Division of Labour and Manufacture', Marx refers to the famous passage at the beginning of *The Wealth of Nations* in which Smith describes what a great number and variety of industries contribute to the satisfaction of the wants of an ordinary workman in a 'civilized' country. Marx notes that the entire passage 'is copied almost word for word from B. de Mandeville's Remarks to his *Fable of the Bees: or Private Vices, Publick Benefits*'.[20] an observation later found also in Edwin Cannan's commentary[21] on Smith's text, as well as in Kaye's introduction to his edition of the *Fable*.[22]

The same can be said for the other important aspect of Mandeville's thought, his theory of the function of *luxury*[23] (it is well known that this problem was debated throughout the eighteenth century, from the point of view of ethics as well as economics: one has only to think of Montesquieu). The function of luxury[24] was to assure a constant stimulus to production, and so fulfil the rôle of the motive force of the economic system: and if it is not in this case certain that Mandeville influenced Smith, he certainly did, at least partially, influence Hume[25] (not to speak of the influence he had on the thought of Malthus, and even on Keynes's theory of 'effective demand', revealed in Chapter XXIII of the *General Theory of Employment, Interest and Money*.)

To leave aside more marginal aspects and come to the heart of the matter: the theme around which all the motifs so far described converge and knit together is the question of *capitalist accumulation*. Mandeville's

---

[19] J. Viner, op. cit., p. 99. And cf. F. B. Kaye, op. cit., pp. cxxxix, cxl, cxli.

[20] K. Marx, *Capital*, Moscow, 1961, Vol. I, Chapter 14, p. 354.

[21] cf. A. Smith, *The Wealth of Nations*, ed. Edwin Cannan, London, 1904; new edition, London, 1961, Vol. I, p. 7, n.

[22] F. B. Kaye, op. cit., p. cxxv.

[23] ibid., p. cxxvi, where Kaye recalls Mandeville's well-known influence on Voltaire (*Le Mondain* and *Défense du Mondain ou l'Apologie du Luxe*).

[24] cf. Schumpeter, *History of Economic Analysis*, op. cit., pp. 324–5 n.

[25] cf. Johnson, op. cit., pp. 295 ff., in which he describes Hume's critical attitude towards Mandeville. See also the whole chapter devoted to 'Idleness and Luxury'.

work certainly does not contain an organically developed theory of 'economic development'.[26] Yet the most significant aspects of his thought are moving in this direction, and conspiring to the same end. The division of labour determines the 'skill' and 'ability' of the workman, and with it the increase in the productivity of labour. The resulting impulse towards 'art' and 'ingenious labour' shakes the mind of man out of its lethargy and plunges it into ferment: it solicits the development of science and technology.[27] In turn, this increased productivity of labour brings an increase in exports, which for its part implies an expansion in the employment of labour in domestic manufacturing, and better opportunities for investment. Finally, since 'buying is bartering', and if a nation refuses to accept goods in payment for its own manufactures, other nations can no longer trade with it,[28] free exchange rather than trade monopoly is therefore the rule. The overall outlook emerging from this mass of correlations and effects within the system was to find its highest expression in Smith: civilization is production and trade;[29] technical skill, individual initiative and the spirit of competition are the legs on which the 'civilization' of humanity advances.

This relation of Mandeville's to the problems of 'economic development' is no fiction; witness the fact that the place in *Capital* where Marx deals with him at greatest length is the chapter devoted to the 'General Law of Capitalist Accumulation.'[30] The problem Marx confronts at the beginning of this chapter is that of the 'growing demand for labour power which accompanies capital accumulation', when the technical composition of capital remains the same: obviously this is particularly true before the take-off of the Industrial Revolution. In such circumstances, Marx points out, '*growth of capital* involves growth of its variable constituent or of the part invested in labour-power': '*the accumulation of capital is, therefore, increase of the proletariat*'.[31] He immediately adds: 'Classical economy grasped this fact so thoroughly that Adam Smith, Ricardo, etc. . . . inaccurately identified accumulation with the con-

---

[26] This is simply demonstrated by the indeterminate nature of Mandeville's concept of 'productive labour' (not to be confused, of course, with the concept of the *productivity* of labour), a characteristic noted by Marx in his *Theories of Surplus Value*, Moscow, 1964, Vol. I, pp. 171 and 376.

[27] cf. Johnson, op. cit., Chapter 13, ' "Art" and "Ingenious Labour"', pp. 259-77.

[28] cf. M. Dobb, *Studies in the Development of Capitalism*, p. 240.

[29] cf. Joseph Cropsey, *Politics and Economy (An Interpretation of the Principles of Adam Smith)*, The Hague, 1957, pp. 94-5.

[30] Marx, *Capital*, Vol. I, Chapter 15, pp. 612 ff.   [31] ibid., p. 614.

sumption, by the productive labourers, of *all* the capitalized part of the surplus product, or with its transformation into additional wage-labourers.' He follows this with a long quotation from Mandeville.[32]

Looking at the passages of the *Fable* quoted by Marx, it is at once clear that they propound the very 'paradox' on which the whole of Mandeville's work hinges: but this time with a particular and much more historically determinate significance. 'Private vices' are 'public benefits' – this means not only that *good is born of evil*, that the immorality of individuals, their egoisms in competition with one another, produce culture and the 'civilizing' of society as a whole; it also means that *wealth is born of poverty* (note this new formulation), well-being from distress, that *what produces prosperity is wage labour*; or again that *the wealth of a nation consists of a mass of toiling poor*, a nation being the richer the more numerous its proletarians, the more cheap and abundant the labour that capitalist investment has at its disposal. True wealth, in short, is not gold or silver but labour paid by the day – the only inexhaustible gold mine yet discovered. As Mandeville writes,

From what has been said, it is manifest, that, in a *free nation*, where *slaves* are not allowed of, the *surest wealth consists in a multitude of laborious poor*; for besides, that they are the never-failing nursery of fleets and armies, without them there could be no enjoyment, and no product of any country which could be valuable. To make *the society happy* and people easier under the meanest circumstances, *it is requisite that great numbers of them should be ignorant as well as poor* . . .[33]

This is the ultimate meaning of Mandeville's 'paradox': what 'economic development', i.e. capitalist accumulation, needs, is an abundance of cheap wage labour; to make 'society' (i.e. those who do not work) happy, the majority must be ignorant as well as poor. In short, a nation is rich when it has at its disposal a mass of laborious poor. And since 'the only thing . . . that can render the labouring man industrious, is a moderate quantity of money, for as too little will, according as his temper is, either dispirit or make him desperate, so too much will make him insolent and lazy . . .', it is in the interest of all rich nations 'that the greatest part of the poor should almost never be idle, and yet continually spend what they get'. In fact, 'those that get their living by their daily labour . . . have nothing to stir them up to be serviceable but their wants which it is prudence to relieve, but folly to cure'.[34]

[32] For Marx's quotations from Mandeville, see Mandeville, op. cit., Vol. I, pp. 193–4 and Vol. II, p. 287. [33] Marx, *Capital*, Vol. I, p. 615. [34] ibid., pp. 614–15.

Poverty, then, is both a necessary condition of wealth, and the source of it. The formula is not a frivolous paradox, but expresses *'the antagonistic character of capitalist accumulation'*,[35] and it is therefore not surprising that it had a very successful career after Mandeville. Destutt de Tracy, whom Marx calls 'the fish-blooded bourgeois doctrinaire', puts it more brutally: 'In poor nations the people are comfortable, in rich nations they are generally poor.'[36] And the same goes for culture as for wealth.

The progress of social wealth [writes Storch, as quoted by Marx[37]] begets this useful class of society . . . which performs the most wearisome, the vilest, the most disgusting functions, which takes, in a word, on its shoulders all that is disagreeable and servile in life, and procures thus for other classes leisure, serenity of mind and conventional dignity of character.

In a word: development through exploitation, progress and enrichment *on the basis of social inequality*, the promotion of 'ability', technology and 'civilization' by means of class oppression. These formulae also lie at the roots of Kant's philosophy of history: and in them – who would ever have suspected it! – Kant reflects and expresses the meaning of *historical development* on the basis of capitalist conditions.

In the *Critique of Judgement* he says:

Skill can hardly be developed in the human race, otherwise than by means of inequality among men. For the majority, in a mechanical kind of way that calls for no special art, provide the necessaries of life for the ease and convenience of others who apply themselves to the less necessary branches of culture in science and art. These keep the masses in a state of oppression, with hard work and little enjoyment . . .[38]

And again there is Mandeville's own argument (noted by Kant in the *Critique of Practical Reason* too), in which – as it says in the last pages of *Anthropologie in pragmatischer Hinsicht* – historical evolution is presented as 'salutary' but also 'rude and harsh', and the meaning of the work carried out by the human race down the generations seems to express 'the realization of the unintended but once present never failing good from the constantly and internally discordant evil'.[39] *Good* from *evil*: Mandeville's own formula! 'The character of the human race,' Kant continues, ' . . . is that of . . . a multitude of persons living one after another and one beside

---

[35] ibid., p. 646.   [36] ibid., p. 648.   [37] ibid., p. 647.

[38] Kant, *Critique of Judgement*, Oxford, 1952, p. 95.

[39] Kant, *Anthropologie in pragmatischer Hinsicht*, 1798, in *Werke* in six volumes, ed. Wilhelm Weischedal, Darmstadt, 1964, Vol. 6, p. 683.

another, unable to *do without* peaceful coexistence, yet also unable to *avoid* being constantly hateful to one another . . .; a coalition always threatened with dissolution, but on the whole progressing towards a world-wide *civil society* (cosmopolitanism)';[40] in short, the specific coalition or society of *ungesellige Geselligkeit,* unsociable sociability, the society of rivalry and competition.

To return to Mandeville, the employment of labour is therefore as high as possible, but wages must be kept low. Since, as Kaye also points out,[41] 'national wealth, indeed, consists not in money, but in "a Multitude of laborious Poor" ', it is clear that to Mandeville not only does the prospect of 'abolishing poverty' appear 'ruinous', but so does the system of aid to the poor through the old charity schools (see his *Essay on Charity, and Charity-Schools*). The poor – 'the vile and brutish part of mankind' as defined by William Petty – must not be helped with charity but shut up in work-houses, the concentration camps of the 'enlightened bourgeoisie'. Charity makes men lazy and troublesome; work makes them sober and virtuous.

Here too we should note the change from medieval times, to which I have already referred, in the relationship between ethics and economics. In the Middle Ages, when 'it was believed that the poor represented Our Lord', the main admonitions, writes Tawney, were directed against cupidity without charity; now, on the contrary, they deal not only with the 'improvidence' and 'idleness' of the poor, but with those who would give them aid.[42] Obviously this is a new way of looking at things:

Upon the admission that distress was the result, not of personal deficiencies, but of economic causes, with its corollary that its victims had a legal right to be maintained by society, the growing individualism of the age turned into a frigid scepticism. . . . That the greatest of evils is idleness, that the poor are the victims, not of circumstances, but of their own 'idle, irregular and wicked courses', that the truest charity is not to enervate them by relief, but so to reform their characters that relief may be unnecessary – such doctrines turned severity from a sin into a duty, and froze the impulse of natural pity with the assurance that, if indulged, it would perpetuate the suffering which it sought to allay.[43]

This, be it noted, is the fusion of the ethic of *puritanism* and the *utilitarianism* of nascent political economy. Just as the *moralist* affirmed that facile indulgence was the ruin of character, so the economist showed

[40] ibid., p. 687.
[42] Tawney, op. cit., pp. 261 and 265.
[41] Kaye, op. cit., pp. lxix–lxx.
[43] ibid., pp. 264–5 and 266–7.

how ruinous it was in economic and financial terms. In a famous passage of the 1848 *Manifesto*, Tawney recalls, Marx observes that 'the *bourgeoisie*, wherever it got the upper hand, put an end to all feudal, patriarchal idyllic relations, pitilessly tore asunder the motley feudal ties that bound man to his "natural superiors", and left remaining no other bond between man and man than naked self-interest and callous cash payment'. 'An interesting illustration of his thesis', Tawney goes on, 'might be found in the discussions of the economics of employment by English writers of the period between 1660 and 1760. Their characteristic was an attitude towards the new industrial proletariat noticeably harsher than that general in the first half of the seventeenth century, and which has no modern parallel except in the behaviour of the less reputable of white colonists towards coloured labour.'[44]

III

I shall cut short the inquiry here and draw some conclusions. Mandeville's 'paradox' – 'private vices' are 'public benefits' – evidently means that, though each man pursues his own *selfish* interests, the total result is national prosperity and the well-being of *society* as a whole. In this sense, it has often been pointed out, Mandeville appears to anticipate Smith's theory of the 'invisible hand': an appeal to that effect of Providence (an authority several times invoked in the *Theory of Moral Sentiments* and *The Wealth of Nations*), which miraculously brings forth *general harmony* from the chaos of private interests struggling against one another. Jacob Viner, as we have seen, viewed the relationship between Mandeville and Smith in this light, in other words as one of continuity. Many other authors, before and since, have done the same. In *Economic Doctrine and Method*, Schumpeter – to use a well-known name – appears to have the same interpretation:

In Mandeville's *Fable* is contained the best and most lucid presentation of the idea that the selfish interest of the individual performs a social function in the economic sphere. Now there were sufficient other sources for similar thought, but many a phrase in Adam Smith points to the fact that he was influenced by Mandeville in particular.[45]

On the other hand, two facts seem to militate against (or at least to modify) this theory. The first is that Mandeville does not seem very

---

[44] ibid., p. 269.   [45] J. A. Schumpeter, *Economic Doctrine and Method*, 1954, p. 66.

enamoured of Providence: his relationship with Pierre Bayle is significant in this respect, for – as Mandeville himself recognized – he used him much more than he acknowledged in the text.[46] The second is that, as is well known, Mandeville's paradox was heavily criticized by Smith in his *Theory of Moral Sentiments*.

Although there are still undeniable points of contact between Smith and Mandeville, I would hold that their respective theories of 'harmony' reveal a certain difference worthy of note. This is also important for that complex problem (which I can only touch on here), the *vexata quaestio* of the consistency or inconsistency of the Smith of the *Theory of Moral Sentiments* (the theorist of 'sympathy' and benevolence) with the Smith of *The Wealth of Nations* (the author who states that, 'it is not from the benevolence of the butcher, the brewer, or the baker that we expect our dinner, but from their regard to their own interest'; and that 'we address ourselves, not to their humanity but to their self-love, and never talk to them of our own necessities but of their advantages').

It is I think undeniable that Smith's critique of Mandeville in this work is weak, and characterized, I would say, by a certain rhetorical vacuity – one, moreover, which Leslie Stephen's severe analysis has discovered in the *Theory* as a whole.[47]

Let me say immediately that I agree completely with those who have remarked that the Smith of the *Theory* cannot be reduced to the level of a Hutcheson; and I also agree that Leslie Stephen exaggerates, at least where he writes that 'Smith, in fact, is a thorough representative of that optimistic Deism which we have seen illustrated by Shaftesbury and Hutcheson' and concludes that 'Hutcheson, Smith's predecessor in the chair of Moral Philosophy in Glasgow, was in this respect nearer to Smith than was Smith's friend and teacher, Hume.'[48] In his classic 1904 introduction to *The Wealth of Nations*, Edwin Cannan has shown with a

---

[46] cf. C. Louise Thijssen-Schouten, 'La diffusion européenne des idées de Bayle' in *P. Bayle, Le Philosophe de Rotterdam, études et documents publiés sous la direction de P. Didon*, Paris, 1959, p. 157. Cf. also Kaye in the *Index to the Commentary*.

[47] L. Stephen, *History of English Thought in the Eighteenth Century*, London, 1962 (first edition 1876), Vol. II, p. 65, where Stephen observes of Smith's *Theory*: '. . . it is impossible to resist the impression, whilst we read his fluent rhetoric, and observe his easy acceptance of theological principles already exposed by his master Hume, that we are not listening to a thinker really grappling with a difficult problem so much as to an ambitious professor who has found an excellent opportunity for displaying his command of language, and making brilliant lectures.'

[48] ibid., p. 50.

wealth of illustrations that even in the *Theory* Smith had already developed an explicit critique of Hutcheson, precisely on the basis of the argument that sufficient attention had not been given in his system to *personal interest*, nor to the reasons for our approval of the more modest virtues of 'prudence', 'vigilance', 'circumspection', etc.[49] Moreover, except for Kaye himself,[50] all the more recent authors, including Macfie, who have tried to stress the continuity between the *Theory* and *The Wealth of Nations*, against the perhaps more traditional thesis of an antithetical contrast between them, appear to go along with this argument.[51]

Nevertheless, conceding all this and recognizing that I need to go still further into the matter, the fact remains, in my opinion, that Smith's polemic against Mandeville in the *Theory* is quite weak: quite weak because, as we shall see, he is wide of the mark. He writes:

It is the great fallacy of Dr Mandeville's book to represent every passion as wholly vicious, which is so in any degree and in any direction. It is thus that he treats every thing as vanity which has any reference, either to what are, or what ought to be the sentiments of others; and it is by means of this sophistry, that he establishes his favourite conclusion, that private vices are public benefits. If the love of magnificence, a taste for the elegant arts and improvements of human life, for whatever is agreeable in dress, furniture or equipage, for architecture, statuary, painting and music, is to be regarded as luxury, sensuality, and ostentation, even in those whose situation allows, without any inconveniency, the indulgence of those passions, it is certain that luxury, sensuality and ostentation are public benefits: since without the qualities upon which he thinks proper to bestow such opprobrious names, the arts of refinement could never find encouragement, and must languish for want of employment. Some popular ascetic doctrines which had been current before his time, and which placed virtue in the entire extirpation and annihilation of all our passions, were the real foundations of this licentious system. It was easy for Dr Mandeville to prove, first, that this entire conquest [of ascetism] never actually took place among men; and secondly, that if it was to take place universally, it would be pernicious to society, by putting an end to all industry and commerce, and in a manner to the whole business of human life.[52]

It is true that a little further on, Smith recognises that there must still be some grain of truth in Mandeville's system: 'how destructive soever

[49] Cannan's introduction to A. Smith, *Wealth of Nations*, op. cit., p. xlii.

[50] Kaye, op. cit., pp. cxli and cxlii n.

[51] For a brief indication of this, see L. Bagolini, *La simpatia nella morale e nel diritto*, Bologna, 1952, pp. 95 ff., as well, of course, as the older but still useful book by L. Limentani, *La morale della simpatia*, Genoa, 1914, pp. 187 ff.

[52] A. Smith, *Theory of Moral Sentiments*, Edinburgh, 1759, pp. 485–6.

this system may appear, it could never have imposed upon so great a number of persons, nor have occasioned so general an alarm among those who are the friends of better principles, had it not in some respects bordered upon the truth'.[53] And yet I persist in thinking that Joan Robinson is right in noting that 'after Mandeville's sharp satire', Smith's reply 'is rather flat and feeble'.[54] It is feeble, I would add, not in style or literary quality, but in substance.

Smith attempts to prove against Mandeville that individual passions or *interests* are not always and not necessarily *vices*, that is, passions *harmful to the interests of others*. In and for itself this argument does not raise a frown. In fact it is evident that no one could ever reasonably think of banning the interests of individuals, of extinguishing their passions. 'Among the savages', Rousseau himself admits, 'personal interest has as loud a voice as with us.' But what Smith does not see is that, independently of the degree of historical consciousness which Mandeville himself may have had, the argument of the *Fable* is not an argument about individual interests and passions *in general* (whatever the form of society in which they develop), but rather an argument about personal passions and interests *when*, and in a society in which, individuals are in *competition with one another*. Wherever there is a cohesive community (Rousseau's '*sauvages*' or Marx's 'primitive communism'), individual interests and passions, far from harming anyone, can be turned to the advantage of others. But they inevitably become quite another thing when this community no longer exists and *competition* is dominant. Personal interest has a loud voice in each case, but, as Rousseau points out, '*it does not say the same things*'. In the one case, individual interest, solidary and homogeneous with the interests of others, is in fact only *one* aspect, or a specification, of the *common interest*; but in the other, where such a 'community' does not exist, it is an interest which collides with that of others and can be achieved only by harming them: only if it operates, in effect, as immorality and injury.

Of course he who is rich can provide himself, as Smith says, with pleasant clothes, furniture, etc., without giving the appearance of 'ostentation' or 'luxury'. But the problem is precisely to look at the derivation of this wealth. And since, as Smith himself recognizes, 'in a civilized country the poor provide for their own wants and for the immense luxury of their masters', and 'the income which goes to sustain the pomp of the indolent lord has all been gained from the toils of the peasant', it seems

[53] ibid.   [54] J. Robinson, *Economic Philosophy*, London, 1964, p. 22.

difficult to deny the fact that this wealth, though devoted to such honest pleasures, is a *vice*, in that it presupposes the ruin and oppression of others.

'Civil society' is the society of free competition. In this social formation, Kant writes, though himself extolling 'civil society',

> *animality* is still earlier and fundamentally stronger than pure humanity in their expressions, and the domesticated animal is of more use to man than the wild beast only in so far as it is *weakened*. The will of the individual is always ready to break out into hostility towards his fellow men, and always seeks, in its effort to attain unrestricted freedom, not only to be independent, but to dominate other beings by nature his equals.[55]

I believe that it is precisely this wildness or animal nature that Mandeville, 'an honest man with a clear mind', describes with such amazement (and not perhaps without a touch of aesthetic pleasure). He was confronted with this extraordinary spectacle – stranger than the unforeseen emergence of an atoll in the Pacific – of the full unfolding of the new society: a phenomenon which he sees with the wondering 'naïvety' of a man seeing things for the first time and reporting them faithfully, but drawing down on himself – from Smith included – the accusation of producing a 'licentious' system.

There is furthermore a specific piece of evidence that Smith was wide of the mark in his critique: when, as in *The Wealth of Nations* and especially in the sections devoted to free competition, he stops discussing human passions and interests *in general* and turns more directly to the examination of individual relationships in *this* society, he is obliged to return to Mandeville (as Cannan[56] and many other authors[57] have noted, in relation to the passage about the brewer, the baker, etc.). He at least has to temper and mitigate a little Mandeville's unrestrained individualism and the 'naturalistic' competition of egoisms, disguising them in Hutcheson's principle of 'freedom': as in the famous passage in which Smith writes that

> the natural effort of every individual to better his own condition, when suffered to exert itself with freedom and security, is so powerful a principle, that it is alone, and without any assistance, not only capable of carrying on the society to wealth and prosperity, but of surmounting a hundred impertinent obstructions with which the folly of human laws too often incumbers its operations.[58]

---

[55] I. Kant, *Anthropologie*, op. cit., pp. 681–2.   [56] E. Cannan, op. cit., p. xlvi.
[57] Including recently, A. L. Macfie, *The Individual in Society*, op. cit., p. 116.
[58] A. Smith, *Wealth of Nations*, op. cit., p. 490.

The difference between Smith and Mandeville begins to become clear at this point. For Mandeville, the selfish activity of man is a *vice*: a vice he certainly rejoices in, as against the hypocrisy and bigotry of priests and puritans, yet still a vice, at least in the sense that the individuals – being in competition with one another – seem to him to be intent on deceiving and swindling one another. For Smith, on the other hand, the selfish activity of the individual (in the face of which, he shows, it would be useless to appeal to 'good will' and 'humanity') tends to appear as a positive factor, almost a 'virtue'. This is precisely because he takes it for granted that, in pursuing his *private* interests, the individual is collaborating in the promotion of the *general* interest. In the first case, *negative* factors produce a positive result; in the second case, the positive result arises from the sum of the partial factors which in themselves are already *positive*.

The consequence of this is worth further study. Mandeville does not know, and in a certain sense is uninterested in knowing, how black turns to white and good to evil. He restricts himself to ascertaining the *de facto* situation, and thus gives us a *paradox*, which according to the dictionary is a 'reasoning containing within itself a contradiction which it appears impossible to resolve'. In short, he presents us with a *problem*, without even claiming to provide an answer, already satisfied with the 'scandal' and intellectual provocation of simply spelling out the problem. Smith, on the contrary (at least where he differentiates himself from Mandeville), does give us a true *theory of harmony* of his own; that is, not the contradiction but the solution, or rather a solution without a problem, since if partial factors ('selfish interests') must already be seen as positive elements, the sum of them must also be positive. This is one side of the story. The other, however – i.e. where he is under Mandeville's influence and holds to the *contradiction* the latter formulated – is that Smith brings into his own analysis the *problem*, i.e. the contradictory nature of capitalist development. Indeed, he not only brings it in but articulates and deepens it (even if, understandably, he then often gives way to the temptation to combine the problem with an *apparent* solution, by recourse to the 'invisible hand' and the intervention of Providence).

In the first case, we have Smith the scientist; in the other, the Smith who anticipates the 'harmonies' of 'vulgar economics' and above all the utilitarian optimism of Bentham,[59] with its 'felicific calculus' and the

[59] On Bentham's relations to Smith, cf. Élie Halévy, *The Growth of Philosophical Radicalism*, 1928 (first French edition 1901), Vol. I, Part I, pp. 3–151, 'The Youth of

banal apologetics of 'the greatest happiness of the greatest number'. In the first instance, Smith seems to be the heir to the highest line of English empiricism – the line starting from Hobbes,[60] the Hobbes to whom Mandeville owes not a little. Otherwise, however, Smith appears (as Stephen has stressed, though too one-sidedly) to follow Hutcheson – who was in fact responsible for the famous formula, 'the greatest happiness of the greatest number'[61] – and through Hutcheson, Shaftesbury, the theorist of the doctrine of 'universal harmony'. (Stephen correctly points out that 'the typical representatives of the two (opposed) schools of thought [in English ethics] in the early part of the [eighteenth] century were Shaftesbury and Mandeville'.)[62] In this doctrine, with man appearing as a moment in the divine cosmic Totality, there can be no conflict between 'interest' and 'virtue' ('Thus God and Nature fixed the general Frame, and bade Self-love and social be the same'). This is the doctrine of 'universal harmony', which, as we know, links Shaftesbury to the Cambridge Platonists, i.e. to Hobbes's most resolute opponents.[63]

To conclude: there were not two theories of 'harmony' but one, since Mandeville's 'paradox', rigorously interpreted, does not contain a theory of 'harmony' proper, but if anything the opposite, if it is true, as I have tried to show, that not only does he formulate the problem without giving an answer, but he formulates an *insoluble* problem: i.e. how the common interest can be obtained while preserving selfish interests, how society can be preserved at the same time as unsociableness. This is a point which I think Myrdal has understood very well – i.e. that *The Fable of the Bees* does not offer a theory of 'harmony' (which always arises from the denial of any opposition of interests), but that rather, 'Mandeville, no doubt, was among the first to have exposed this fiction'.[64] I would add

Bentham'. For the survival in Ricardo of the 'theory of harmony', cf. Vol. III, pp. 19 ff. As for the relationship between Smith and Mandeville, Halévy's position on the problem can be summed up by quoting these lines: 'The economic doctrine of Adam Smith is the doctrine of Mandeville set out in a form which is no longer paradoxical and literary, but rational and scientific. The principle of the identity of interests is not perhaps a principle which is true to the exclusion of all others, but it is a principle which can always be applied, in a general if not in a universal way, in the sphere of political economy' (Vol. I, p. 90).

[60] cf. F. Jonas, *Geschichte der Soziologie*, Hamburg, 1968, Vol. I, p. 99.
[61] L. Stephen, op. cit., Vol. II, p. 51.   [62] ibid., p. 67.
[63] cf. E. Cassirer, *The Platonic Renaissance in England*, London, 1953, pp. 157 ff.
[64] G. Myrdal, *The Political Element in the Development of Economic Theory*, p. 45. On p. 44, Myrdal had already noted what to my mind is the essential point – that in the doctrine of 'harmony', 'the possibility of conflicts of interest is simply ignored'.

that it was no accident that Mandeville was such a resolute opponent of Shaftesbury.

According to liberalism, writes Myrdal, 'whenever someone increases his income, all benefit. For he can only succeed by offering to his fellows better and cheaper services than his rivals.' In classical liberalism, 'this argument had an almost religious character. Adam Smith gave it immortal expression in the words that the individual is "led by an invisible hand to promote an end which was no part of his intention".' Mandeville, however, in his work, 'destroyed the unqualified doctrine as far as British moral philosophy is concerned', in that he brought to light the conflict of interests, showing that 'acquisitiveness has its roots in such immoral qualities as the desire for power, ambition, the love of luxury, etc.'[65]

Economics and ethics, in short, cannot be combined in this society. Private interest cannot be reconciled with the common interest (or the interest of others) but contradicts it. Since the individual cannot gain or satisfy his own passions and interest without ruining or harming another, it seems to me that the least we can do is to recognize with Joan Robinson that 'Mandeville has never been answered', and that 'after more than two hundred years' bourgeois economists are still brooding over this 'squinting morality'.[66] The least! For the most would be to recognize that Mandeville's paradox – his thesis that good is born of evil and that 'the surest wealth lies in a mass of labouring Poor' – is and always will be a paradox, i.e. a *rationally* insoluble problem, at least until the day when it is decided to solve it . . . *practically.*

In Kant's *Anthropologie* there is a remark about Rousseau which I find admirable for its penetrating understanding. He writes, 'One should not take the hypochondriac (ill-willed) description Rousseau gives of the human race, as it emerges from the state of nature, as an invitation to return to it and to the forest, but rather grasp its real meaning as an expression of the difficulty our species has in advancing along the trail constantly approaching its destination.'[67] A little further on, speaking of the evils denounced in Rousseau's work, Kant points out: '*civilization with inequality and mutual subjection*'.[68]

Carefully examined, this formulation proves all-embracing: progress through exploitation; the development of science and technology through wage-labour; the creation of wealth and well-being out of and by means of destitution; the development of culture, on the basis of mass ignorance

---

[65] ibid., pp. 44–5.   [66] J. Robinson, op. cit., p. 23.
[67] op. cit., p. 680.   [68] ibid., p. 324.

and obscurantism. In a word, it is Mandeville's own paradox (which in Rousseau, of course, is not a cause for rejoicing but for execration): it is the expression (still very general yet pertinent) of the antagonistic nature of accumulation and development in the conditions of a competitive society.

Faced with this paradox, which he was the first to sense in its 'rational' insolubility, Rousseau was defeated, even in his inner life. But Marx, coming afterwards and hence in much more favourable historical circumstances, was able to carry the original intuition further. Capitalist accumulation is antagonistic in character. It is full of contradictions. The development of capitalism cannot overcome these contradictions. But if it does not overcome them, capitalism still 'creates the *form* in which they can operate'.

The meaning of the argument is clear. In spite of inequality and mutual subjection, capitalism is development and *civilization*. The contradiction does not paralyse it: if anything it makes it move. Capitalism is a river which can carve out its own channel. Mandeville and Smith are therefore in a sense right to celebrate it. On the other hand, if it is 'civilization', it is still true that capitalism is so *through inequality and oppression*; and that it is therefore a progress which does not humanize man but exacerbates his predatory animal nature.

These two aspects of the contradiction, taken together, allow us to understand both the continuing intellectual fascination that *The Fable of the Bees* and *The Wealth of Nations* exercise on us, and the dissatisfaction and profound moral unease they still arouse. This not only means that if the 'moral conscience' of today wishes to cure its 'squint', it must look to Rousseau's *Discourse* rather than to these two works; but also that if it wants to complete the cure, and at the same time, find confirmation in an understanding of the actual situation, it must go on from the *Discourse* to *Capital*: until at last it is fully appeased, not by contemplation but by 'subversive praxis'.

Part Four

Lenin's *State and Revolution*

The basic theme of *State and Revolution* – the one that indelibly inscribes itself on the memory, and immediately comes to mind when one thinks of the work – is the theme of the revolution as a *destructive* and *violent* act. The revolution cannot be restricted to the seizure of power, it must also be the destruction of the old State. 'The point is whether the old State machine shall remain, or be *destroyed*,' says Lenin.[1] *Sprengen, zerbrechen*, destroy, smash: these words capture the tone of the text. Lenin's polemic is not directed against those who do not wish for the seizure of power. The object of his attack is not *reformism*. On the contrary, it is directed against those who wish for the seizure of power but not for the destruction of the old State as well. The author he aims at is Kautsky. But not, let it be clear, the Kautsky who was to emerge after 1917 (in *Terrorism and Communism*, for example), but rather the Kautsky of the writings devoted to the struggle against opportunism: the Kautsky who *wants* revolution, and yet *does not want* the destruction of the old State machine.

At first impression the text seems an implacable but sectarian essay, primitive, steeped in 'Asiatic fury' – a kind of hymn to 'violence for violence's sake'. What seems to emerge from it it is a reduction of revolution to its most elementary and external features: the capture of the Winter Palace, the Ministry of the Interior in flames, the arrest and execution of the political personnel of the old government. It was precisely this interpretation that ensured the success of *State and Revolution* throughout the Stalin era, for more than a quarter of a century from 1928 to 1953, not only in Russia but in all the Communist Parties of the world. The revolution is violence. Kautsky is a social-democrat because he does not want violence. It is impossible to be a Communist if your aim is not the violent seizure of power. Until 1953, any militant in a Communist Party (the Italian Party included) who had dared to cast doubts on this necessity of violence would have found himself in the same position as

[1] Lenin, *State and Revolution*, in *Selected Works*, op. cit., Vol. II, p. 355.

anyone today who expresses doubts about the 'peaceful, parliamentary road'.

I shall not be so stupid as to suggest that Lenin was *against* violence. He was in favour of a violent insurrection, just as in June 1917 he had supported the peaceful development of the revolution. He was for one or the other, according to the circumstances. But on one point his thought was immutable: in each and *every* case, the State machine must be *destroyed*.

The ways in which the revolution can be achieved are to some extent contingent: they depend on a constellation of events which it is useless to discuss beforehand. Nor does the amount of bloodshed in itself indicate the thoroughness of the revolutionary process. The essential point of the revolution, the *destruction* it cannot forgo (and of which violence is not in itself a sufficient guarantee) is rather the destruction of the bourgeois State as a power *separate* from and *counterposed* to the masses, and its replacement by a power of a new type. This is the essential point.

According to Lenin, the old State machine must be destroyed because the bourgeois State depends on the *separation* and *alienation* of power from the masses. In capitalist society, democracy is, at best, 'always hemmed in by the narrow limits set by capitalist exploitation'. 'The majority of the population is debarred from participation in public and political life.' All the mechanisms of the bourgeois State are restrictions that 'exclude and squeeze out the poor from politics, from active participation in democracy'.[2] A socialist revolution that maintained this type of State would keep alive the *separation* between the masses and power, their *dependence* and subordination.

If the socialization of the means of production means that, emancipating itself from the rule of capital, the society becomes its own master and brings the productive forces under its own conscious, planned control, the political form in which this economic emancipation can be achieved can only be one based upon the initiative and self-government of the producers.

Here we have the really basic theme of *State and Revolution*. The destruction of the bourgeois State machine is not the Ministry of the Interior in flames, it is not the barricades. All this may take place, but it is not the essential point. What is essential to the revolution is the destruction of the diaphragm that separates the working classes from power, the emancipation and self-determination of the former, the transmission of power

[2] ibid., pp. 333–4.

directly into the hands of the people. Marx said that the Commune had proved that 'the working-class cannot simply lay hold of the ready-made state machinery, and wield it for its own purposes'. It cannot: for the aim of the socialist revolution is not 'to transfer the bureaucratic-military machine from one hand to another'[3] but to transfer power directly into the hands of the people – and that is impossible if this machine is not first smashed.

These few lines require the most serious reflection: the socialist revolution does not consist in transferring 'from one hand to another' the military-bureaucratic machine; the destruction of the military-bureaucratic state machine is, according to Marx, 'the preliminary condition for every real people's revolution', and, comments Lenin, a 'people's revolution' is one in which 'the mass of the people, its majority, the very lowest social groups, crushed by oppression and exploitation, rise independently and place on the entire course of the revolution the impress of *their* own demands, of *their* attempts to build in their own way a new society in place of the old society that is being destroyed'.[4]

The sense of the passage is clear. The destruction of the old machine is the destruction of the *limits* imposed on democracy by the bourgeois State. It is the passage from a 'narrow, restricted' democracy to full democracy. And, adds Lenin, 'full democracy is *not*, qualitatively, the same thing as incomplete democracy'. Behind what might seem formally a difference in quantity, what is actually at stake is 'a gigantic replacement of certain institutions by other institutions of a fundamentally different type.'[5]

The significance of the polemic against Kautsky emerges here too. The clash with Kautsky is important because it reveals a dilemma which has since become the crux of the whole experience of the workers' movement after Lenin. Kautsky wished for the seizure of power but not the destruction of the State. What is essential, he said, is purely and simply to take possession of the State machine which is already there, and to use it for one's own ends. Anyone who reflects on the diversity of the two formulae will find, behind the innocent verbal difference, a far more substantial and profound divergence. For Lenin, the revolution is not only the transfer of power *from one class to another*, it is also the passage from *one type of power to another*: for him, the two things go together because the working class that seizes power is the working class that governs itself.

[3] ibid., pp. 293–4.
[4] ibid., p. 295.   [5] ibid., p. 298.

For Kautsky, on the other hand, the seizure of power does not mean the construction of a *new power*, but simply the promotion to the use of the *old* power of the political personnel who *represent* the working class, but are not themselves the working class. For the former, socialism is the self-government of the masses: in socialism, says Lenin, 'the *mass* of the population will rise to taking an *independent* part, not only in voting and elections, *but also in the everyday administration of the State*. Under socialism *all* will govern in turn and will soon become accustomed to no one governing.'[6]

For the latter, socialism is the management of power *in the name* of the masses. For Lenin, the socialist revolution has to destroy the old State because it must destroy *the difference between governors and governed itself*. For Kautsky, the State and its bureaucratic apparatus is not to be destroyed, because bureaucracy, i.e. the difference between governors and governed, cannot be suppressed and will always survive. For Lenin, the revolution is the end of all masters; for Kautsky, it is merely the arrival of a new master.

I repeat, the Kautsky against whom Lenin directed this polemic was still a Marxist, holding firmly to the class conception of the State. His political vision, indeed, had a rigidly *ouvrierist* cast. As with all the Marxists of the Second International, his class position was, in fact, so strict that it often turned into a closed corporatism. What Lenin wrote in opposition to Plekhanov *et al.*, on Marx's concept of the 'people's revolution', could easily have been extended to Kautsky as well.

And yet, despite its rigid class standpoint, Kautsky's idea of *power* already contained the germ of all his subsequent developments. The State that must not be destroyed but which can be taken over and turned to one's own ends, the military-bureaucratic machine that is not to be dismantled but transferred 'from one hand to another', is already embryonically a State 'indifferent' in class nature: it is a technical or 'neutral' instrument, a mere means that can do good or ill, according to who controls it and uses it.

Hence the theory of the simple seizure, without at the same time the destruction-transformation of power, contains the germ of an *interclass* theory of the State. Or rather it is a perennial oscillation between two extreme poles: a reckless subjectivism that sees the essence of the revolution and socialism in the promotion to power of particular *political personnel*, who are, as we know, the party bureaucracy; and an inter-class

[6] ibid., p. 357.

conception of the State. The first pole gives the so-called Rakosi-type regime: the 'dictatorship of the proletariat' *by decree*, which can then in due time evolve towards the conception of . . . the 'State of the whole people'. The second pole gives the mandarins of social-democratic bureaucracy: the Scheidemanns, Leon Blums, Mollets, Wilsons, who – while serving the bourgeois State, and precisely because they are serving the bourgeois State – believe that they are thereby serving the interests of the *whole* society, the 'general' and 'common' interest.

The aim of our political struggle, wrote Kautsky, is 'the conquest of State power by winning a majority in parliament, and by raising parliament to the rank of master of the government'.[7] Parliament – evidently – has existed hitherto, will continue to exist hereafter, indeed must always exist. Not only is it independent of classes, but even of historical epochs. This is the acme of inter-classism. Kautsky's formula (and that of his present-day imitators) does not suggest even as a hypothesis that the parliamentary regime might be linked in some way to the class structure of bourgeois society. This formula makes *tabula rasa* of the whole of Marx's critique of the modern representative State. Furthermore, insofar as it is prepared to concede that the parliamentary regime has any class character whatsoever, it identifies this not in the regime itself *as such* but in its abuses: electoral frauds, *trasformismo*, 'pork-barrelling', *sottogoverno*, etc.[8] It stresses these 'anomalies' all the more willingly in that they allow it to invoke the 'true parliament', 'true mirror of the nation', which Togliatti, too, foretold: the only utopianism which the 'old foxes' can envisage.

To win a parliamentary majority and convert parliament into the master of the government. The essential question for Kautsky is who is in control in parliament; simply a change, even if a radical one, in the government's political personnel. That it is possible and necessary to go further, that the essential point is precisely to destroy the distinction between governors and governed – Kautsky cannot even imagine such a thing. His formula is parliament as 'master of the government'; Lenin's is the people as 'masters of the parliament' – i.e. the suppression of parliament as such.

We must make sure that we understand properly this Leninist critique

---

[7] ibid., p. 358.

[8] *Trasformismo* is the process whereby opposition forces, or their leaders, are absorbed into the ruling elite. *Sottogoverno* is the practice prevalent in Italy, whereby the party in power bypasses sections of the State administration by setting up parallel bureaucratic organizations directly dependent upon itself.

of the parliamentary system. It is not a primitive and sectarian critique, the impotent critique of Bordiga, the denunciation of parliament as a 'fraud', of political democracy as a 'fraud', etc. This latter is the critique that has prevailed historically in the Communist tradition. It is an elementary critique which, failing to give a class analysis of liberal democracy or to grasp the organic way in which its growth is linked to that of the capitalist socio-economic order, denounces parliament and the modern representative State in subjectivist terms as if it were an institution consciously 'invented' by the ruling class to fool the people (rather as, according to Voltaire, religion is an invention of the priests). The superficiality and impotence of this critique emerges clearly when we remember that from it has descended precisely the nihilistic contempt for the problem of *democracy* and of the *power structure* in a socialist society that has permeated the whole experience of Stalinist and post-Stalinist political circles to this day. In *State and Revolution*, on the contrary, Lenin's critique of parliament succeeds for the first time – and, note, for the first time within Lenin's own thought (hence the crucial importance of this text, which is far and away his greatest contribution to political theory) – in restoring some of the basic lines of Marx's critique of the modern representative State. So much so that, just as on the level of political practice *State and Revolution* coincides with Lenin's first real penetration and discovery of the significance of the soviet (which had first emerged much earlier, during the 1905 Revolution, but which he had long failed to understand), so on the level of political theory *State and Revolution* coincides with his discovery that the 'dictatorship of the proletariat' is not the dictatorship of the party but the Paris Commune, the very same Commune that, even as late as the early months of 1917, Lenin had still regarded as only a form, though an extreme one, of 'bourgeois democratism'.

The difference between the two viewpoints is so radical that whereas in the first case the critique of parliament becomes a critique of *democracy*, in Lenin's case, on the contrary, the critique of parliament, i.e. of *liberal* or *bourgeois* democracy, is a critique of the *anti-democratic* nature of parliament – a critique made in the name of that infinitely 'fuller' (and hence qualitatively different) democracy, the democracy of the soviets, the only democracy that deserves the name of socialist democracy.

Marxist literature since Marx knows nothing that could even remotely compete with the seriousness of the critique of parliament contained in *State and Revolution*; nor, at the same time, anything pervaded with such a profound democratic inspiration as that which animates Lenin's text from beginning to end. The 'imperative mandate', the permanent and constant revocability of representatives by those they represent, the demand for a legislative power which would be 'a working, *not* a parliamentary body, executive and legislative at the same time' and in which, hence, the representatives 'have to work, have to execute their own laws, have themselves to test their results in real life, and to account directly to their constituents'.[9] All this is no 'reform' of parliament (as imagined in the extremist folklore of some tiny sects, prey to party bureaucracy, but 'implacable' in their denunciations of Lenin's parliamentarianism!); it is rather the *suppression* of parliament, and its replacement by representative organs of a 'council' or 'soviet' type: to refer again to Lenin's own words, it is 'a gigantic replacement of certain institutions by other institutions of a fundamentally different order'.

Hence the destruction of the State and its replacement by institutions of 'proletarian democracy', i.e. by the self-government of the mass of producers. Lenin's line of thought is so rigorous that he does not hesitate to draw the most extreme conclusions from this: the socialist State itself – in so far as socialism (i.e. the first phase of communist society) still has need of a State – is a remnant of the bourgeois State.

The State withers away insofar as there are no longer any capitalists, any classes, and, consequently, no *class* can be *suppressed*. But the State has not yet completely withered away, since there still remains the safe-guarding of 'bourgeois right' [i.e. of the principle of 'to each according to his labour' rather than according to his needs] which consecrates actual inequality.[10]

Hence 'in its first phase . . . communism *cannot* as yet be fully mature economically and entirely free from traditions or traces of capitalism. Hence the interesting phenomenon that communism in its first phase retains "the narrow horizon of bourgeois right".' And since 'bourgeois right in regard to the distribution of *consumer* goods inevitably presupposes the existence of the *bourgeois State*, for right is nothing without an apparatus capable of *enforcing* the observance of the standards of right. It follows,' concludes Lenin, 'that under communism there remains for a time not only bourgeois right, but even the bourgeois State without the bourgeoisie!'[11]

As we see, the level of development of socialism is here measured by the

[9] ibid., pp. 301–2.
[10] ibid., p. 339.   [11] ibid., pp. 342–3.

level of development of democracy. The further the withering away of the State has advanced and the self-government of the masses has been extended, the more progress has been made in the transition from socialism to communism. Communism is not the Volga–Don Canal plus the State. It is not 'swathes of forest windbreaks' plus the police, concentration camps and bureaucratic omnipotence. Lenin has a different idea. But precisely because this idea is still today only an *idea*, we should reject all taboos and speak frankly.

State and Revolution was written in August and September 1917 at the height of the revolutionary process. None of Lenin's writings have a 'contemplative' character. This is less than ever the case with *State and Revolution*. Lenin embarked upon it so as to decide what to do in the on-going revolution. He was a realist who did not trust to 'inspiration', to the political improvisation of the moment, but aspired to act with a full consciousness of what he was doing. This was the moment and this the man of which *State and Revolution* was born. And yet we only have to look around today to see that the relation between this *idea* of socialism and socialism as it exists is not much different from the relationship between the Sermon on the Mount and the Vatican.

The answer we must accept – but which we should give thoughtfully and calmly, without dramatization – is the answer we all know: the countries we call socialist are only socialist metaphorically. They are countries which are no longer capitalist. They are countries where all the principal means of production have been nationalized and are state-owned – but not *socialized*, which is quite different. They are those 'links' in the world imperialist chain that have broken (and so far this chain has broken at its weakest links). This is true of China, of the 'people's democracies', not to speak of the Soviet Union. None of these countries is really socialist, nor could they be. Socialism is not a national process but a world process. This tremendous process – which today is above all the disintegration of the world capitalist system – is precisely the process we are living and which, simply in terms of its totally unprecedented proportions, obviously cannot reach harbour in a single day. The process is visible to everybody. Only the purblind 'concreteness' of Social-Democracy, convinced that it will be in the saddle for all time, can grant itself the luxury of ignoring it. This social-democratic illusion is the fate of anyone who thinks the idea of *State and Revolution* is outdated. There are few writings more timely or more relevant. Lenin is not outdated. National socialism, the 'construction of socialism in one country', these are outdated. Communism, said Marx, cannot exist as a 'local event': 'The proletariat can thus only exist on the *world-historical* plane, just as communism, its activity, can only have a world-historical existence.'[12]

[12] Marx and Engels, *The German Ideology*, London and Moscow, 1965, pp. 46–7.

Marxism: Science or Revolution?

Marxism as science or Marxism as revolution? There was and there still is this alternative. To resolve it is not so easy as is often thought. I shall begin with the first horn of the dilemma – Marxism as a science. The broad outlines of the argument might be presented as follows. Marxism is a theory of the *laws* of development of human society. In *Capital*, Marx has studied and analysed the laws governing the development of capitalist production, he has taken this 'mechanism' to pieces and described it. As a scientific doctrine, Marxism essentially consists of the discovery of objective causal relationships. It discovers and analyses the laws which make the system work, describes the contradictions which undermine it from within and signal its destiny. But insofar as it is a work of science and not ideology, *Capital* will not allow this analysis to be tainted with 'value judgements' or subjective choices: instead it makes only 'judgements of fact', objective judgements, affirmations which in the last analysis are universally valid. Scientific propositions are in the indicative. They do not advance 'choices' or finalities. It is impossible to deduce imperatives from the objective and impartial statements of science. This is the well-known argument developed by Hilferding in the preface to his *Finance Capital* (the argument of more or less all the orthodox Marxism of the Second International), 'Marxism is only a theory of the laws of development of society.' 'These laws, which obtain their general formulation in the Marxist view of history, are applied by Marxist economics to the epoch of commodity production.' 'Marxism, which is a scientifically logical and objective doctrine, is not bound to value judgements.' The task of Marxism as a science is to 'describe causal relationships'. Though they are always being confused, 'socialism' and 'Marxism' are *not* the same thing. Socialism is an end, a goal, an objective of political will and action. Marxism, on the other hand, being a science, is objective and impartial knowledge. One can accept the science without desiring the end. 'To recognize the validity of Marxism', says Hilferding, 'does not at all mean to make value judgements, much less to point out a line of practical action. It is one thing to recognize a necessity, and quite another to put oneself at the service of that necessity.'

This view clearly allows no room for a link between *science* and *class consciousness*, between science and ideology, let alone for the 'partisanship' of science. Socio-economic development is seen as a process unfolding before the observer and the scientist like the movement of the stars. 'Economic laws' are objective laws, external to classes and independent of our wills just like the laws of nature (see Stalin, *Economic Problems of Socialism in the Soviet Union*). The 'law of value' is like the law of the fall of heavy bodies. More or less present in this conception is always a 'theory of breakdown'. The laws of the capitalist mode of production inescapably lead the system to its end. The extinction of capitalism is inevitable. It is made fatal and almost automatic by the explanation of its own laws. Nuances and slight variations apart, this was more or less the view which prevailed in the Third International too. While it existed, and above all with Stalin, all that was added was the criterion of 'partisanship' (an element anyway already latent in Lenin). But apart from the blind and sectarian way in which it was advanced, this criterion was only juxtaposed to that of naturalistic objectivism. Juxtaposed, never mediated with it: i.e. united with it only by paste and string.

This 'physicalist' position, in infinitely more cultivated and refined forms, is still the dominant one among the next Marxist economists. The case of Oskar Lange is typical, and still more so is that of Maurice Dobb (who in general is a very serious scholar). Dobb sees the law of value as a law which allows us to reconstruct, unify, order and explain all the major mechanisms and movements of the system.

Only with the work of Adam Smith, and its more rigorous systematization by Ricardo, did Political Economy create that unifying quantitative principle which enabled it to make postulates in terms of the general equilibrium of the economic system – to make deterministic statements about the general relationships which held between the major elements of the system. In Political Economy this unifying principle, or system of general statements cast in quantitative form, consisted of a theory of value.

This passage stresses above all the ultimate social neutrality of the law of value. The law makes it possible to relate together the most important quantitative factors of the system, to establish certain quantifiable relationships between them – just as the law of universal gravitation does in its own field (Dobb's very example). But what does not come out here is the particular, 'fetishistic' or 'alienated' nature of the quantitative factors related together by the law. For Marx, commodities and capital have not always existed, and what is more, their existence must come to an end. Apart from the relationships *within* the system, Marx analyses and criticizes the system itself. He discusses why the product of labour takes the form of a 'commodity'; why human labour is represented by the 'value' of 'things'; he discusses why (that is, under what conditions) capital exists and reproduces itself. Dobb, on the other hand, argues a little like Smith and Ricardo, who see the commodity as the 'natural' and inevitable form of the products of labour and the *market* as an institution which must always exist, and who present the law of value as a law of permanent quantities or factors (often, in fact, confusing it with the problem of the 'measurement' of values).

There is no reason to dwell on this point here. Suffice it simply to note that for Marx too the law of value is an objective law, a law operating independently of consciousness and even 'behind the backs' of men; except that for him a quite peculiar kind of objectivity is involved. It is, so to speak, a false objectivity and one which must be abolished. The laws of the market – Marx writes – are a 'natural necessity' for men. The movements of the market are as unpredictable as earthquakes. But this is not because the market is a 'natural' phenomenon. What has taken the objective form here of *things* and interactions between things is really nothing but the social relationships of men to each other. 'These formulae,' Marx writes, 'bear it stamped upon them in unmistakable letters that they belong to a state of society, in which the process of production has the mastery over instead of being controlled by him.' A little earlier he had pointed out: 'The life-process of society, which is based on the process of material production, does not strip off its mystical veil until it is treated as production by freely associated men, and is consciously regulated by them in accordance with a settled plan.' And this can obviously come about only through revolution.

In the Ricardian interpretation, then, the law of value tends to be naturalized and appear as a socially neutral law. The laws of nature have no class character. And, by the same token, the production of commodities and the existence of a market have no class character. Hence the constant familiar speeches. The 'market' and 'profit' are not seen as the inevitable survivals of bourgeois institutions in the first phase of socialist society, which is *par excellence* a *transitional* society, but as 'rational criteria or measurements of economic activity', as something positive which must always exist. There is a 'socialist' market and there is 'socialist' profit. The revolution is not made to abolish profit, i.e. to abolish exploitation. The revolution is made only for the pleasure of marching, well drilled and cheering, past a speakers' platform.

Another basic distortion, closely related to the first, is the misinterpretation of the nature and meaning of Marx's work. For Marx, political economy is born with the extension and generalization of commodity production. It is born with capitalism and dies with it (that is with the progressive extinction of its surviving elements in the transitional society); which explains why all Marx's major works have the title or sub-title: 'critique of political economy'. For many Marxists today, however, the contrary is true: there must always be political economy (see the *Manual of Political Economy* produced by the Academy of Sciences of the USSR), just as there will always be law, the State, and those who tell the masses what the masses themselves ought to think and believe.

I must interrupt the argument developed so far in order to look at the problem in another way and from a different angle. Open Marx's first really important writing, the *The Critique of Hegel's 'Philosophy of Right'*. It has a remarkable structure. Not only does the work begin with a critique of the Hegelian *philosophy* of the State, and imperceptibly turn into a critique of the *State*; but in both cases – that is, both on the question of the way Hegel sees the State, and on the question of the State itself – the critique is developed by the use of a single model. Not only is Hegel's *representation* of the reality of the State upside down and 'standing on its head' but, Marx says, so is the actual *reality* generated by the State. 'This uncritical spirit, this mysticism', he writes, 'is the enigma of the modern constitution . . . as well as the mystery of Hegelian philosophy. . . . This point of view is undeniably abstract, but it is the abstraction of the political State as Hegel himself develops it. It is atomistic, too, but it is the atomism of society itself. The point of view cannot be concrete when the object of the point of view is abstract.' In general, an author criticizes another by showing him that things are not as he has described them. He criticizes him in the name of reality and on the basis of reality. But here the procedure seems to be different: the death sentence pronounced on the old philosophy applies at the same time to its *object* too. Marx does not only want to see the end of the Hegelian *philosophy* of the State: he wants to see the actual 'dissolution' of the State. This again is because he understands that not only is the philosophical representation of reality false, metaphysical and 'standing on its head' – but so is reality itself, that is to say, the particular type of social regime which takes the form of the modern representative State or parliamentary government. There is an analogous situation in *Capital*. Here too Marx does not restrict himself to criticizing the 'logical mysticism' of the economists, their 'trinity formula': Land, Capital, Labour. Their 'fetishism' is explained by the fetishism of reality itself, that is of the capitalist mode of production. This is quite evident in a whole series of expressions. *Capital* contains such phrases as: 'the mystical character of commodities', or 'The whole mystery of commodities, all the magic and necromancy that surrounds the products of labour as long as they take the form of commodities'; or finally that the 'mystical veil' is not an invention of the bourgeois interpreters of the 'life-process of society which is based on the process of material production', but actually belongs to this process, which therefore *appears* to political economy as what it really *is*.

In fact, reality itself is upside down. It is therefore not just a question of criticizing the way in which economists and philosophers have depicted reality. It is necessary to overturn *reality* itself – to straighten it up and 'put it back on its feet'. 'Until now the philosophers have only interpreted the world: the point however is to change it.' In the above pages I have looked at Marxism as a science; now I come to Marxism as revolution.

I urge the reader not to get too excited, but to keep his eyes open and use his head. In the argument I have just outlined there is an extremely dubious and even dangerous point. An author criticizes another by appealing to *reality*, showing him that things are not as he had described and depicted them. This is the only correct kind of procedure. But Marx – with Hegel as with the economists – *seems* to be unable to do this: unable to, because the reference criterion – reality – is already itself a counterfeit standard. If this were really so, Marx would only be a prophet (which is not much), and we would be revisionists. On what basis do we say that the reality of capitalism is upside down? According to Bernstein, on the basis of the *moral ideal*. The idea of 'justice', Kant's ethics, tell me that the world should be corrected and reformed. Value and surplus value are mere words. Socialism is the product of good wishes. Change the minds of men! Abandon scientific socialism for utopian socialism. Reality is not important. 'Facts' are of no account. Reality is denied to make room for the realization of the ideal. Reason is Revolution. The contemporary Bernstein seems to lie to the left – in the petty-bourgeois anarchism of Marcuse and of all those who have taken him seriously.

I must stop here a moment to put some order into the argument. Reality is certainly upside down – otherwise revolution would not be necessary. On the other hand, Marxism also needs to be a science: if not there would be no *scientific* socialism, only messianic aspirations or religious hopes. In short, if Marx is a scientist, he has to measure his ideas and those of others against the facts, to test hypotheses experimentally against reality. In simpler and more familiar terms, this means that when Marx criticizes Hegel, the economists and all the reality of capitalism, he still has to do it in the name of reality and *on the basis of reality*. The criterion of his critique, in short, cannot be the *ideal* (which is still the ideal of X or Y). It must be a criterion drawn from and rooted in reality. If I may summarize this briefly, I would say that there are *two realities* in capitalism: the reality expressed by Marx, and the reality expressed by the authors he criticizes. I shall now try to demonstrate this as simply and quickly as possible, by examining the relationship between capital and wage labour.

I shall begin by seeing how this relationship looks from the point of view of the capitalist. The capitalist invests his money in the purchase of spindles, cotton and labour. He finds these things on the market, that is as *commodities*. He buys them as anyone might buy a whip, a horse and a carriage. After making these purchases (suppose he buys at no more than their actual value), the capitalist then puts the worker to work at the spindles to transform the cotton into thread. At this point, Marx says, 'the labour process is a process between things that the capitalist has *purchased, things that have become his property*'. 'The product of this process belongs, therefore, to him, just as much as does the wine which is the product of a process of fermentation completed in his cellar.'

The capitalist's eye, accustomed to synthesis and the overall view, does not deign to distinguish between the various things he has bought. From his point of view, wage labour is a *part* of capital, in the same way as machinery and raw materials: it is the 'variable' part of capital, the 'wages fund', as distinct from the part invested in the purchase of means of production. The fact that besides reproducing his own value, i.e. the wage, the wage labourer produces surplus value, is a happy circumstance which raises no theoretical problem for the capitalist. To him, this fertility of labour appears directly as the *productivity of his own capital*: the capital of which labour is itself a part, being one of the purchases. This is, as we know, the thesis of all non-Marxist economists, what Marx calls the fetishism of political economy. It is not only labour which produces value, but capital too. Wages pay for the productivity of the former, profits pay the latter. Land produces the harvest; capital or machinery produce profits; labour produces wages. To each his own. Then let harmony be established once and for all, and let the factors of production collaborate.

You will say that this is the 'bosses' point of view. But the important thing to understand is that more than a subjective point of view is involved: it is a point of view which corresponds in a certain sense to the actual courses of things. The working class reproduces its own means of subsistence, and at the same time produces surplus value (i.e. profit, rent and interest); with its labour it provides the revenues of all the basis classes of society. And – *as long as it is kept down* – the working class is in fact only a cog in the mechanism of capitalism. Capital is produced by labour: labour is the cause, capital the effect; the one the origin, the other the outcome. And yet not only in the accounting of the enterprise, but in the real mechanism, the working class appears only as 'variable capital' and as the wages fund. The 'whole' has become the 'part', and the part the whole. Such is the reality 'on its head' already mentioned: the reality which Marx not only rejects as a criterion and yardstick, but which he wants to overthrow and invert.

Think of the American working class. It is only a cog of capital, a part of the capitalist mechanism. More strictly speaking, it is not even a 'class' (it does not have *consciousness* of being a class). It is an agglomeration of 'categories': car workers, chemical workers, textile workers, etc. When it reacts and goes on strike, its relationship to the whole of the social 'mechanism' is like that of a bilious irritated organ to the human body: it demands no more than a pill to make it feel better. This class (though every working class has passed through this stage, and in a certain sense remains in it until it takes power) is, really, a *part* of capital: although (leaving aside the imperialist exploitation of workers in other countries) it is also true that the thing of which it is a *part* (capital) is in its turn a *part* of the value produced by that working class.

The point of view adopted by Marx is in fact the expression precisely of this other reality. Capital, of which wage labour is only the variable component, is in reality part of this its part (which is therefore the 'totality'): it is the product of 'living labour'. Without then repeating Bernstein's moralism or Marcuse's 'utopias', Marx – utilizing an aspect of *reality* – overthrows the arguments of the economists and points to the overthrow of capitalism itself. Marxism is therefore science. It is an analytical reconstruction of the way in which the mechanism of capitalist production works.

On the other hand, as well as being a science, Marxism is revolutionary ideology. It is the analysis of reality from the viewpoint of the working class. This in its turn means that the working class cannot constitute itself as a *class* without taking possession of the scientific analysis of *Capital*. Without this, it disintegrates into a myriad of 'categories'. The working class (dreamers awake!) is not a *given* factor, it is not a product of nature. It is a destination point: the product of *historical action*, i.e. not only of material conditions but also of *political* consciousness. In short, the class becomes a class when, going beyond economistic spontaneism, it develops the consciousness of being the protagonist of a revolution which emancipates not only the workers but the whole of society. This consciousness, through which the class constitutes itself in political organization and takes its place at the head of its allies, cannot be derived from anywhere but *Capital*. It is in this sense, I think, that Lenin said that building the party also requires something 'from without'.

Index